CW00556067

STRUCTURED
DERIVATIVES

STRUCTURED DERIVATIVES

A Handbook of Structuring, Pricing and Investor Applications

MEHRAJ MATTOO

FT
PITMAN
PUBLISHING

London . Hong Kong . Johannesburg . Melbourne
Singapore . Washington DC

To Farah

PITMAN PUBLISHING
128 Long Acre, London WC2E 9AN
Tel: +44 (0)171 447 2000
Fax: +44 (0)171 240 5771

A Division of Pearson Professional Limited

First published in Great Britain 1997

© Mehraj Mattoo 1997

The right of Mehraj Mattoo to be identified as author
of this work has been asserted by him in accordance
with the Copyright, Design and Patents Act 1988.

ISBN 0 273 61120 8

British Library Cataloguing in Publication Data
A CIP catalogue record for this book can be obtained
from the British Library.

1 3 5 7 9 10 8 6 4 2

Typeset by Pantek Arts, Maidstone, Kent
Printed and bound in Great Britain by
Creative Print and Design Wales, Ebbw Vale Gwent

*The Publishers' policy is to use paper manufactured
from sustainable forests.*

About the Author

Mehraj Mattoo is currently a Director of Financial Products at the Canadian Imperial Bank of Commerce based in Singapore. Prior to joining CIBC in 1995, Dr. Mattoo was a Director at NatWest Markets based in London and Hong Kong. At NatWest, he worked in the areas of risk management and structured derivatives for over eight years. He received his MBA and Ph.D (Financial Economics) degrees from the University of London. A former NatWest research fellow at the University of London, he is also the recipient of the Diploma of Imperial College (DIC).

CONTENTS

PREFACE

Structured Derivatives is a comprehensive guide to a wide variety of over-the-counter or structured financial derivatives and their applications in investment management. The products covered in the book include interest rate forwards, foreign exchange forwards, interest rate swaps, cross currency swaps, equity swaps, interest rate options – caps, floors, swaptions, bond options etc., currency options, equity options and a range of 'second generation' derivatives such as barrier options, look back options, digital options, average rate options and quantos. The book includes a comprehensive guide to using structured derivatives in investment management. It provides the necessary tools to structure, price and unbundle a variety of structured investment products.

Divided into two parts, the book contains;

- An in-depth study of the theoretical principles of valuing forwards, swaps and options
- A comprehensive description of structured derivatives
- A practical, step-by-step guide to pricing forward rate agreements, forward FX contracts, interest rate swaps, cross currency swaps, equity swaps, caps, floors, swaptions, bond options, equity options, currency options and a range of exotic options
- A detailed discussion on product strategies and applications in various market conditions
- A review of the principles of financial engineering in investment management
- A practical guide to creating synthetic securities
- A practical guide to creating and pricing structured assets and off-balance-sheet structures
- A survey of derivative applications in portfolio management including duration and convexity management.

While the book provides all the necessary theoretical tools for structuring and valuing a variety of derivatives, it is written for practitioners engaged in investment management and hence has a strong applied bias. Fund managers, insurance companies, pension funds, hedge funds, finance companies, banks and cash rich corporates will find the book particularly useful. The book can also be used by MBA students specializing in Finance to gain a deeper understanding of the theory and practice of structured derivatives.

ACKNOWLEDGEMENTS

In writing this book, I have drawn on the pioneering work of a number of scholars and practioners who have helped advance our understanding of derivatives and their role in asset and liability management. Their numbers are too many to be mentioned here, but to all of them I owe an intellectual debt.

I am indebted to my wife for her help in putting this book together. This book is a result as much of her understanding and patience as it is of my effort. The time spent on this book truly belonged to her.

Over the course of time, a number of individuals have helped shape my intellectual and professional life. I am especially grateful to Mr Gerry Salkin (Director, Centre for Quantitative Studies, Imperial College, London) and Dr Martin Owen (CEO, NatWest Markets) for first introducing me to the world of financial derivatives.

Finally, I would like to thank FT-Pitman Publishing for commissioning me to write this book. My thanks are due to Richard Stagg, Amelia Lakin, Elizabeth Truran, Kim Whiting and Peter Drew.

Mehraj Mattoo
Singapore

1

INTRODUCTION

Economic background to the
development of derivatives

What is a derivative?

What is a structured derivative?

Overview of the book

The last two decades have witnessed a fundamental change in the financial environment in which corporate borrowers and institutional investors operate. The cataclysmic changes were brought about as a result of two major sets of external forces – the globalization of competition in product and factor markets and the deregulation and integration of financial markets – coupled with unparalleled advances in technology.

By all measures the financial environment is more risky today than it was two decades ago. The financial certainties of the past have given way to today's volatile markets. Unpredictable movements in interest rates and exchange rates present risks that no borrower or investor can ignore. The financial markets have responded to this increased volatility by 'engineering' financial instruments and strategies that allow borrowers and investors to hedge against market risks. These risk management products – more popularly known as derivatives – have come to dominate international financial markets in many ways. For example, a large proportion of Euro-issues are swaps driven and asset swaps constitute an integral part of fixed income investments.

The risk management role of derivatives, however, represents only one side of the coin. In recent years derivatives have increasingly been used to speculate in various financial and commodity markets. Derivatives, for example, provide an easy way of assuming geared positions and obviate the need to operate in the underlying cash markets.

Derivatives are also increasingly used to assume measured risk as part of a conventional investment programme and to gain access to regulated or restricted markets. Derivatives, in these cases, are embedded in conventional asset and liability products. Risk and return characteristics can be altered either to exploit a market anomaly or to express a view that is different from the market view. The role of derivatives in creating structured assets and liabilities is the dominant theme of today's financial markets. The trend toward structured products represents a major new application for derivatives. This book is aimed to provide the tools for the creation of structured products for investors.

ECONOMIC BACKGROUND TO THE DEVELOPMENT OF DERIVATIVES

After a long period of general price stability, Western economies began to experience unexpected and unprecedented price increases in the

1950s. A precursor to this growing price uncertainty was the 'great depression' of the 1930s. This period was characterized by competitive devaluations and protectionism to bolster individual economies. The international economic policy making at the end of World War II was, therefore, dominated by two considerations: to facilitate the reconstruction of war-ravaged European economies and to prevent a return to the competitive devaluations and protectionism of the 1930s. To achieve these objectives the International Monetary Fund (IMF) was established to 'police' a system of fixed exchange rates known universally as the Bretton Woods system, after the small New Hampshire ski resort where the agreement was signed in 1944.

Under the Bretton Woods system the member countries undertook to maintain convertibility and to preserve a fixed exchange rate for their currency. The fixed exchange rate was to be maintained until unambiguous evidence of fundamental disequilibrium appeared. At that point it was expected to devalue or revalue, as the case may be. In other words, a new 'fixed' parity would be established. Convertibility turned out to be a good intention rather than a realistic objective. For, among the major economic powers, only the USA permitted full freedom of capital movements. As far as the objective of keeping exchange rates fixed was concerned the Bretton Woods system was a success. Changes in the major parities were few and when they did prove inevitable, tended to be relatively small, relative to changes that were to be witnessed since the 1970s. In fact, until the process of breakdown began in the late 1960s there were only two market trends: the decline in the value of the British pound, with two devaluations in 1948 and 1967, and the rise of the Deutschmark, as the German economy recovered and the competitiveness of US trade decreased.

Having provided the world with the much needed stability after the war, the Bretton Woods system began to disintegrate in 1968. The system worked on a principle known as the Gold Exchange Standard. Under this arrangement the USA operated a gold standard under which it pledged to keep the dollar price of gold fixed at $US35 per ounce by guaranteeing to exchange gold for US currency on demand via the so-called 'Gold Window'. Other countries then fixed their currencies in terms of dollars, devaluing or revaluing as necessary to maintain equilibrium. In 1968 an unofficial free market in gold began to operate from which central banks were barred. Effectively there now existed a two-tier gold price, making the official price of monetary gold unrealistic. The system finally broke down on 15 August 1973 when the American president Mr Nixon announced the closing of the Gold Window. A new attempt to patch up the system in the form of the Smithsonian Agreement also failed within twelve months.

Thus, the first big jolt to the stability of post-war financial markets came in 1973 with the ending of the Bretton Woods system of fixed exchange rates. One of the main reasons for the failure of the system was rising inflation. Instead of deflation, which had been feared by the participants at the original Bretton Woods conference, the 1950s and 1960s witnessed steadily accelerating world-wide inflation; slow at first but quite rapid from 1967 onwards. Controlling inflation, therefore, assumed a high priority for the governments of the main industrialized countries. Since most of these governments found it difficult to reduce public spending, the main burden of inflation fighting fell on monetary policy. Governments aimed at controlling the quantity of money and worried less about the level of interest rates. Consequently interest rates became much more volatile. Exchange rates moved in line with changes in interest rates as flows of short-term capital, seeking the highest return, came to dominate the foreign exchange markets.

Figures 1.1 and 1.2 provide dramatic evidence of fluctuations in interest and exchange rates since the 1970s. These fluctuations exposed borrowers and investors to unprecedented risks. Eliminating or even minimizing these risks would be prohibitively expensive and in many cases impossible without the new tools of risk management – the derivatives. Derivatives provide a liquid and efficient way of transferring financial risks to third parties who are more willing to assume such risks either because it provides a hedge to their exposure or because they are willing to speculate.

WHAT IS A DERIVATIVE?

A derivative is a financial instrument which derives its value (hence 'derivative') from the value of other more basic securities and variables. The underlying securities and variables include common stock, bonds, stock indices, bond indices, currencies, interest rates and so on. Derivatives also exist on commodities and commodity indices. These include precious metals, agricultural produce, oil and indices such as the CRB.

Derivatives are also called contingent claims because their value is contingent on the value of an underlying security. For example, the value of a stock option is contingent on the price of the stock on which it is written.

In efficient and complete financial markets derivative securities are redundant since in such a world the payoffs or cash flows from a derivative security can be perfectly replicated by a dynamic hedging strategy. For example, the payoff from a stock option can be replicated by a dynamic strategy involving, say, Government issued bills and the underlying stock on which the option is written.

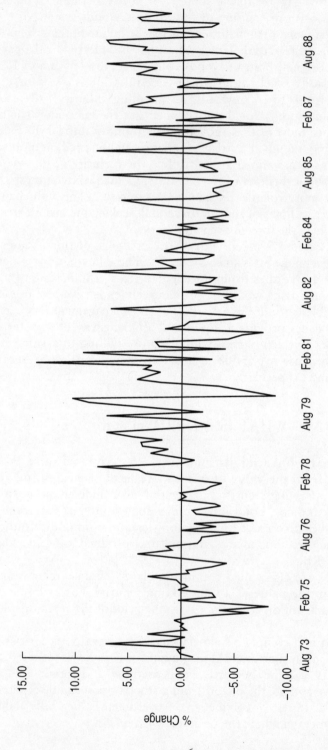

Fig 1.1 Interest rate volatility: Monthly changes in 5-year USD Treasury yields

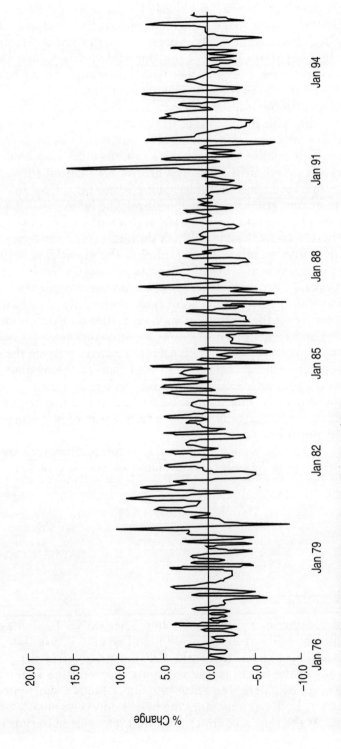

Fig 1.2 Exchange rate volatility: Monthly changes in spot US$/DM

In reality, however, there are all kinds of frictions that exist in financial markets that would make replication of payoffs associated with a particular derivative prohibitively expensive and, in some cases, impossible. The first important economic function of derivatives, therefore, is that they complete markets. In other words derivatives create payoffs unattainable from conventional financial instruments.

Derivatives also provide an efficient mechanism for risk allocation from those who wish to avoid risk to those who are more willing to assume it. The willingness to assume risk may be driven by perceived potential for speculative gain or because of an underlying offsetting position. For example when a cotton grower sells cotton forward in the futures market he has an underlying position in cotton and does not wish to assume risk of price fluctuations. The buyer of such a contract is hoping to benefit from a rise in price of cotton in the spot market. This is a classic example of risk shifting.

Derivatives also maintain the liquidity in the underlying security, give access to markets that would otherwise be inaccessible and reduce transaction costs. Because derivatives allow investors to assume leveraged positions in the underlying security or commodity, they have the effect of increasing the trading in such securities and commodities. Institutional and regulatory restrictions bar investors from participating in many markets. In many such cases derivatives provide the only way of assuming an indirect position in these markets. Derivatives also allow investors to assume exposure to cash markets at a fraction of the costs involved in cash transactions. Better liquidity, transparency and tighter spreads make derivatives a cost effective way of balancing asset and liability portfolios.

While derivatives come in a wide variety of forms, often with confusing labels, they can be broadly classified into four generic categories:

• forwards,
• futures,
• swaps, and
• options.

Forward contracts

A forward contract is a particularly simple derivative. It is an agreement to buy or sell a security or commodity at a future date (the delivery date) for a given price (the delivery price). The party who agrees to buy in the future is said to hold a long position in the contract. The party who agrees to sell in the future holds a short position in the contract. Each party assumes the risk of non-performance by the other party. At the time a contract is entered into, the delivery price is chosen so that the value of the contract to either party is zero. Therefore, no money changes hands at the time the contract is entered into. Subsequently, however, the value of the contract can become positive or negative depending on changes in the forward price.

Figure 1.3(A) depicts the terminal value of a forward contract in which the holder agrees to buy the underlying security at a delivery price of F and the actual spot price at delivery is S. Notice that this value is given by S-F. For a short position the reverse is true Fig 1.3(B).

Two of the most important forward contracts are the forward foreign exchange contract and the forward rate agreement. A large number of banks and investment firms make market in currency and interest rate forward contracts.

Futures contracts

A futures contract, like a forward contract, is an agreement between two parties to buy or sell a security or a commodity at a future time for a given price. Futures contracts are fundamentally similar to forward contracts in that they too establish a price today for a transaction that will settle at a future date. However, unlike forward contracts, futures contracts are traded in centralized and established exchanges. Moreover, unlike forward contracts, futures contracts specify standardized quantities and delivery dates. Futures contracts allow participants to realize gains and losses daily, while forward contracts are settled only at delivery. Futures contracts require participants to set aside a certain proportion of the nominal value of the contract in a 'margin' account held by a broker. Futures contracts are marked-to-market every day to determine their settlement price. Extra margin calls are made if an adverse price movement results in the margin account

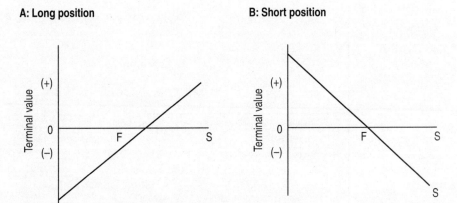

Fig 1.3 Terminal value of a forward contract

falling below the 'maintenance' margin. Maintenance of margin accounts ensures the solvency of the futures exchange. In a forward contract, each party assumes the credit risk of the other party.

Futures are used for a variety of reasons. Businesses use futures to hedge against future changes in security prices, commodity prices, interest rates, exchange rates and various indices. Speculators transact futures in the hope of profiting from favorable future price movements. A third category of futures users – arbitrageurs – trade simultaneously in futures and the underlying securities to profit from price discrepancies between the futures and cash markets.

Figure 1.4 depicts the payoffs for long and short futures contracts held to expiration.

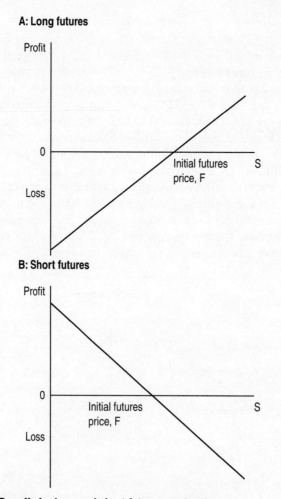

Fig 1.4 Payoffs for long and short futures contracts

Swaps

Interest rate and cross currency swaps form the largest segment of the derivatives market. Swaps are also the most recent derivative instrument. An interest rate swap is an agreement between two parties, one of whom is usually a bank, to make to each other periodic payments calculated on the basis of specified interest rates and a notional principal amount. Typically, the payment to be made by one party is calculated using a floating rate index (such as LIBOR), while the payment to be made by the other party is determined on the basis of a fixed rate of interest or a different floating rate index (basis swap). In the case of an interest rate swap all payments are made in the same currency and no exchange of principal takes place.

Currency swaps involve exchange of periodic payments calculated on the basis of specified interest rates in designated currencies and a notional principal amount. The interest payments may be fixed, floating or a combination of fixed and floating. Currency swaps usually involve exchange of principals.

Corporates and investors have become interested in swaps primarily as a result of;

- attractive arbitrage opportunities between the various capital markets around the world which can significantly lower the cost of their funds,
- the sharp and unpredictable shifts in exchange and interest rates which can reduce their profits significantly or eliminate them altogether, and
- adverse market conditions or regulations making certain otherwise standard capital market transactions difficult or impossible.

Interest rate and currency swaps are effectively multi-period forward contracts bundled into a single contract. Borrowers use swaps to manage interest rate and currency exposure on newly issued or existing debt. By combining a new issue with a swap, a borrower can raise funds in a market in which it enjoys a comparative advantage even when it may not be the market for required type of funding. Similarly, swaps allow investors to separate the decision on issuers and the type of debt issued.

Figure 1.5 depicts payoffs (net present value or NPV) for pay and receive swaps on interest payment. A pay swap is the one in which you pay a fixed rate against receiving a floating index. A receive swap, on the other hand, is a swap in which you receive a fixed rate of interest against paying a floating index.

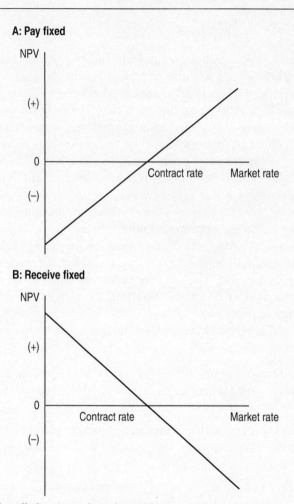

A: Pay fixed

B: Receive fixed

Fig 1.5 **Payoffs for pay and receive swaps**

Options

Unlike other derivative securities that obligate the parties to buy or sell an underlying commodity or a security at a future date, an option contract gives the buyer of the contract the right to buy or sell a security or commodity within a specified period of time. The seller of an option contract, however, is obligated to buy or sell the underlying security or commodity should the buyer of the contract choose to exercise the option.

An option contract that grants to the holder the right to buy an underlying security or commodity is referred to as a call option. Put options, on the other hand, convey the right to sell. An American style option refers to a contract that can be exercised any time up to expiration. A European style option, on the other hand, can only be exercised at expiry. The specified price at which the underlying security or commodity may be bought (in the case of a call option) or sold (in the case of a put option) is called the exercise price or the strike price. The buyer of an option pays the option seller (writer) an amount of money called the option premium or option price at the time of purchasing the option.

Option contracts are traded on a variety of underlying securities and commodities. Options exist on common stocks (stock options), foreign currencies (currency options), government bonds (bond options), interest rates (interest rate options), swaps (swaptions), commodities (commodity options) and futures (futures options). Options are traded on organized exchanges as well as over-the-counter.

Figure 1.6 depicts the payoffs for a call and a put on a stock at their expiration date. Notice that part of the payoff for a call looks similar to the payoff of a forward or a futures contract purchased. The major difference is that while the payoffs on forward and futures contracts can become negative (symmetric payoff) and therefore result in losses, payoffs on options contracts purchased are downside protected (asymmetric payoff). In other words, the purchaser of an option has effectively entered a forward contract to buy (in the case of a call option) or sell (in the case of a put option) a security or a commodity at a specified price at a future date and has simultaneously purchased an insurance policy for protection against potential losses arising from the forward contract. The combination of the forward contract and the insurance against potential losses arising from the forward contract constitutes an option contract.

In the case of a call, the option premium, C, paid to the seller represents the insurance premium for the risk that would arise if the price of the underlying stock fell below the exercise price of E (shaded area). In the case of a put, the premium of P represents the insurance premium for the risk that would arise if the price of the underlying stock rose above the exercise price of E (shaded area).

WHAT IS A STRUCTURED DERIVATIVE?

From our brief description of the four generic types of derivatives it should be clear that those derivatives that trade on organized exchanges are commoditized instruments. In order to facilitate trading, exchanges fix the terms for each contract. Thus all futures contracts and exchange traded options have fixed attributes in terms of delivery dates, contract size, strike rates and so on. Such derivatives cannot, therefore, be tailored to specific hedging or investment requirements.

Forward contracts, swaps and OTC options, on the other hand, are negotiated derivatives and can, therefore, be 'tailored' or 'structured' to the requirements of an individual investor or borrower. It is these 'structured' derivatives that this book deals with. When evaluating structured bonds or considering portfolio management through the use of derivatives, an investor will invariably be dealing with structured rather than exchange traded derivatives.

Moreover, it is easier to evaluate the economics of exchange traded derivatives because the underlying markets are liquid and transparent. A structured derivative, on the other hand, can be a complex package

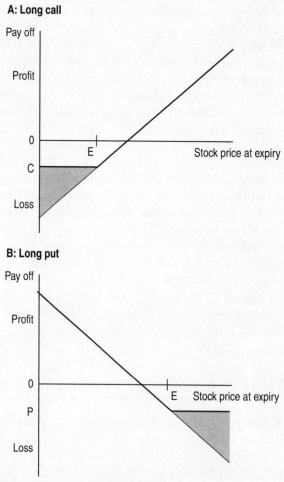

Fig 1.6 Payoffs for a call and put on a stock at their expiration date

14

with odd payoffs whose price cannot be readily established. For an investor, the ability to reverse engineer and price a structured derivative or a structured asset is crucial not only to evaluate its true worth but also to understand the potential risks involved.

It needs to be emphasized that while for corporates and investors structured derivatives provide the ultimate tools for risk and return management, for traders standardized exchange traded derivatives often form the benchmark for the valuation and hedging of such packages. An understanding of exchange traded derivatives is therefore necessary to fully understand structured derivatives in various forms.

OVERVIEW OF THE BOOK

This book aims to provide investors with the necessary theoretical foundations for structuring, valuation and hedging of structured derivatives and assets. It also aims to develop a framework for structured derivative applications in investment management.

The book is divided into two parts. Part I provides the necessary theoretical foundations for the economic analysis and valuation of structured derivatives. Emphasis is placed on practical implications of the underlying theory particularly in the context of the market convention for each type of the structured derivative. A comprehensive introduction to the principles of valuation in Chapters 2 and 3 lays the theoretical foundation for various types of derivatives covered in the book. The book covers interest rate and foreign exchange forward contracts, interest rate swaps, cross currency swaps, equity swaps, interest rate options, currency options and equity options.

Part II of the book deals with the application of structured derivatives in investment management. Chapter 11 develops the principles of financial engineering in investment management. Chapter 12 provides a practical guide to creating synthetic securities using derivative products. Finally, Chapter 13 surveys general derivative applications in portfolio management.

References

Bank for International Settlements, *Recent Innovations in International Banking*. Basel, Switzerland, 1986.

Beckstrom, R., 'The Development of the Swap Market', in *Swap Finance*, 1, Boris Antl, ed., London: Euromoney publications, 1986.

Bock, D.R., 'Fixed-to-Fixed Currency Swap: The Origins of the World Bank Borrowing', in *Swap Financing Techniques*, Boris Antl, ed., London: Euromoney, 1985.

Miller, M., 'Financial Innovation: Achievements and Prospects', *Journal of Applied Corporate Finance*, Winter 1992.

Park, Y.S., 'Currency Swaps as a Long Term International Financing Technique', *Journal of International Business Studies*, 15:3, Winter 1984, pp. 47–54.

Price, J.A.M., 'The Technical Evolution of the Currency Swap Product', in *Swap Finance*, 1, Boris Antl, ed., London: Euromoney publications, 1986.

Putman, B. and Wilford, D.S., *The Monetary Approach of International Adjustment*, New York: Praeger, 1986.

Rawls, S.W. and Smithson, C.W., 'The Evolution of Risk Management Products,' *Journal of Applied Corporate Finance*, Winter 1989, pp. 18–26.

Stevenson, M., 'The Risk Game: A Survey of International Banking'. *The Economist*, 21 March, 1987.

Tufano, P., *The Essays on Financial Innovation*, Ph.D Dissertation, Harvard University, 1989.

Williamson, J., *The Open Economy and the World Economy*. New York: Basic Books, 1983.

2

PRINCIPLES OF FIXED INCOME VALUATION

Time value of money

The term structure of interest rates

Forward exchange rates

Summary

Before we begin to consider the pricing and applications of various derivative securities it is important to understand the fundamental principles of valuation. The discussion in this chapter will be couched in general terms so as to facilitate understanding of the principles involved. Specific valuation techniques will be described in later chapters. We begin by describing the key concepts underlying financial securities valuation.

TIME VALUE OF MONEY

In an economy in which time preferences of individuals, corporations, financial institutions and governments result in positive rates of interest, the time value of money is a key concept. For example, investors will place a higher value on a security that promises returns over the next five years than on a security that promises identical returns for years six through ten. Consequently, the timing of expected future cash flows and the level of interest rates are extremely important for a security's value.

In investment valuation, the time value of money is captured through two simple but important notions: compounding and discounting. These two notions are central to understanding the mathematics of securities valuation.

The future value, FV, of an investment, I, made today will grow to

$$FV = I \left(1 + \frac{r}{m}\right)^{mn} \qquad (2.1)$$

where r is the periodic rate of interest, n is the number of years to maturity and m is the frequency of compounding per year. For example, an investment of $100 for four years at an interest rate of 10 percent compounded bi-annually will grow in four years to:

$$FV = \$100 \left(1 + \frac{0.10}{2}\right)^{8} = \$147.74$$

Now suppose the interest was compounded quarterly instead of bi-annually as in the previous example. The future value of the investment in this case will be:

$$FV = \$100 \left(1 + \frac{0.10}{4}\right)^{16} = \$148.45$$

In the limit, if interest were compounded continuously, our compounding formula given in (2.1) will assume the following form:

$$FV = Ie^{rn} \qquad (2.2)$$

where e is approximately equal to 2.71828 and is given by

$$e = \lim_{m \to \infty} \left(1 + \frac{1}{m}\right)^m \qquad (2.3)$$

where ∞ is the sign for infinity.

For our above example, the future value, assuming continuous compounding, will be

$$FV = \$100 \, (2.71828)^{0.10 \times 4} = \$149.18$$

In complex mathematical models, such as those developed for the valuation of options, interest rates are assumed to be continuously compounded. This assumption makes such models mathematically easier to handle.

The notion of compounding helped us to determine the future worth of an investment given the initial amount of investment and the relevant rate of interest. When valuing financial securities we are generally interested in knowing the present value of future cash flows. The present value, PV, of a nominal sum received n years from today is given by

$$PV = \frac{C}{\left(1 + \frac{r}{m}\right)^{mn}} \qquad (2.4)$$

where

C = cash flow received at time n
r = the rate of interest
m = number of times interest is compounded per year
n = number of years to maturity

For example, the present value of a sum of \$100 to be received at the end of year four when the interest rate is 10 percent compounded bi-annually is

$$PV = \frac{\$100}{\left(1 + \frac{0.10}{2}\right)^8} = \$67.68$$

To see the effect of more frequent compounding let us assume that the interest is compounded quarterly in the above example. The present value in this case will be

$$PV = \frac{\$100}{\left(1 + \dfrac{0.10}{4}\right)^{16}} = \$67.36$$

When interest is compounded continuously, the present value of a cash flow, C, at the end of year n is

$$PV = \frac{C}{e^{rn}} \tag{2.5}$$

In solving present value problems, it is useful to separate the interest factor from the cash flow to be discounted so that formula (2.4) can be rewritten as

$$PV = C\left[\frac{1}{\left(1 + \dfrac{r}{m}\right)^{mn}}\right] \tag{2.6}$$

The term in brackets is generally referred to as the discount factor and the interest rate, r, is sometimes called the discount rate.

Equation (2.6) provides the basis for valuing longer term securities such as bonds. For money market instruments, where interest is generally quoted on the simple basis, the issue of bringing in the compounding effect does not arise. For such securities the discount factor is defined as

$$\frac{1}{1 + r\,\dfrac{D}{b}} \tag{2.7}$$

where r is the quoted interest rate, D is the number of days between the valuation date and the maturity date and b is the interest basis, i.e. 360 or 365. Consider an interest-bearing USD certificate of deposit paying an interest rate of 10 percent with 95 days to maturity. What will be the value of this CD if the face value were $100?

Using Equation (2.7) we have

$$\$100\left[\frac{1}{1 + 0.10 \times \dfrac{95}{360}}\right] = \$97.428$$

It is important to note the difference between money market and bond market securities valuation methods. The difference arises because while in the case of the former, interest is quoted and paid on a simple basis, in the case of the latter interest is quoted and paid on a compound basis. A quoted compound interest rate implies that both principal and interest are re-invested periodically at the quoted rate. A simple interest rate is calculated and paid at maturity.

An m times compounded interest rate can be converted into an annually compounded rate as

$$r_{ann} = \left(1 + \frac{r_m}{m}\right)^m - 1 \qquad (2.8)$$

where r_{ann} is the annually compounded interest rate, r_m is the m-period compounded rate and m is the frequency of compounding. An annually compounded rate can also be converted into an m-period compounded rate by using

$$r_m = m\left[(1 + r_{ann})^{\frac{1}{m}} - 1\right] \qquad (2.9)$$

THE TERM STRUCTURE OF INTEREST RATES

In describing the notions of compounding and discounting we implicitly assumed that there was only one interest rate prevailing in the market with which to compound or discount a cash flow. In general, this assumption does not represent reality.[1] In practice, there are several interest rates prevailing in an economy at any point in time. There are interest rates applicable to investments of different maturities. For example, there is an interest rate applicable to a one-year investment which is generally different from interest rates applicable to investments of other maturities such as a ten-year investment. Then there are interest rates that apply to government bonds while there are others that apply to risky corporate bonds or swaps. The term structure of interest rates represents the relationship between interest rates and the time to maturity. The representation of interest rates along the dimension of credit risk is referred to as the risk structure of interest rates. In this section we will ignore the effects of credit risk on securities valuation.

To most investors the term structure of interest rates is synonymous with the yield curve for government securities. Government securities form the benchmark for pricing other securities in the market. At any time there is a series of government securities trading in the market that will be priced more or less in accord with a set of discount rates and the associated implied forward interest rates. The most popular way of representing the term structure is the set of yields to maturity on the most recently issued (on-the-run) government securities.

Yield-to-maturity

Yield to maturity of a bond is the single discount rate that equates the

---

[1] Strictly speaking, this assumption only holds when the yield curve is flat.

price of the bond with the present value of its future cash flow. It is the rate, Y, that solves the bond pricing equation:

$$P = \sum_{t=1}^{mn} \frac{\frac{C}{m}}{\left(1 + \frac{Y}{m}\right)^t} + \frac{B}{\left(1 + \frac{Y}{m}\right)^{mn}}$$ (2.10)

where
   P = current price of the bond
   C = the coupon
   m = frequency of interest compounding per year
   B = the face value of the bond
   Y = yield to maturity

Yield to maturity is a useful summary measure of a bond's return. It is indeed the most popular measure used both by traders and investors. However, it suffers from some major shortcomings that reduce its usefulness in valuing other securities. First, it assumes that the bond will be held to maturity and that all intermediate cash flows will be invested at this rate. In reality, this assumption is unlikely to hold so that the realized return on a bond will almost certainly be different from its yield to maturity. Second, in a term structure context, even for a homogeneous class of bonds there will not be a unique yield to maturity for a given maturity sector because bonds of the same maturity but carrying different coupons will generally have different yields to maturity.

Despite its shortcomings yield to maturity is commonly used to analyze the returns of fixed income securities of different maturities. However, for valuation of other securities yield to maturity is an inappropriate measure because, by definition, it assumes that investors use the same discount factor to value all cash flows of a bond irrespective of their timing. This assumption would only hold if the yield curve were flat, i.e. if yields on bonds of all maturities were equal. In reality, however, yield curves can assume a variety of shapes.

It is easy to see why yield to maturity cannot be used to value other securities if we note that it is not the yield to maturity that determines a bond's price. In fact it is the other way around. Yield to maturity is a measure that is dependent on a known price for the bond. To value other securities we therefore need to look at other factors (measures of value) that determine bond prices at any point in time. As discussed below, spot rates provide the answer.

Spot rates

The spot rate of interest for a given maturity is defined as the yield to maturity on a zero coupon bond of that maturity. Since spot rates are unique to a maturity, they express the time value of money in an accurate fashion. At any point in time, demand and supply forces for capital combine to determine spot rates for each period in time. These rates are then used to value packages of future cash flows. Bonds are just one example of these packages of cash flows. Other financial packages of cash flows such as interest rate swaps can also be valued using spot rates. We will have more to say about that later. Here, let us rewrite our bond pricing Equation (2.6) to correspond to spot discount rates.

$$P = \sum_{t=1}^{mn} \frac{\frac{C}{m}}{\left(1 + \frac{r_t}{m}\right)^t} + \frac{B}{\left(1 + \frac{r_{mn}}{m}\right)^{mn}} \tag{2.11}$$

where r_t is the spot discount rate for time t. Note that, unlike the implicit use of a single discount rate in the yield to maturity calculation, a different spot rate is used to discount each cash flow.

Application of Equation (2.11) to value any financial security would be trivial if zero coupon bonds for various maturities traded in the market. In reality, however, zero coupon bonds are not issued with any regularity by governments and businesses. Even where zero coupon bonds exist, they may not span the whole term structure. Fortunately, it is possible to infer spot rates from the prices of regular (coupon-bearing) bonds or, equivalently, from their yields to maturity.

To analyze the returns of various securities or portfolios it may be desirable to construct the yield curve or the term structure of spot rates from all government bonds that are currently available with various terms to maturity. Regression techniques are usually employed to construct such a curve. For valuation purposes, however, the term structure given by the most recently issued (on-the-run) risk free bonds of various maturities is more suitable since liquidity and other considerations such as tax and call features usually distort the true time value aspects of off-the-run bonds. For such bonds, spot rates can be calculated using the following iterative formula:

$$r_n = \left[\frac{1 + Y_n}{1 - Y_n \sum_{t=1}^{n-1} \left(\frac{1}{1 + r_t}\right)^t} \right]^{\frac{1}{n}} - 1 \tag{2.12}$$

where

r_n = n-period spot rate
Y_n = yield to maturity of the n-period bond.

Equation (2.12) must be solved iteratively to obtain spot rates for all maturities. Notice that the yield to maturity of a one-period bond (such as one-year bonds if annual compounding is assumed) is, by definition, the one-period spot rate since there are no intermediate cash flows hence no re-investment risk. Therefore, Equation (2.12) is used to obtain spot rates for subsequent periods. It should also be noted that Equation (2.12) is exact only for par bonds, i.e. bonds whose yield to maturity is equal to its coupon rate. For non-par bonds Equation (2.12) will result in an error. The magnitude of the error will depend on the extent of deviation from the par. For the purposes of constructing spot yield curves from recently issued bonds, however, Equation (2.12) will be fairly accurate. Table 2.1 contains zero coupon yields calculated from par bond yields using Equation (2.12).

Table 2.1 Zero Coupon Yield Curve

Term (years)	Par Bond Yield	Zero Coupon Yield
1	9%	9%
2	9.3%	9.316%
3	9.6%	9.639%
4	9.8%	9.86%
5	9.9%	9.97%

Spot rates not only allow us to value any arbitrary set of cash flows, they can also be used to impute the market expectations of how interest rates are likely to behave in future. Expected future rates, or forward rates as they are called, are important for derivatives valuation.

Forward rates

A spot interest rate applies to financial commitments such as loans made today and repaid at some later date. As we have seen, at any point in time there can be a one-year spot rate, a two-year spot rate and so on, applicable to financial commitments of these terms. A forward rate, on the other hand, is the interest rate on money to be loaned in the future for a given period with the contract made today. Thus, at any time there can be a forward rate for one-year loan beginning in one year, another one in two years and so on. There can also be a forward rate for a two-year loan beginning in one year's time or later.

The importance of forward rates in forward contracts is obvious. Forward rates also provide investors with the market consensus on expected future spot rates. This consensus may or may not be in accord with an individual investor's views. Investment strategies can be devised that incorporate the disparity of views between an individual investor's expectations of future interest rates and that of the market consensus, i.e. forward rates.

Forward rates can be implied from spot rates in a straightforward way if the data are suitably spaced. Spot rates and forward rates are, by definition, related according to the following formula:[2]

$$(1 + \tilde{r}_{i,\,t-i})^t = \frac{(1 + r_t)^t}{(1 + r_{t-i})^{t-i}} \qquad (2.13)$$

Where $\tilde{r}_{i,\,t-i}$ is the i-period forward rate for money to be loaned t-i periods from now. If this relationship does not hold at any point in time, arbitrage opportunities will arise. Consider two alternative investment strategies:

1 Invest in a two-year zero coupon bond at 7 percent per year.
2 Invest in a one-year bond at 6 percent and enter into a forward contract to lend the proceeds from the bond for one year at the end of year one at the forward rate $\tilde{r}_{1,\,1}$.

We can easily establish that a two-year bond with a face value of 100 must sell for $\left[\frac{1}{(1+0.07)^2}\right]$ $100 i.e. $87.344. Thus, if we invest $87.344 for two years at an annual rate of 7 percent it will grow in two years' time to $87.344 $(1+0.07)^2$ = $100. However, the payment on a two-year bond can be considered the result of investment for two years at two potentially different rates. Thus, under the second alternative, the initial investment of $87.344 would grow to $87.344 $(1 + r_1)$ at the end of year one and $87.344 $(1+r_1)$ $(1 + \tilde{r}_{1,1})$ at the end of the second year. Since we know that the one-year rate, r_1, is 6 percent and that the value of the investment in two years must be $100 we can infer the forward rate, $\tilde{r}_{1,1}$, from the following equation

$87.344 $(1 + r_1)$ $(1 + \tilde{r}_{1,1})$ = $100

or

$87.344 $(1 + 0.06)$ $(1 + \tilde{r}_{1,1})$ = $100

$\tilde{r} = 8.01\%$

Therefore, the implied forward rate for money loaned in one year's time for a period of one year is 8.01 percent. If this rate were greater than 8.01 percent investors would use the second investment alternative because they would be assured of earning more than 7 percent on a two-year investment. If this rate were less than 8.01 percent, investors could make a risk-free profit by borrowing for one year and simultaneously selling a one-year forward contract and investing for two years at the two-year spot rate.

---

[2] In general

$\dfrac{d_{t1}}{d_{t2}} = 1 + \tilde{r}_{t1,\,t2}$ where $\tilde{r}$ is expressed in terms of time $t1$ and $t2$ and d is the discount factor for $t1$ and $t2$.

Notice that spot rates are a geometric average of forward rates, while forward rates can be thought of as the marginal cost of borrowing or lending over a future period of time. It is important to distinguish between implied forward rates from the spot rates expected to prevail in the future. In fact, there is much debate among economists on the point of relationship between forward rates and the spot rates expected to prevail in the future. This debate is at the heart of economists' attempt to explain the term structure or the shape of the spot rate yield curve.

Historically, positively sloped yield curves have been more common. When the curve is positively sloped, long-term spot rates exceed short-term spot rates implying that forward rates are higher, the further in the future a financial commitment begins. Such yield curves tend to be associated with periods of normal or low short-term interest rates.

In periods when short-term rates are high and 'sticky', the yield curve may assume a flat shape implying that all forward rates are roughly the same.

In periods of high inflation when tighter monetary policy may result in abnormally high short-term interest rates, the yield curve may be falling or 'humped.' A negatively sloped yield curve implies that forward rates are generally smaller, the further in the future a financial commitment begins.

Figure 2.1 shows the general relationship among par yields; spot rates and forward rates in the rising, flat and falling yield curve environments.

Term structure theories

Three theories that attempt to explain the shape of the yield curve have received the widest attention. They are:

1 The expectations theory
2 The liquidity preference theory, and
3 The preferred habitat theory.

The expectations theory postulates that forward rates represent the market consensus of the expected futures spot rates.[3] Thus, a rising yield curve suggests that future interest rates will be higher while a falling yield curve suggests that future interest rates will be lower. The theory implies that:

---

[3] There are several versions of expectations hypothesis, some of them at odds with each other. We will have more to say about these when describing the continuous time term structure models for option pricing.

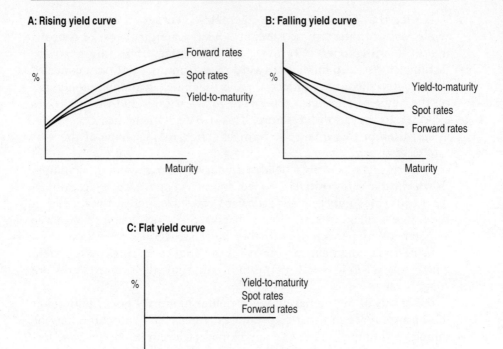

Fig 2.1 Par, spot and forward interest rate relationships

- the implied forward rates are unbiased estimators of futures spot rates,
- the expected holding period returns over any period will be the same for all bond investment strategies, and
- yields on long-term bonds are equal to an average of the present yield on a short-term bond plus expected future yields on short-term bonds after rolling over. In other words, long-term spot rates are an average of current short-term spot rates and a sequence of forward rates or expected spot rates. This last implication is believed to account for the observed tendency of short-term yields to fluctuate more than the long-term yields as shown in Figure 2.2.

The expectations hypothesis has been challenged on several counts. First, while its general approach is reasonably consistent with experience, its implication that upward sloping curves are as likely as downward sloping curves is contrary to empirical experience. Second, the assumption that all bonds are perfect substitutes for all investors is inconsistent with investor behavior in the real world. Third, the theory assumes that investors are risk neutral which is also at odds with reality.

Fig 2.2 Monthly volatility of US Treasury bills/bond yields

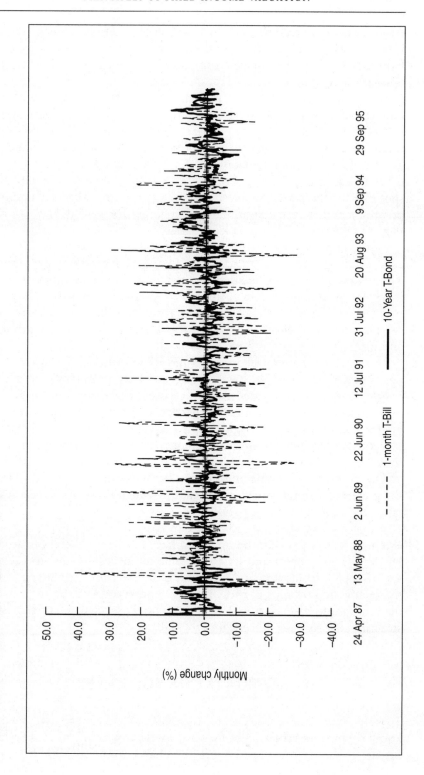

Despite these shortcomings, as we will note when describing interest rate options valuation using continuous time models, the expectations hypothesis plays the same pivotal role that risk neutrality does for option pricing.

The proponents of the liquidity preference theory agree with the importance of expected future spot rates but place more weight on the effects of the risk preferences of market participants. This theory postulates that risk aversion will cause forward rates to be systematically greater than expected spot rates, usually increasing with maturity. In other words it implies that each forward rate will equal the expected spot rate for the period in question plus a premium, called the liquidity premium, and that this premium will be larger for periods that are further into the future.

Liquidity preference theory explains the observed shapes of the yield curves with greater consistency than does the expectations hypothesis. The primary criticism levelled against it is that it assumes that all investors prefer short-term securities to long-term securities. In practice, that need not be the case. There are certain investor classes such as pension funds who have a natural preference for long-term bonds and for whom short-term bonds pose higher risk.

The preferred habitat theory takes the above criticism into account. It postulates that investors have strong maturity preferences and that bonds of different maturities trade in separate and distinct markets. The demand and supply of bonds of a particular maturity are little affected by the prices of bonds of neighbouring maturities. Sometimes this theory is relaxed to assume that investor habitats are not fixed thereby creating some dependence among yields in nearby maturities.

The liquidity preference model can be considered a special case of the preferred habitat model in the case in which investors have a habitat of the shortest holding period.

While empirical evidence backs up each of the theories to some extent, tests suggest that the preferred habitat theory receives relatively less validation. The liquidity preference hypothesis seems to receive some support from empirical evidence. It is, however, difficult to assess the relative importance of these theories in determining the term structure. It should also be noted that none of these theories of the term structure incorporates uncertainty formally.

FORWARD EXCHANGE RATES

To value currency forward contracts and currency swaps we need to know the current structure of forward foreign exchange rates. Forward foreign exchange rates can be inferred from current spot interest rates in any two currencies and their spot exchange rate using the interest rate parity theorem. The interest rate parity theorem holds that the ratio of the forward and spot exchange rates will equal the ratio of foreign and domestic interest rates. The theorem can be expressed as the following equation:

$$\frac{X_t}{X_0} = \left[\frac{1 + \left(\frac{n}{N}\right) r_{ft}}{1 + \left(\frac{n}{N}\right) r_{dt}}\right] \tag{2.14}$$

or

$$X_t = X_0 \left[\frac{1 + \left(\frac{n}{N}\right) r_{ft}}{1 + \left(\frac{n}{N}\right) r_{dt}}\right]$$

where

X_t = forward exchange rate for time t expressed as units of foreign currency per unit of domestic currency

X_0 = spot exchange rate expressed as units of foreign currency per unit of domestic currency

r_{ft} = foreign spot interest rate for time t

r_{dt} = domestic spot interest rate for time t

n = number of days up to forward date

N = number of days in a year

For example, if the one-year foreign spot interest rate is 10 percent while the one year domestic spot interest rate is 5 percent and the spot exchange rate is 2, the forward exchange rate at the end of one year will be

$$X_1 = 2 \left[\frac{1 + 0.10}{1 + 0.05}\right] = 2.095$$

i.e. 2.095 units of foreign currency per unit of domestic currency.

Equation 2.14 also suggests that, in the absence of market imperfections, risk adjusted expected real returns on financial assets will be the same in foreign markets as in domestic markets. Equilibrium among the spot exchange rate, forward exchange rate and the domestic and foreign spot interest rates is achieved through covered interest arbitrage.

When the foreign interest rate is higher than the domestic interest rate (positive differential) the forward exchange rate will be at a discount from the foreign currency's point of view. In other words, the foreign currency will be expected to depreciate against the local currency. Reverse will be the case when interest differentials are negative.

SUMMARY

This chapter has provided a primer on the principles of fixed income valuation. In an economy that is characterized by positive interest rates, the time value of money is a key concept of valuation. The time value of money is captured through two simple but important notions: compounding and discounting. These concepts are central to understanding the mathematics of securities valuation.

Interest rates can be expressed along several dimensions. The most important dimension, however, is the time to maturity. Interest rates for various terms to maturity form the term structure of interest rates or simply the yield curve. For the valuation of arbitrary packages of cash flows the term structure of par yields, i.e. yields-to-maturity on par bonds, is less useful than the term structure of spot or zero coupon yields. Zero coupon yields allow investors to value any arbitrary set of cash flows. Spot notes also allow us to imply forward rates. Spot rates in two currencies in conjunction with the current exchange rate allow us to calculate the forward foreign exchange rate.

References

Baumol, W.S. and Quandt, R.E., 'Investment and Discount Rates under Capital Rationing', *Economic Journal*, June 1965, pp. 317–29.

Fama, E.F., 'The Information in the Term Structure', *Journal of Financial Economics*, December 1984, pp. 509–28.

Fama, E.F., and Miller, M.H., *The Theory of Finance*, New York: Holt, Rinehart and Winston, 1972.

Fisher, I., 'Appreciation and Interest', *Publications of the American Economic Association*, August 1896, pp. 23–9, 91–2.

Hick, J.R., *Value and Capital*, 2nd edn, London: Oxford University Press, 1946.

Hirshleifer, J., *Investment, Interest and Capital*, Englewood Cliffs, N.J.: Prentice Hall, 1970.

Lutz, F.A., 'The Structure of Interest Rates', *Quarterly Journal of Economics*, November 1940, pp. 36–63.

Malkiel, B.G., 'Expectations, Bond Prices and the Term Structure of Interest Rates', *Quarterly Journal of Economics*, May 1962, pp. 197–218.

Meiselman, D., *The Term Structure of Interest Rates*. Princeton, N.J.: Princeton University Press, 1966.

Nelson, C., *The Term Structure of Interest Rates*, New York: Basic Books, 1972.

Sharpe, W.F., *Investments*, 3rd edn, Englewood Cliffs, N.J.: Prentice Hall, 1985.

3

PRINCIPLES OF OPTIONS VALUATION

General properties of option prices

A primer on binomial distribution

A one-period option pricing model

Multiperiod binomial option pricing

Continuous time option pricing

Black and Scholes option pricing model

Summary

So far, we have been concerned with valuation in an absolute sense. That is, our aim has been to determine a specific value for a series of expected cash flows promised by a security. The fixed income valuation tools, as we have seen, allow us to value any arbitrary set of cash flows. As we will note later, these tools are sufficient to value derivative securities with symmetric payoffs such as forward contracts and swaps. To value derivatives with asymmetric payoffs, such as options, we need to develop a framework for relative valuation since the payoffs of an option are relative rather than absolute.

To make matters easy, we will restrict our analysis to European style calls and puts which can only be exercised at their expiration date. This type of option differs from American style calls and puts that can be exercised at any time up to and including their expiration date. American style options introduce additional complications to the valuation and, thereby, tend to cloud the underlying principles. Much of the valuation framework can be developed either in terms of a call or a put, but, given the popularity of call options we will begin our exposition with these options and then show how the valuation techniques can be applied to puts. To develop the valuation framework, we will assume that the underlying security is a non-dividend paying stock. Not only are such options easier to value, they also provide greater insight into the economic principles involved.

A European style call option gives its buyer the right to buy the underlying stock at the expiration date at a given price (the strike price). The buyer of the call pays a price (option premium) to the seller of the call for this privilege. The seller of the call, on the other hand, undertakes to sell the underlying stock at the expiration date at the given (strike) price should the buyer choose to exercise the option. The buyer of the call will only exercise the option if it results in an economic gain. Otherwise the option will expire worthless. The value of the call option at its expiration date is simply

$$C_T = \text{Max}(S_T - E, 0) \tag{3.1}$$

and the value of a put at its expiration date is

$$P_T = \text{Max}(E - S_T, 0) \tag{3.2}$$

where

C_T = value of the call at the expiration date T
P_T = value of the put at the expiration date T
S_T = market price of one share of the underlying stock at time T

E = exercise price

Suppose an investor buys a call option giving the investor the right to buy one share of XYZ stock at its expiration date at a strike price of $100. Now if the price of XYZ stock at the option expiration date is greater than its strike price of $100 the investor will exercise the option. Otherwise the call will expire worthless. Suppose at expiration XYZ stock trades at $150. What will be the value of the call? Equation (3.1) gives

$$C_T = \text{Max}(S_T - E, 0)$$
$$= \text{Max}(150 - 100, 0)$$
$$= \$50$$

That is, the investor exercises the call option to buy the underlying stock at the strike price of $100 and immediately sells it at the current market price of $150 to make a gain of $50.

In the case of puts, the investor will exercise the option if the price of the underlying stock at the expiration date is below the strike price.

The possible values of calls and puts at expiration are depicted graphically in Figure 3.1. Notice that, in the case of call options, the option has a positive value when the stock price exceeds the exercise price and increases linearly with the increase in the price of the underlying stock. Similarly, in the case of puts, the option has a positive value when the price of the underlying stock is below the strike price and rises linearly with the fall in the stock price.

To determine the gain or loss to the purchaser of a call or a put we must take into account the premiums paid for the option. This gain or loss is simply the difference between the value of the option at its expiration and the amount of premium paid. Figure 3.2 shows the possible payoffs to the call and put option purchasers at expiration where C and P represent option premium paid for calls and puts respectively.

The corresponding gains and losses for the call and put option sellers are depicted in Figure 3.3. Notice that the payoffs to option sellers

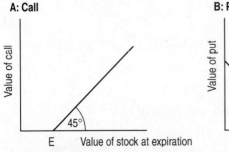
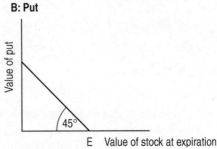

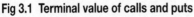

Fig 3.1 Terminal value of calls and puts

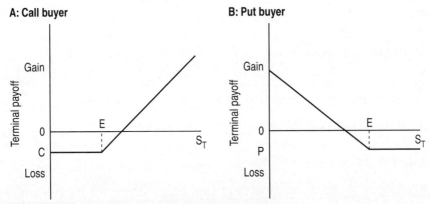

Fig 3.2 Terminal payoff to call and put option buyers

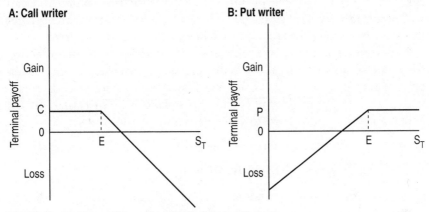

Fig 3.3 Terminal payoff to call and put option sellers

are a mirror image of the payoffs to option buyers. In other words options are a zero sum game.

GENERAL PROPERTIES OF OPTION PRICES

Before we proceed to describe various option valuation methods it will be useful to consider some of the general features of option valuation. While we will restrict the discussion to stock options, the underlying principles can be easily extended to other types of options.

Factors affecting the option price

From our discussion so far, it is easy to establish that the value of calls and puts on stock must depend on the following three variables:

- stock price, S
- exercise price, E
- time to expiration.

In addition to these three (obvious) factors there are two other important (but less obvious) factors that affect the option's value. These are:

- the instantaneous variance of the rate of return on the underlying stock (stock price volatility)
- risk-free rate of interest.

Remember that calls and puts are contingent claims. In other words, the call holder gains only under the condition that the stock price exceeds the exercise price at expiration (for European options) or on early exercise (for American options). Therefore, the holder of a call will prefer more volatility to less. The greater the volatility, the greater the probability that the stock price will exceed the exercise price.

Risk-free rate of interest is the least intuitive of all factors affecting the value of an option. As we will note later, however, it is a crucial pricing parameter because, within the Black and Scholes pricing framework, risk-free interest rate is the appropriate rate of return on the hedge portfolio that is used to value calls and puts on stock.

Arbitrage bounds on options pricing

Using arbitrage arguments, we can define various boundary conditions that a precise options valuation model must satisfy. For stock options, some of the important restrictions are briefly described below.

1 Options are securities with limited liability. That is because an option holder's liability is limited to the premium paid for the option. Hence, the value of an option can never be negative. That is

   $C \geqslant 0$ and $P \geqslant 0$

2 On its expiration, the value of a European call must be either $S_T - E$ or zero. That is because the option holder will exercise the option only if the stock price is greater than the exercise price of the call option. Formally,

   $C = \max(S_T - E, 0)$

   Similarly, the value of a European put at its expiration must be either $E - S_T$ or zero. That is

   $P = \max(E - S_T, 0)$

3 Since an American option can be exercised at any time up to its expiration date, it must be worth at least its intrinsic value at any point in time to avoid the opportunity of risk-free profit that could be made by buying the option and exercising it immediately. That is,

$$C' \geqslant S - E$$
$$P' \geqslant E - S$$

4 Since an American option offers greater flexibility in terms of the timing of exercise, it must be worth at least the same as a European option with similar terms, but that can be exercised only at expiration. That is,

$$C' \geqslant C$$

and

$$P' \geqslant P$$

where C' and P' are premiums for American calls and puts respectively.

5 Since the right to buy a security cannot be worth more than the value of the security itself, the price of the call option cannot exceed the security price. That is,

$$C \leqslant S$$

Similarly, the value of a European put cannot exceed the exercise price of the option because that is what it would pay at expiration should stock price, S, drop to zero. That is,

$$P \leqslant E$$

Put-call parity

Put-call parity refers to the relationship between the price of a put and the price of a call written on the same stock and with the same exercise price and expiration date. It can be shown that the payoff of a European call at its expiration date can be replicated by a long position in the stock and a put written on the same stock.

To show this precisely, let us consider two portfolios. The first portfolio consists of a long position in the call and the second portfolio comprises a stock purchased at price S; a European put purchased at price P, and a borrowing of $PV(E)$ to finance the transaction. The payoffs for the two portfolios are given below:

Portfolio strategy	Payoff at expiration	
	$S_T < E$	$S_T > E$
(a) Buy call	0	$S_T - E$
(b) Buy share	S_T	S_T
Buy put	$E - S_T$	0
Borrow	$- E$	$- E$
Net payoff on (b)	0	$S_T - E$

Since the two portfolios have the same payoff under all scenarios, they must initially cost the same. Hence we have the put-call relationship:

$$C = S + P - PV\ (E)$$

and

$$P = C - S + PV\ (E)$$

A PRIMER ON BINOMIAL DISTRIBUTION

We know that the value of a stock option depends crucially, among other things, upon the price of the underlying stock at its expiration. Any option pricing model must therefore assume a sensible description of stock price at option expiration. In this section we will describe the basics of such a distribution. Consider a game of chance in which, on n successive turns, a ball is drawn from an opaque urn containing 100 balls of which k are black and 100-k are white.[1] After each drawing the ball is replaced so that the composition of balls in the urn remains the same for each trial. Suppose the rules of the game allow you to bet only at the beginning of the game. Thereafter, in each trial, for every $1 initially bet you receive $u for every dollar accumulated up to then if a black ball is drawn or $d if a white ball is drawn. We assume that $u > d$.

Let q denote the probability of drawing a black ball and $p = 1-q$ denote the probability of drawing a white ball. Further let the experiment be repeated n times and let x denote the total number of black balls that will be drawn in the n repetitions of the experiment. In terms of this notation the basic problem is to find the probability distribution of the random variable x. In problems of this type, it is assumed that the n trials are independent and therefore multiplicative. A sequence of independent trials, such as in our example, in which the probability of a particular event, such as drawing the black ball, is the same for all trials is called a sequence of Bernouli trials in honour of a Swiss mathematician who pioneered the study of probability distributions.

---

[1] See Kendall and Stuart (1967) for an excellent introduction to the binomial distribution.

To find the probability distribution of x we first calculate the probabilities of all possible sequences of outcomes and then add the probabilities of those sequences that yield the same value of x. To explain this point let us turn to our game of chance. Suppose you decide to bet $1 in this game. The possible outcomes after three drawings can be shown in the form of a tree diagram (Figure 3.4).

The tree shows that after the first trial there are two possible outcomes; you either receive $u or $d. At the end of the second trial there are three possible outcomes (sequences); $uu, $ud or $dd. Similarly, at the end of the third trial the possible outcomes are $uuu, $uud, $udd or $ddd. If we assume $u = 1.2$ and $d = 0.8$ then after three games you are faced with four possible outcomes; your $1 could have grown to $u^3 = (1.2)^3 = 1.73$ or $(1.2)^2 0.8 = 1.152$ or it could have fallen to $1.2 (0.8)^2 = 0.77$ or $(0.8)^3 = 0.51$.

Notice that these outcomes follow a pattern. This pattern becomes clear if we represent the outcomes in the form of what is known as Pascal's triangle. In this triangle, each row is constructed from the sum of the numbers in the adjacent two columns in the row immediately above it.

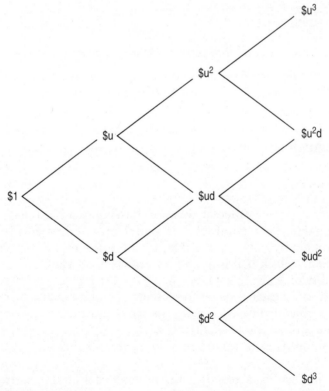

Fig 3.4 Bernouli trails

Number of trials (n)	Pascal's triangle
0	1
1	1 1
2	1 2 1
3	1 3 3 1
4	1 4 6 4 1

The numbers in the rows of Pascal's triangle are the coefficients for a binomial expansion, $(a+b)^n$. For example, if $n=3$ and we wish to know the coefficients in $[q+(1-q)]^3$, they are 1,3,3,and 1 from row four of Pascal's triangle; that is

$$1q^3 + 3q^2(1-q) + 3q(1-q)^2 + 1(1-q)^2$$

This enumeration can be easily confirmed from the above tree diagram. Notice that the sum of the numbers in each row is 2^n.

For large numbers Pascal's triangle becomes cumbersome. Given that our problem is to figure out various possible outcomes and not the order in which they occur, this is a combination problem of choosing j things from n things. The coefficients of various sequences are given by:

$$\binom{n}{j} = \frac{n!}{(n-j)!\,j!} \tag{3.3}$$

$\binom{n}{j}$ is the number of combinations of n things chosen j at a time.[2] For example, what are the possible ways of drawing two black balls in three trials ($n=3$) in our game of chance? The answer can be found using Equation (3.3)

$$\binom{3}{2} = \frac{3!}{(3-2)!\,2!}$$

$$= \frac{3.2.1}{(1)2.1} = \frac{6}{2} = 3$$

That is, there are three different ways of drawing two black balls in a three trial game. In general, the binomial probability of any one sequence containing j drawings of black balls, given that the probability of drawing a black ball is q, and $n-j$ drawings of white balls, given the probability of drawing a white ball is $(1-q)$, is $q^j(1-q)^{n-j}$.

In general, since each sequence represents one of the mutually exclusive ways in which the desired event can occur and each such sequence has the same probability of occurring, i.e. $q^j(1-q)^{n-j}$, it follows that the desired probability is obtained by adding this probability as many

---

[2] The term $n!$ (read n factorial) is the product of all numbers from n down to 1.

times as there are sequences. This number of sequences, as noted above, is given by $\binom{n}{j}$; therefore, the probability of $x_n = j$ or the probability of obtaining j black balls out of n is obtained by[3]

$$x_n = \frac{n!}{j!\,(n-j)!} q^j\,(1-q)^{n-j} \tag{3.4}$$

This formula gives the probability of obtaining j black balls in n Bernouli trials where the probability of occurrence in a single trial is q. The random variable x is commonly called the binomial variable and Equation (3.4) gives the binomial distribution.

A ONE PERIOD OPTION PRICING MODEL

To develop the framework for option pricing we make very restrictive assumptions to begin with. In particular we assume a simple dynamics for the underlying stock price over the term of the option. The objective of this section is not to develop a complete option pricing model but rather to provide an insight into the fundamental principles that underlie such valuation.

In this section we will develop a simple approach to price an option with one period to expiry to buy one share of the underlying stock currently trading at S.[4] We will assume that at the end of one period the price of this stock can go up by a factor of u to Su (with probability q) or fall by a factor of d to Sd (with probability $1-q$). Thus, there are only two possibilities for the end-of-period stock price. Further, we also make the following simplifying assumptions;

1 Investors can borrow or lend money at the risk free rate of r per period.[5]

2 Investors can buy and sell short any fraction of the underlying stock.[6]

Consider an option to buy one share of stock with a current price, S, of $100. Suppose the option has one period to expiry[7] and that at the end

---

[3] See P J Hoel.

[4] This section utilizes the brilliant approach originated by William Sharpe, Professor of Finance at Stanford University.

[5] We require $u > 1 + r > d$. If these inequalities did not hold, there would be opportunities for riskless arbitrage involving trading in the underlying stock and borrowing or lending at the risk free rate.

[6] In practice, a share of stock is not divisible. This assumption is made for convenience of mathematical exposition.

[7] The period is arbitrary.

of this period the stock price can go up by 25 percent (u=1+0.25 = 1.25) or fall by 25 percent (d=1-0.25 = 0.75). Thus, at the end of the period the price can either be Su= \$100(1.25) =\$125 or Sd = \$100 (0.75) = \$75. What would a call option written on this stock with an exercise price, E, of \$100 cost today? To answer this question we employ the key insight provided by Black and Scholes that the payoff structure of this particular option contract at its expiration can be exactly duplicated by a levered portfolio consisting of a specific proportion of the underlying stock and certain amount of one-period borrowing.

If we can construct such a portfolio and show that it is risk-free under all scenarios, we can determine a unique price for the option. This price must be acceptable to all investors irrespective of their views on the direction of the underlying stock's price movements.

Given our assumptions about the future price of the underlying stock we can easily determine the end-of-period range of values for the call option in our example. Since we have assumed that the underlying stock can only assume two possible values at the option's expiration, it follows that the call option can also have only two possible values at the expiration date associated with each of the assumed prices for the underlying stock. Thus, if the stock price at expiration turns out to be Su the option will be worth

C_u = Max ($Su - E$, 0)

= Max (125–100, 0) = \$25

Similarly, if the stock price at expiration turns out to be Sd, the option will be worth

C_d = Max ($Sd - E$, 0)

= Max(75–100, 0)=\$0

It is convenient to depict the end-of-period values for the stock prices, Su and Sd, and the associated end-of-period call values, C_u and C_d in terms of the tree diagram in Figure 3.5.

Now consider forming a riskless hedge portfolio consisting of one short call option and h shares of the underlying stock.[8] The initial cost of establishing the position will be hS minus the option premium, C, received from writing one call i.e. $hS - C$. The end-of-period values of the position will be either $hSu - C_u$ if the stock price moves up to Su or $hSd - C_d$ if the stock price moves down to Sd. This portfolio will be riskless only if the end-of-period payoffs are the same irrespective of

---

[8] Traded options are generally traded in multiples of 100 shares of stock per option. To simplify our derivation we assume that each option contract gives the holder the right to buy or sell one share of the underlying stock.

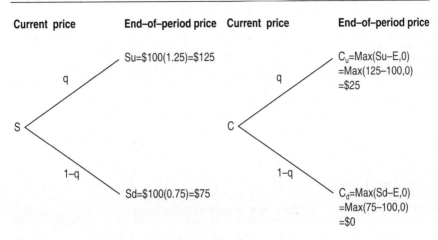

Fig 3.5 End-of-period stock prices and call values

whether the stock price moves up to *Su* or down to *Sd*. This condition can written as

$$hSu - C_u = hSd - C_d$$

The proportion of stock or the hedge ratio, *h*, can be implied from this equation. Solving for *h* we obtain

$$h = \frac{C_u - C_d}{Su - Sd} \qquad (3.5)$$

The hedge ratio for our example will therefore be

$$h = \frac{\$25 - \$0}{\$125 - \$75} = 0.50$$

A useful insight into the hedge ratio can be gained by plotting the relationship between the possible end-of-period call prices and the possible end-of-period stock prices. Figure 3.6 depicts this relationship for our example. Notice that since there are only two possible outcomes, both of them lie on a straight line which means that the end-of-period returns on the call and the underlying stock are perfectly correlated. It is, therefore, possible to hedge the returns on one security with the returns on the other security and thereby eliminate all risk. The proportion of underlying stock necessary to hedge exposure on a call option sold is simply the ratio of the difference between the end-of-period call prices and the end-of-period stock prices, i.e. the slope of the straight line as depicted in Figure 3.6.

Thus, for every call option sold we need to buy half a share of the underlying stock to ensure that the differences in the payoffs of the two positions are exactly equal. The end-of-period values for this portfolio

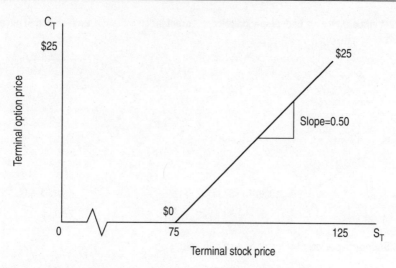

Fig 3.6 Relationship between end-of-period stock and call prices

will be \$37.50 irrespective of whether the stock price rises to \$125 or falls to \$75 as shown in Table 3.1.

Table 3.1 End-of-period payoffs of the hedge portfolio

	End-of-period stock price = \$125	End-of-period stock price =\$75
Value of 1/2 share held long	\$62.50	\$37.50
Value of one call sold	–\$25.00	\$0.00
Net Portfolio Value	\$37.50	\$37.50

By choosing h such that the end-of-period values of the portfolio are the same irrespective of whether the stock price moves up or down, we have established a risk-free or 'hedged' position. To avoid arbitrage, any net investment in the portfolio must, therefore, earn the risk free rate of interest for the period. In other words the initial cost of establishing this position $hS-C$ must grow at the risk free rate to be equal to the end-of-period value of the hedge portfolio. That is[9]

$$(hS - C)(1 + r) = hSu - C_u \tag{3.6}$$

---

9 or, equivalently

$$(hS - C)(1 + r) = hSd - C_d$$

46

By rewriting the arbitrage condition given by Equation (3.6) we can figure out the value of the call option, C, that must prevail today as under

$$C = \frac{[hS(1+r) + C_u - hSu]}{1+r} \tag{3.7}$$

Assuming risk-free interest rate of 10 percent for the term of the call we have for our example

$$C = \frac{[0.50(\$100)(1+0.10)+\$25-0.5(\$125)]}{1+0.10} = \$15.91$$

where
    $S = \$100$
    $u = 1.25$
    $Su = \$100(1.25) = \$125$
    $r = 0.10$ or 10%

Equation (3.7) can be simplified by substituting h from Equation (3.5)

$$C = \frac{C_u\left(\frac{(1+r)-d}{u-d}\right) + C_d\left(\frac{u-(1+r)}{u-d}\right)}{1+r} \tag{3.8}$$

If we let

$$p = \frac{(1+r)-d}{u-d}$$

and

$$1 - p = \frac{u-(1+r)}{u-d}$$

then

$$C = \frac{C_u p + C_d(1-p)}{1+r} \tag{3.9}$$

Using Equation (3.9) for our base case example we have

$$C = \frac{\$25\left[\frac{(1+0.10)-0.75}{1.25-0.75}\right] + \$0\left[\frac{1.25-(1+0.10)}{1.25-0.75}\right]}{1.1} = \$15.91$$

which is the same as given by Equation (3.7).

p can be regarded as the hedging probability. It has the properties of a probability because it is always between zero and one. In fact it can be

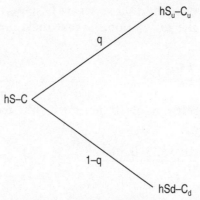

Fig 3.7 The payoff for a risk-free hedge portfolio

shown that p is the value q would assume in equilibrium if investors were risk neutral. For example, a risk neutral investor would require only the risk-free rate on a stock investment of S that will grow to Su with probability q and fall to Sd with probability $(1-q)$ at the end of the period. That is

$$S(1+r) = Suq + (1-q)Sd$$

or

$$q = \frac{(1+r) - d}{u-d} \tag{3.10}$$

Thus, for a risk neutral investor $p=q$ and Equation (3.8) can be interpreted as the expectation of the call option's discounted future value in a risk neutral world.[10] Parameters u and d represent the volatility of the underlying stock price.

For our base case example, the value of the call option today is $15.91. We can now show that, given our assumptions, this must be the consensus price for the call irrespective of whether the purchaser is bullish or bearish on the underlying stock. Any deviation from this price will result in opportunities for risk-free profit. Consider the net investment required to create our hedge portfolio, $hS-C$, i.e. $34.09 $(0.50($100)-$15.91=$34.09)$. Suppose the investor borrows this amount to create the hedge portfolio. The net investment of the investor in the portfolio is now zero and therefore, to avoid arbitrage, the net cash flows to the investor at the expiration of the option must, under all scenarios, also be zero as shown in Table 3.2.

---

[10] This does not imply that in equilibrium the required rate of return on call is the risk-free rate.

Table 3.2 Expiration value of the zero cost hedge portfolio

	Current value	Value if $S_T=\$125$	Value if $S_T=\$75$
Value of 1/2 stock bought	−$50.0	$62.50	$37.50
Value of call option sold	$15.91	−$25.0	$0
Borrowing at 10%	$34.09	−$37.50	−$37.50
Net value of portfolio	$0	$0	$0

Table 3.2 can be rearranged to show that an appropriately leveraged portfolio consisting of a position in the underlying stock and a borrowing duplicates the payoffs of the call option at its expiration date as shown in Table 3.3.

Table 3.3 Cash flows of a duplicating portfolio

	Current value	Value if $S_T=\$125$	Value if $S_T=\$75$
Value of 1/2 stock bought	−$50.0	$62.50	$37.50
Borrowing at 10%	$34.09	−$37.50	−$37.50
Net value of duplicating portfolio	−$15.91	$25.0	$0
Value of call option bought	−$15.91	$25.0	$0

Notice that the net value of the duplicating portfolio matches the payoffs of a call option under all scenarios. By constructing a duplicating portfolio that is risk-free under all scenarios, we are able to determine a unique price for the option. This price must be acceptable to all investors irrespective of their views on the direction of underlying stock's price movements.

To prove that the fair price of the call option must be $15.91, suppose the option sells for $10. We can, in this case, buy the underpriced call option and sell the underlying stock in the proportion given by the hedge ratio to make riskless profit. We would buy a call option and sell (short) half a share of the underlying stock and lend $34.09 to generate a riskless profit of $5.91 as shown in Table 3.4.

Table 3.4 Arbitrage profit from mispriced call option

	Current value	Value if $S_T=$125$	Value if $S_T=$75$
Value of 1/2 stock	$50.00	−$62.50	−$37.50
Value of call option	−$10.00	$25.00	$0
Lending at 10%	−$34.09	$37.50	$37.50
Arbitrage gain	$5.91	$0	$0

The strategy results in a net cash inflow of $5.91 today with no further obligation at the expiry of the option. As investors spot this arbitrage opportunity, the buying pressure on the call option will force its price up to its fair level. If, on the other hand, the price of the call option was greater than its fair price, say $20, we could sell the overpriced call, buy the underlying stock in the proportion given by the hedge ratio and borrow $34.09 to generate a riskless profit of $4.09 as shown in Table 3.5. In this case the selling pressure will force the price of the call to its fair level.

Table 3.5 Arbitrage profit from mispriced call option

	Current value	Value if $S_T=$125$	Value if $S_T=$75$
Value of 1/2 stock	−$50.00	$62.50	$37.50
Value of call option	$20.00	−$25.00	$0
Borrowing at 10%	$34.09	−$37.50	−$37.50
Arbitrage gain	$4.09	$0	$0

Equation (3.9) has a number of notable features:

1 It does not depend on q the probability of an upward price movement. This means that even if investors disagree in their subjective probabilities about an upward or downward movement in the stock price, they will still agree on the value of the call relative to its other parameters; S, u, d, E and r.
2 The value of the call option does not depend on an investor's attitude to risk. The only assumption is that investors prefer more wealth to less.
3 The only random variable on which the option value depends is the price of the underlying stock.

50

We were able to value a call option because of our ability to construct a properly proportioned hedge portfolio that gave exactly the same payoffs irrespective of the price movement in the underlying stock.[11] Arbitrage arguments were then used to prove that the call price given by our method was the fair market price for the option. We were able to construct the hedge portfolio fairly easily because we assumed that the underlying stock price could assume only two values at option's expiry date. This assumption is clearly unrealistic but it allowed us to demonstrate the economic principles that underlie option valuation. The question arises can we always construct a hedge (or duplicating) portfolio to be able to value an option by our method? The answer to this question depends on the assumptions made about the possible range of stock prices at option's expiration date and their likelihood of occurrence, i.e. its probability distribution. We assumed that the stock in our example followed a binomial probability distribution in which only two end-of-period price outcomes were possible. When the time interval between the creation of the hedge portfolio and the expiry of the option is long, such as a year or even a month, the binomial stock price model is clearly unrealistic. What if we were to divide the option period into a number of smaller time periods, say a week or even a day. Clearly, as we do so, the binomial model provides a better characterization of observed stock price movements. In the limit, mathematically speaking, if these time intervals were to be the shortest possible time interval, say a microsecond, the binomial process becomes a diffusion process. We will have more to say about this process later.

Now, suppose we divide the time period in our above example into twenty equally spaced intervals. Can we still create a hedge portfolio and therefore determine the fair value of the option? Yes, to a fair degree of accuracy depending on the time intervals, it is still possible to construct a hedge portfolio for the call option as above. But because each interval is now shorter than the life of the call option, the hedge portfolio must be periodically rebalanced to take into account any price changes as well as the option's residual life. The following section develops this multiperiod binomial approach to option pricing.

MULTIPERIOD BINOMIAL OPTION PRICING

The one-period binomial option pricing technique described above is clearly unrealistic because it assumes that the stock price can only have two end-of-period values. When the period between the option's pur-

---

[11] Or, equivalently, the duplicating portfolio that generates exactly the same payoffs as the underlying call option.

chase date and its expiry is months or even years, this assumption will result in serious mispricing. However, if we divide this period into smaller intervals a more realistic description of stock price movements can be obtained. The question of option valuation now becomes a multiperiod problem. In terms of the terminology used when discussing Bernouli trials, the problem is simply equivalent to playing a game of chance with multiple trials. As noted previously, we can still use the same arbitrage arguments to value an option. However, in this case, since each portfolio corresponding to a single sub-interval has a shorter life than the life of the option, the hedge portfolio must be periodically rebalanced to take into account any price changes as well as the option's remaining life.

First, consider a call option with two periods before expiration. Let us suppose that the current price of the underlying stock is S dollars and that over each period it can either go up by a factor of u with probability q or down by a factor of d with probability $(1-q)$. Thus, at the end of the first period, the stock price will either be Su or Sd. At the end of the second period (in this case corresponding to option's expiry date) the stock price can again either go up by u or down by d. At this point, therefore, the stock price will either be Suu (if it goes up both the times), Sud (if it goes up in one period and down in the other) or Sdd (if it goes down both the times). As pointed out in our description of Bernouli trials, the order of a sequence of outcomes is irrelevant. Thus, $Sud = Sdu$.

Purchasing an option with two periods to expiry is analogous to playing the game of chance twice. The drawing of a black ball in that case can be likened to the event of rising stock price and the drawing of a white ball to the event of falling stock price. The price of a call option on the above stock can be similarly denumerated.

Let C be the current price of the call with two periods to expiration. At the end of period one it can either be worth C_u or C_d depending on whether the stock price goes up or down. At its expiry, the call will be worth C_{uu} if the stock rises in both periods, C_{ud} if the stock goes up in one period and down in the other and C_{dd} if the stock price falls in both periods.

The possible movements in the stock price and the related option prices are depicted in Figure 3.8 assuming the current stock price, $S = \$100$, exercise price, $E=\$100$, $u=1.25$, $d=0.75$ and $r=10$ percent.

First, we use Equation (3.9) to derive the value of the option at the end of the current period. It will be C_u or C_d depending on whether the stock price goes up or down and will be given in each case by

$$C_u = \frac{[C_{uu}\,p + C_{ud}\,(1-p)]}{1 + r} \qquad (3.11)$$

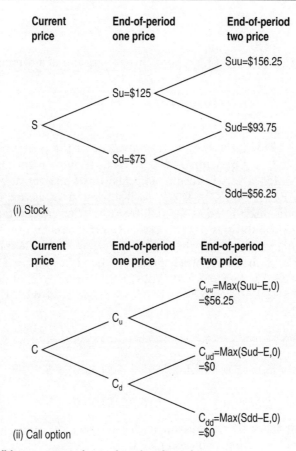

Fig 3.8 Possible movements in stock and option prices

and

$$C_d = \frac{[C_{ud}\,p + C_{dd}\,(1-p)]}{1+r} \qquad (3.12)$$

Again we can construct a hedge portfolio consisting of one short call and hS shares of the underlying stock such that the end-of-period pay-offs are the same irrespective of whether the stock price moves up or down. The functional form of the hedge ratio remains unchanged. To compute the hedge ratio we simply use Equation (3.5) with the new values of C_u and C_d. Note that in the case of an option with more than one period to expiration, the hedge ratio will need to be readjusted for each period to maintain the equivalence of the positions.

Since the hedge ratio has the same functional form in each period, the current value of the call in terms of C_u and C_d will still be

$$C = \frac{[C_u p + C_d (1-p)]}{1 + r}$$

substituting (3.11) and (3.12) into this equation and noting that $C_{du} = C_{ud}$ we obtain

$$C_d = \frac{[C_{uu} p^2 + C_{ud} (1-p) 2p + C_{dd} (1-p)^2]}{(1 + r)^2} \tag{3.13}$$

Equation (3.13) is the two-period equivalent of the one-period pricing formula given by Equation (3.9). The terms within the brackets of Equation (3.13) are a binomial expansion of the terms within the brackets in Equation (3.9). It can be interpreted as the expected two-period payoffs discounted at the risk free rate. The expectation is based on hedging probabilities p and $(1-p)$. Referring to Figure 3.8 we can now compute the value of the call two periods before expiration. At the time of expiration the stock price will be either $Suu = \$100 (1.25) (1.25) = \$156.25$, $Sud = \$100 (1.25) (0.75) = \$93.75$ or $Sdd= \$100 (0.75) (0.75) = \$56.25$. The call prices associated with these stock prices will be

$$C_{uu} = \text{Max } [Suu-E,0] = \text{Max } [\$156.25-\$100,0] = \$56.25$$

$$C_{ud} = \text{Max } [Sud-E,0] = \text{Max } [\$93.75-\$100,0] = \$0$$

$$C_{dd} = \text{Max } [Sdd-E,0] = \text{Max } [\$56.25-\$100,0] = \$0$$

The current price of the option with two periods to expiration can now be obtained using Equation (3.13)

$$C = \frac{[C_{uu} p^2 + C_{ud} (1-p) 2p + C_{dd} (1-p)^2]}{(1 + r)^2}$$

noting that

$$p = \frac{(1 + r) - d}{u - d} = \frac{1 + 0.10 - 0.75}{1.25 - 0.75} = \frac{0.35}{0.50} = 0.70$$

$$C = \frac{[\$56.25 (0.70)^2 + \$0(1 - 0.70) 2 (0.70) + \$0 (1 - 0.70)^2]}{(1 + 0.10)^2} = \$22.78$$

The two-period case can be extended to a multiperiod case using the same recursive procedure. By starting at the expiration date and working backwards we can write the general valuation formula for a call option with n periods to expiration. The n-period generalization of the binomial model is simply the probability of each final outcome multiplied by the value of that outcome discounted at the risk free rate for n-periods. The general form of payoff for a call option can be written as

Max $[Su^j d^{n-j} - E, 0]$

where n is the total number of time periods up to expiration and j is the number of upward movements in the stock price (j=0,1,2,..n). The general form of the probabilities of each payoff is given by the binomial distribution

$$\frac{n!}{n! \, (n-j)!} \, p^j \, (1-p)^{n-j}$$

Multiplying the payoffs by the probabilities and summing across all possible payoffs we have

$$C = \sum_{j=0}^{n} \frac{n!}{j! \, (n-j)!} \, p^j \, (1-p)^{n-j} \, \frac{\max \, [Su^j d^{n-j} - E, 0]}{(1+r)^n} \tag{3.14}$$

which gives the complete general binomial valuation formula.

CONTINUOUS TIME OPTION PRICING

The binomial option pricing model outlined above is a discrete-time pricing model. It assumes that the price of the underlying stock moves either up or down over a discrete length of calendar time, a day, a month or a year and so on. In practice, this is obviously an unrealistic description of price movements over time periods of a month, a week or even a day. For these time intervals there are obviously more than two possible end-of-period stock price outcomes. However, as we consider shorter and shorter time intervals, say an hour, a minute or, realistically, a second, a version of the binomial process which states that the stock price will either move slightly up or down over the next second could provide a better description of observed stock price movements over time. Such a continuous iteration would explain any end-of-day stock price realization given a beginning-of-day price. This version of the binomial stock price process is known as a diffusion process. It assumes that stock prices move continuously in a smooth fashion without any sudden jumps. By restricting the end-of-period (say a second) stock price movements to be slightly up or down we can still use the concept of a hedge portfolio to derive the value of the option. However, since each interval is shorter than the term of the option, the hedge portfolio must be continuously rebalanced to maintain the risk free position as we demonstrated for a two-period binomial option pricing model.

Black and Scholes model for the valuation of stock options is essentially a continuous time version of the discrete option pricing model described above. They assume a general diffusion process model of stock price changes over time. This assumption allowed them to use advanced continuous time mathematics to derive a simple formula to value calls and puts.[12]

Before we describe their model in detail it will be useful to briefly describe the diffusion process assumed by them to derive the option valuation formula.

A Continuous Time Probability Model of Stock Price Changes

A variable, such as the price of a stock, whose value changes over time in an uncertain way is said to follow a stochastic (or probabilistic) process. Stochastic processes can be classified as discrete time or continuous time processes. The example of a discrete time stochastic process is the binomial process described above in which the stock price can only change at fixed points in time. Under a continuous time stochastic process the variable can change continuously over time. Stochastic processes can also be characterized in terms of the nature of change that the variable can undergo. Thus, a discrete variable process can only assume a certain number of discrete values while a continuous variable can assume any value.

The stock price changes over time have been shown by various studies to be random. The first to propose this was Louis Bachelier in his doctoral thesis in 1900. This random walk hypothesis postulates that each successive change in stock prices is independent. This has led to the formulation of the efficient markets hypothesis which states that information is widely available to investors and that all relevant information is already reflected in security prices. The weak form of the efficient markets hypothesis states that the sequence of past price changes contains no information about the magnitude or direction of future changes. In other words markets have no memory.

The stochastic process that corresponds to the weak form of market efficiency is the Markov process. It is a particular type of stochastic process in which the past history of the variable is irrelevant to future changes. The Markov property of stock prices states that all relevant

---

[12] The continuous time option pricing model developed by Black and Scholes is easier to use than the binomial model which requires an iterative approach to work out the value of the option. Binomial model, however, can be used to value options of greater complexity than would be possible with the simple Black and Scholes formula.

information is captured in the current price. Black and Scholes use a particular type of Markov process, called a Weiner process, to describe changes in the stock price. This stochastic process is also referred to as Brownian motion (used to describe the motion of a particle in physics).

The general Weiner process for a variable, X, can be described by considering a change in this variable, ΔX, over a very short time interval of length Δt;

$$\Delta X = \alpha \, \Delta t + b \, \Delta z \qquad\qquad (3.15)$$

where a and b are constants and $\Delta z = \varepsilon \sqrt{\Delta t}$ where ε is a random sample from a standardized normal distribution, i.e. a normal distribution with a mean of zero and a standard deviation of 1. It follows that Δz follows a normal distribution with a mean of zero and a standard deviation of $\sqrt{\Delta t}$.

The first term in equation (3.15), $\alpha \Delta t$, implies that S has an expected drift rate of α per unit time, i.e.

$$\alpha = \frac{dX}{dt}$$

or

$$\alpha = \frac{X_1 - X_0}{T_1 - T_0}$$

or

$$X_1 = X_0 + \alpha \, \Delta t$$

where X_0 is the stock price at time T_0 and X_1 is the expected stock price at time T_1.

The second term is Equation (3.15), $b \, \Delta zt$, can be regarded as the element of uncertainty in price X. The amount of this variability (or the rate of variance) is b times a Weiner process.

It follows that ΔX follows a normal distribution with a mean of $\alpha \Delta t$ and a standard deviation of $b \sqrt{\Delta t}$.

As Δt approaches zero, Equation (3.15) takes the form

$$dX = \alpha dt + bdz \qquad\qquad (3.16)$$

Notice that this generalized Weiner process assumes constant expected drift and variance rates. The constant expected drift assumption of this model suggests that investors will require different returns at different stock prices which is not the case in reality. This assumption therefore needs to be replaced by the assumption that the expected drift in a stock price, expressed as a proportion of the price, is constant. Similarly, it can be reasonably assumed that investors are equally uncertain about price changes at all levels of stock prices. Therefore, again we can express this by assuming that the variance rate as a proportion of the stock price is constant. Equation (3.16) can now be modified to express the price dynamics for stock price change, dS, as under:

$$dS = \mu\, Sdt + \sigma\, Sdz$$

or

$$\frac{ds}{S} = \mu dt + \sigma dz \qquad\qquad (3.17)$$

where μ is the expected rate of return and σ is the stock price volatility over the instant.

Equation (3.17) is an Ito process for the stock price S with an instantaneous expected drift rate μS and instantaneous variance rate $\sigma^2 S^2$. It is the most widely used model of stock price behavior. This model in essence assumes that percentage changes in the stock price, i.e. $\dfrac{dS}{S}$ are normally distributed with mean μdt and standard deviation $\sigma\sqrt{dt}$. When percentage changes in a variable are normally distributed the variable itself is log-normally distributed.

BLACK AND SCHOLES OPTION PRICING MODEL

As noted above, the Black and Scholes model is a continuous time version of the binomial option pricing model. That is, if we hold the calendar time between now and the option's expiration date constant (say six months) and divide it into more and more binomial trials (say 180 trials, each corresponding to daily changes in stock prices), we can have a close approximation of the Black and Scholes pricing model. This is not surprising because as the number of binomial trials, n, approaches infinity, the probability distribution for percentage changes in the price of the stock approaches the normal distribution.

As stated before, the key to the Black and Scholes option pricing model is the idea of a 'riskless hedge'. To derive the pricing formula Black and Scholes make the following assumptions:

1 Trading takes place continuously.

2 Investor can freely buy and sell securities short.

3 The short term interest rate, r, is known and is constant over time and investors can freely borrow and lend at this rate.

4 The stock pays no dividends.

5 The markets are frictionless. There are no transactions costs for buying or selling the stock or the option.

6 The stock price follows a random walk in continuous time with a variance rate proportional to the square of the stock price. Thus the distribution of possible stock prices at the end of any finite interval is lognormal.

As in the case of the binomial model, consider forming a hedge portfolio consisting of stock and call options on that stock. If we let

N_S = Quantity of stock in the hedge portfolio
N_C = Quantity of call options in the hedge portfolio

then the value of the hedge portfolio, H, at any time is given by

$$H = N_c\, C + N_s\, S \tag{3.18}$$

where S is the price of the stock and C is the price of a call to purchase one share of the stock.

In a short instant of time, where N_s and N_c are fixed, the only source of change in Equation (3.18) is the change in the price of the stock and the option. Using basic calculus the change in the value of the hedge position, dH, is given by the derivative of Equation (3.18)

$$dH = N_c\, dC + N_s\, dS \tag{3.19}$$

where dC and dS are changes in the price of the stock and the call option respectively.

By assumption (6) above, the stock price is assumed to follow an Ito process:

$$dS = \mu S\, dt + \sigma S dz \tag{3.20}$$

where dz is a Weiner process and μ and σ are drift rate and volatility respectively.

Because the stock is assumed to follow a continuous Ito process and the option is assumed to be a function of the stock price and time, therefore, we can employ Ito's lemma to express the change in the call price, dC, as

$$dC = \left(\frac{\delta C}{\delta S}\mu S + \frac{\delta C}{\delta t} + \frac{1}{2}\frac{\delta^2 C}{2S^2}\sigma^2 S^2 \right) dt + \frac{\delta C}{\delta S}\sigma S dz \tag{3.21}$$

Notice that both S and C are affected by the same underlying source of uncertainty namely dz. In other words, the underlying Weiner process for S and C are the same. It follows that by choosing an appropriate portfolio consisting of the stock and the call, the only source of uncertainty in Equation (3.21), dz, can be eliminated at least instantaneously.

Consider a portfolio consisting of a short position in one call (N_c = -1) and a long position in the stock of $\frac{dc}{ds}$ then (3.19) yields

$$dH = \left(-\frac{\delta C}{\delta t} - \frac{1}{2} \frac{\delta^2 C}{\delta S^2} \sigma^2 S^2 \right) dt \qquad (3.22)$$

All stochastic terms in Equation (3.21) have been eliminated in Equation (3.22). Now if the quantities of the stock and the option are adjusted continuously in the prescribed way as stock and option prices change over time, then the return on the hedge portfolio becomes certain. To avoid arbitrage, therefore, this portfolio must earn the risk free rate of interest. That is

$$dH = rHdt \qquad (3.23)$$

where r is the risk-free interest rate.

Substituting (3.18) and (3.22) into (3.23) results in the fundamental Black and Scholes partial differential equation for the value of the call option:

$$\frac{\delta C}{\delta t} + rs\frac{\delta C}{\delta S} + \frac{1}{2} \frac{\delta^2 C}{\delta S^2} \sigma^2 S^2 = rC \qquad (3.24)$$

The solution to a particular option valuation problem using Equation (3.24) will depend on the boundary conditions. For European call and put options the required boundary conditions of (3.24) are those at the expiration date of the option. For such options Black and Scholes were able to derive a closed form analytical solution by transforming (3.24) into the heat equation from physics for which the solution is known.

For a European call option the Black and Scholes pricing formula is given by

$$C = SN(d1) - Ee^{-rT} N(d2) \qquad (3.25)$$

where

$$d1 = \frac{1n + \left(\frac{S}{E}\right) + \left(r + \frac{1}{2} \sigma^2\right)T}{\sigma\sqrt{T}}$$

and

$$d2 = d1 - \sigma\sqrt{T}$$

The terms $N(d1)$ and $N(d2)$ are the cumulative probability for a unit normal variable z. [13] That is, it is the probability

$$N(d1) = \int_{\infty}^{d1} f(z)dz$$

where $f(z)$ is distributed normally with mean zero and standard deviation of one. $1n$ is the natural logarithm, e is the exponential

---

[13] That is, $N(d)$ is the probability that a normally distributed random variable, X, will be less than or equal to d.

(e=2.7183), T is time to maturity and σ^2 is the instantaneous variance of the stock price which is the measure of volatility of the stock.

From Equation (3.25) we note that the value of the call is equal to the stock price, S, minus the discounted value of the exercise price, Ee^{-rT}, each weighted by a probability. The stock price is weighted by $N(d1)$ which is also the hedge ratio. For each call written, the riskless hedge portfolio contains $N(d1)$ shares of stock. On the other hand the discounted value of the exercise price is weighted by $N(d2)$ which can be interpreted as the probability that the option will finish in the money.

The value of a European put, P, can be derived in a similar way to a European call. The result is

$$P = Ee^{-rT} N(-d2) - SN(-d1) \tag{3.26}$$

where P is the value of a European put and $d1$ and $d2$ are as defined above.

For American style option contracts, where there is some chance of early exercise, it is not possible to derive analytical solutions unless it can be, a priori, proved that a rational investor will not exercise the option before its expiry date. It can be shown that in the case of a non-dividend paying stock it is never optimal to exercise an American call option before its expiration date. In this case, therefore, European call option pricing formula can be used. An American put option, on the other hand, has a chance of early exercise and therefore the valuation problem must be solved using numerical techniques such as an iterative binomial method.

Although Equation (3.25) looks daunting it has an intuitive explanation given above and can be used relatively easily, It depends on observable parameters such as the current stock price, S, the exercise price, E, the risk free rate of interest, r, and the volatility which can be estimated from market data using simple statistical techniques. To demonstrate its application consider the call option that we valued earlier using the one-period binomial option pricing method. In that case we had:

S=\$100
r=0.10 or 10%
E=\$100

Now suppose the undefined period in our binomial example is equal to one year so that $T = 1$. The only other parameter needed to use the Black and Scholes option pricing formula is an estimate of the stock price volatility, σ, for the option period of one year. Recall that in the case of the binomial model we assumed that stock price could go up or down by 25 percent over the next period. This is equivalent to an annual volatility of 25 percent in the case of the Black and Scholes model. Using this information we can compute the value of the call as

$$C = SN\,(d1) - Ee^{-rT}\,N\,(d2)$$

where

$$d1 = \frac{ln + \left(\frac{S}{E}\right) + \left(r + \frac{1}{2}\sigma^2\right)T}{\sigma\sqrt{T}}$$

$$d1 = \frac{ln + \left(\frac{100}{100}\right) + (\,0.10 + 0.5\,(0.25)^2)\,(1)}{0.25\sqrt{1}}$$

$$= \frac{0.0 + 0.131}{0.25} = 0.525$$

and

$$d2 = d1 - \sigma\sqrt{T}$$
$$= 0.525 - 0.25 = 0.275$$

Substituting these values into the call option formula, we have

$$C = SN\,(0.525) - Ee^{-rT}\,N\,(0.275)$$

Recall that $N(d1)$ and $N(d2)$ are cumulative probabilities for a unit normal variable. Therefore $N(d1)$ is the cumulative probability from minus infinity to + 0.525 standard deviations above the mean which is zero for the standard normal variable. This is shown in Figure 3.9 by the shaded area. A ready reckoner for the area under the normal curve appears as Appendix 1 of this book which shows the cumulative probability from minus infinity to 0.525 to be approximately 0.70. Repeating the same procedure for $N(d2)$ we observe a cumulative probability of approximately 0.608 from minus infinity to 0.275.

Substituting these probabilities into the call option formula we get

$$C = \$100(0.70) - \$100(2.7183)^{-(0.10)(1)}\,(0.608)$$

$$= \$70 - \$100(0.9048)(0.608) = \$14.98$$

This value compares reasonably well with our earlier value of $15.91 derived using the simple one-period binomial option pricing model. It can be shown that the price given by the binomial model will approach the Black and Scholes price as we increase the number of binomial steps or trials.

While the cumulative probabilities can be directly obtained from the Normal Distribution Table given at Appendix 1, it is desirable if we

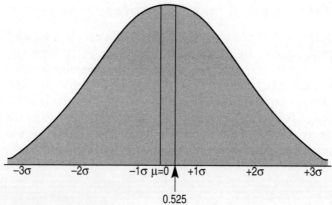

Fig 3.9 Probability distribution of d1

can calculate the cumulative probability directly. A procedure for computing cumulative probability can be employed to value options using a simple computer model.

The probability that a drawing from a unit normal distribution will be less than d is given by the integral

$$N(d) = \int_{-\infty}^{d} \frac{1}{\sqrt{2\pi}} e^{\frac{-z^2}{2}} dz \qquad (3.27)$$

While this integral can be evaluated directly using numerical procedures, it is easier to use a polynomial approximation. One such approximation is

$N(d) = 0.5 + w \qquad$ for $d \geqslant 0$

$N(d) = 0.5 - w \qquad$ for $d < 0$

where

$$w = 0.5 - k\,(0.436184m - 0.120168m^2 + 0.937298m^3)$$

$$k = \frac{1}{\sqrt{2\pi}} e^{\frac{-d^2}{2}}$$

$$m = \frac{1}{1 + [0.33267\,abs(d)]}$$

$abs\,(d) =$ Absolute value of d

Delta – the measure of price sensitivity

We noted above that the term $N(d1)$ in Black and Scholes call option pricing formula given by Equation (3.25) is the hedge ratio of the call. That is, for each call written, the riskless hedge portfolio contains $N(d1)$ shares of stock. Delta, therefore, provides a valuable measure of the option's exposure to the price fluctuations of the underlying stock. A call with a delta of 0.5 is five times as sensitive to price changes in the underlying stock as the one with a delta of 0.1. Put options have a negative delta because the value of the put is inversely related to the value of the underlying stock. Traders use delta to hedge their option positions with the underlying stock. By purchasing the underlying stock in proportion to the delta, a trader can hedge his exposure to a call sold on the stock.

It is obvious from Equation (3.25) that delta is a kind of probability, ranging in value from 0 to 1 for calls and –1 to 0 for puts. A deep-out-of-the-money option has a delta that is very close to zero. That is because the probability that the option will be exercised is low.

Since delta provides a a first order (or linear) approximation of the true price sensitivity of the option (which is non-linear), traders need to adjust the delta hedge as the underlying price changes. The second-order effect is captured by gamma which measures the sensitivity of an option's delta to changes in the value of the underlying stock. Gamma is measured in terms of change in the option's delta per unit change in the value of the underlying stock.

SUMMARY

Option valuation is an exercise in relative valuation. Since options represent a right but not an obligation for the buyer, they result in asymmetric payoffs. It is the asymmetric nature of option payoffs that requires a different framework for valuation than that used for fixed income valuation.

An important breakthrough in option valuation is the Black and Scholes pricing model originally developed for stock options. The key insight of the Black and Scholes model is the concept of instantaneous risk free hedge. The assumption of risk neutrality allows the use of simpler techniques to value options. The binomial option pricing model is simple and extremely versatile. Not only can it be used to value simple European calls and puts, it can also be used to value American calls and puts as well as more complex options.

References

Black, F. and Scholes, M., 'The Pricing of Options and Corporate Liabilities', *Journal of Political Economy*, May–June 1973, pp. 637–59.

Boyle, P. and Emmanuel, D., 'Discretely Adjusted Option Hedges', *Journal of Financial Economics*, September 1980, pp. 259–82.

Brennan, M. and Schwartz, E., 'The Valuation of American Put Options', *Journal of Finance*, May 1977, pp. 449–62.

Cox, J. and Ross, S., 'The Valuation of Options for Alternative Stochastic Processes', *Journal of Financial Economics*, Jan–Mar 1976, pp. 145–66.

Cox, J., Ross, S. and Rubinstein, M., 'Option Pricing: A Simplified Approach', *Journal of Financial Economics*, September 1979, pp. 229–63.

Cox, J. and Rubinstein, M., *Options Markets*, Englewood Cliffs, N.J.: Prentice Hall, 1985.

Drezner, Z., 'Computation of the Bivariate Normal Integral'. *Mathematics of Computation*, 32, January 1978, pp. 277–9.

Feller, W., *An Introduction to Probability Theory and its Applications,* Vol 1, 3rd edn, New York: John Wiley and Sons, 1968.

Geske, R. and Johnnson, H., 'The American Put Option Valued Analytically', *Journal of Finance*, December 1984, pp. 1511–24.

Geske, R. and Roll, R., 'On Valuing American Call Options with the Black-Scholes European Formula', *Journal of Finance*, 1984, pp. 443–55.

Hoel, P.J., *Finite Mathematics and Calculus with Applications to Business*, New York: John Wiley & Sons, 1974.

Kendall, M.G. and Smart, A., *The Advanced Theory of Statistics*, London: Charles Griffin & Co, 1967.

Merton, R., 'The Theory of Rational Option Pricing', *Bell Journal of Economics and Management Science*, Spring 1973, pp. 141–83.

Rendleman, R. and Bartler, B., 'Two-State Option Pricing', *Journal of Finance*, December 1979, pp. 1093–1110.

Roll, R., 'An Analytic Valuation Formula for Unprotected American Call Options on Stocks with Known Dividends', *Journal of Financial Economics*, November 1977, pp. 251–8.

Rubinstein, M., 'The Valuation of Uncertain Income Streams and the Pricing of Options', *Bell Journal of Economics*, Autumn 1976, pp. 407–25.

Smith, C., 'Option Pricing Review', *Journal of Financial Economics*, Jan–March 1976, pp. 1–51.

Stoll, H.R., 'The Relationship between Put and Call Option Prices', *Journal of Finance*, December 1969, pp. 802–24.

Whaley, R., 'On Valuation of American Call Options on Stocks with Known Dividends', *Journal of Financial Economics*, June 1981, pp. 207–12.

4

FORWARD CONTRACTS

Forward rate agreements

How is the contract rate derived?

Cash market implied forward rates

Futures implied forward rate

Forward FX contracts

How is the forward FX rate derived?

Summary

Forward contracts comprise a number of agreements in which the underlying transaction takes place at a future date. The most significant feature of forward contracts is the lag in time between the agreement to trade and the trade itself. Forward contracts are common in various spheres of economic activity. Such contracts exist on commodities, deposits, bonds, currencies etc. The most important forward contracts from the point of view of this book are those that relate to deposits and foreign exchange. In this chapter we describe forward rate agreements (FRAs) and forward foreign exchange contracts.

FORWARD RATE AGREEMENTS

Until early 1980s major international banks routinely entered into forward lending and deposit agreements which allowed them to lock-in a fixed rate for a future lending or deposit. Thus, a bank could agree to lend in six months time for a period of twelve months at a fixed rate, the forward rate, that was established today. This arrangement would allow the bank to lock-in a return on its lending but would also create an on-balance-sheet asset attracting regulatory capital.

Forward Rate Agreements (FRAs), also known as Futures Rate Agreements, provide a mechanism to obtain protection against future interest rate changes. Although the basis of an FRA is a notional contract of loan and deposit between two counterparties to be made at a future date, it is important to note that no commitment is made to lend or deposit the principal amount; only the difference between the agreed rate (the 'contract rate') and the actual reference rate (the 'settlement rate') changes hands. FRAs are, thus, essentially OTC form of interest rate futures. This can be made clear by way of the following examples involving forward loans and deposits.

Suppose a company will have $100 million available in three months' time that it would need to invest in a deposit for a period of six months. It is concerned that in three months' time the six-month interest rate may be lower than is implied by the forward rate. Suppose the implied six-month forward rate in three months' time is 10 percent. The company can ensure that it will earn 10 percent return on its deposit to be made in three months' time by selling a 3 × 9 (three-month into nine-month) FRA in which it agrees to make a notional deposit of $100 million in three months for a period of six months at the contract rate of 10 percent. If in three months' time the actual six-month rate is lower than 10 percent, the company will receive the present value of the difference between this rate and the contract rate of 10 percent based on the notional principal amount of $100 million ensuring that the return on its six-month deposit is 10 percent. If, on the other hand, the actual six-month rate is above 10 percent, the company will pay the present value of the difference between this rate and the contract rate to the buyer of the FRA. Thus, while the company is protected against any interest rate falls, it also gives up any opportunity to earn a higher rate of interest.

Now, assume a company will need to borrow $100 million in three months' time for a period of nine months. It is concerned that nine-month interest rate in three months' time may be higher than is implied by the forward curve. The company wishes to fix its cost of borrowing at the currently implied forward interest rate. Suppose the 3×12 FRA is priced at 11.00–11.05. The company can buy this contract and fix its future cost of borrowing at 11.05 percent. If in three months' time the actual nine-month interest rate is greater than the contract of 11.05 percent, the company will receive the present value of the difference between this rate and the contract rate calculated on the basis of the notional principal amount. However, if the actual nine-month interest rate in three months' time is less than 11.05 percent, the company will need to pay the present value of the difference between the contract rate and this rate to the seller of the contract. In either case the company's cost of borrowing is fixed at 11.05 percent.

FRAs are, thus, off-balance-sheet contracts used to lock-in the currently implied forward rate for a given term. Thus, a 3×12 FRA allows the user to lock-in the currently implied nine-month interest rate expected to prevail in three months' time. The 'three' in 3×12 refers to the forward period at the end of which settlement of the FRA takes place while twelve refers to the period at the end of which the underlying loan or deposit will mature. FRAs can also be used to speculate on the direction of future interest rates. A speculator can buy an FRA if the view is that interest rates will rise in the future. The speculator, on the other hand, will need to sell an FRA if the view is that future interest rates will fall. The payoffs to buyers and sellers on settlement date are depicted in Figure 4.1.

Features of FRAs

1 FRAs are OTC derivatives and can, therefore, be tailored to specific requirements in terms of amount, settlement date, etc.

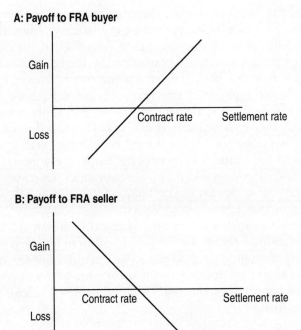

Fig 4.1 Payoffs to buyers and sellers on settlement date

2 Exposure of FRA counterparties to each other is restricted to movements in interest rates.

3 FRAs are off-balance-sheet contracts and are not, therefore, carried on balance sheet unlike forward lending and forward deposits.[1]

4 A FRA contract can be cancelled at any time before the delivery date either by cancelling the original contract or by entering into a matching contract for the residual life of the contract.

Mechanics of FRAs

As stated above, the basis of an FRA is a notional contract of loan and deposit between two counterparties one of which is an intermediary bank. Under the contract the parties agree to indemnify each other against the impact of changes in interest rates on the notional loan and deposit. This is achieved by a cash settlement at maturity of the contract. The settlement amount is computed by reference to the 'contract

---

[1] Forward lending and deposit transactions were common in the interbank markets prior to the introduction of forward rate agreements.

rate' and the 'settlement rate.' Settlement rate is the preagreed reference rate, such as LIBOR, prevailing at maturity. When the settlement rate is higher than the contract rate the seller of the contract – the notional lender – makes a payment to the buyer of the contract – the notional borrower – according to a predetermined formula. This settlement amount represents the value of the difference between the contract rate and the settlement rate as applied to the notional deposit. Conversely, when the settlement rate is lower than the contract rate the buyer of the contract – the notional borrower – makes a payment to the seller of the contract – the notional lender – computed according to a pre-defined formula. Thus, as a simple rule to remember, the borrowers fix the cost of borrowing by buying FRAs whereas investors fix the return on investment by selling FRAs.

The settlement date of an FRA is usually chosen to correspond to the value date of the underlying notional loan and deposit. Since the settlement amount is paid on the value date and not the maturity date of the notional loan and deposit, it is computed on a discounted basis.

For the buyer, the settlement value of a FRA is calculated using the following formula:

$$NPA \times \frac{(R_T - R_f)}{100} \times \frac{D}{b} \times \frac{1}{1 + \left(\frac{R_T}{100} \times \frac{D}{b} \right)} \qquad (4.1)$$

where

NPA = Notional principal amount of the contract
R_f = Contract rate expressed as a percentage
R_T = Settlement rate expressed as a percentage
D = number of days in the contract period
b = interest basis i.e. 360 or 365

For the seller, the settlement value of an FRA is calculated using the following formula:

$$NPA \times \frac{(R_f - R_T)}{100} \times \frac{D}{b} \times \frac{1}{1 + \left(\frac{R_T}{100} \times \frac{D}{b} \right)} \qquad (4.2)$$

Notice that the values given by Equations (4.1) and (4.2) can be both positive as well as negative. In other words, if the settlement rate is lower than the contract rate, the buyer of the contract will need to make a net payment to the seller. If, on the other hand, the settlement rate fixes higher than the contract rate the buyer will receive a net payment. Also notice that the settlement value of a FRA for the buyer of the contract is a mirror image of the settlement value for the seller of the contract. This relationship is depicted in Figure 4.1.

Example

Suppose a company purchased a 3×9 (three-month into nine-month) FRA on 1 January 1995 for settlement on 1 March 1995. The company purchased the FRA with a contract rate of 7 percent in anticipation of a six-month loan that it will raise in three months' time. Suppose the amount of the loan will be $100 million and the maturity date will be 1 September 1995. What will the settlement value of this contract be if the settlement rate, say six month USD LIBOR, on 1 March 1995 was 8 percent. In this case we have

NPA = $100 million
R_f = 7%
R_T = 8%
D = 184 days (1 March 1995 to 1 September 1995)
b = 360

Using formula (4.1) we get

$$100{,}000{,}000 \times \frac{(8-7)}{100} \times \frac{184}{360} \times \frac{1}{1 + \left(\frac{8}{100} \times \frac{184}{360}\right)}$$

$$= 100{,}000{,}000 \times 0.01 \times 0.511 \times \frac{1}{1 + (0.08 \times 0.511)}$$

$$= \$490{,}931$$

Since the settlement value is positive, the buyer of the contract will receive this sum from the seller of the contract. If the settlement value was negative, the buyer of the contract would be required to pay to the seller of the contract an amount equal to the settlement value of the contract. This would, for example, be the case if the settlement rate was lower than the contract rate. Suppose in the above example the settlement rate on 1 March 1995 was 6 percent, i.e. the six-month reference rate had fallen instead of rising. What will the settlement value of the contract in this case be? Using formula (4.1) we have

$$100{,}000{,}000 \times \frac{(6-7)}{100} \times \frac{184}{360} \times \frac{1}{1 + \left(\frac{6}{100} \times \frac{184}{360}\right)}$$

$$= 100{,}000{,}000 \times -0.01 \times 0.511 \times \frac{1}{1 + (0.06 \times 0.511)}$$

$$= (\$495{,}799)$$

In this case, therefore, the buyer will be required to make the settlement payment to the seller of the contract. Notice that while the magnitude of interest rate deviation from the contract rate is equal in both cases, i.e. 1 percent, the settlement value is different in the two cases. Specifically, it is higher when the settlement rate is lower than the contract rate. The reason for this is simply a higher discount factor because of a lower interest rate.

Let us now analyze the impact of the FRA on the underlying borrowing costs for the company. Under the first scenario six-month interest rates have risen to 8 percent – 1 percent more than was implied at the time of purchasing the FRA. The company will, therefore, borrow at a rate of 8 percent for a period of six months. Its interest expense under this scenario is summarized in Table 4.1.

Table 4.1

	Alternative –1 No FRA	Alternative –2 Buy FRA
A. Loan	$100,000,000	$100,000,000
B. Interest at 8%	$4,088,000	$4,088,000
C. Settlement value of FRA	–	$490,931
D. Future value of FRA Settlement amount (at 8% return)	–	$511,000
E. Net interest expense (B–D)	$4,088,000	$3,577,000
F. Effective cost of funding	8%	7%

We can similarly analyze the impact of the FRA on the underlying borrowing cost for the company under the second scenario – that of falling interest rates. Under this scenario six-month settlement rate is 6 percent which is lower than the contract rate of 7 percent. The company will, therefore, borrow at this lower rate for a period of six months. The effective interest expense for the company in this scenario is summarized in Table 4.2.

Table 4.2

	Alternative –1 No FRA	Alternative –2 Buy FRA
A. Loan	$100,000,000	$100,000,000
B. Interest at 6%	$3,066,000	$3,066,000
C. Settlement value of FRA	–	$495,799
D. Future value of FRA Settlement amount (at 6% return)	–	$511,000
E. Net interest expense (B+D)	$3,066,000	$3,577,000
F. Effective cost of funding	6%	7%

Thus, in both cases the effective cost of borrowing is locked-in at 7 percent. However, while in the first case the company stood to lose if it had not purchased the FRA, in the second case it stood to gain if it had not purchased the FRA. That is because in the first case it would need to pay 8 percent for a period of six months on its borrowing, whereas in the second case it would only pay 6 percent.

In deriving the effective cost of borrowing in Tables 4.1 and 4.2 we implicitly assumed that the settlement amount can be invested, when it is positive, and borrowed, when it is negative, at the same rate as the strike rate relevant to the FRA, such as six-month LIBOR. In practice, differences will arise because of the differences in borrowing and lending rates. We have also ignored any brokerage fees that may be involved in the purchase of an FRA. It is important to understand that the settlement value of an FRA bought is the equal but opposite settlement value of an FRA sold. Thus, under the first scenario, while the settlement value of the FRA is a positive $490,931 from the buyer's perspective, it is a negative $490,931 from the seller's perspective.

HOW IS THE CONTRACT RATE DERIVED?

The contract rate of an FRA is the implied forward rate for the term of the underlying notional loan and deposit expected to prevail on the settlement date of the contract. Thus, in a 6×18 FRA contract the contract rate is the twelve-month interest rate expected to prevail in six months' time.

In Chapter 2 we noted that all derivatives with symmetric payoffs must be valued at zero at the time of entering into such a contract. Therefore, at the outset, the contract rate of an FRA is that rate which produces a value of zero. This rate, by definition, must be the forward rate. Forward rates can be implied either from the cash market yield curve[2] or, where they exist, from the futures curve. We will first describe the method using cash market instruments.

CASH MARKET IMPLIED FORWARD RATES

The law of one price driven by arbitrage considerations requires that financial packages that are equivalent must command the same price. An investor wishing to invest for a specific holding period can do so in three ways: invest in assets maturing exactly at the end of the holding

---

[2] That is the market for spot delivery of the underlying security.

period; invest for a shorter term and sell an FRA covering interest rate risk for the residual term; or, invest for a longer term than the holding period and buy an FRA to cover the interest rate risk for this extra period. These three financial packages would be equivalent and must command the same price.[3] This fundamental principle of securities valuation can be described by way of an example. Suppose you wish to invest $100 million for a period of one year. You can easily do so by depositing the money with a bank or by purchasing a fixed income security with one year to maturity. Suppose, for simplicity, in either case you can earn an annual return of 10 percent on your investment. The law of one price requires that you should be able to achieve the same result by investing your money for a shorter term and selling a forward rate agreement to guarantee the return for one year. Suppose you invest for six months at a rate of 8 percent. Simultaneously you enter into a forward deposit contract to lend $100 million in six months' time for a six-month period. The two alternatives are depicted in Figure 4.2.

Ignoring such considerations as credit and liquidity these two investments are equivalent and must therefore yield the same return. Under Alternative-1 you receive a guaranteed return of 10 percent. That is, at maturity you receive $110 million. Arbitrage considerations require that you should not receive more than $110 million at maturity under Alternative-2. Since under this alternative the return is fixed at 8 percent for the first six months, it must be that the return on the forward deposit is such that the redemption value of your investment is $110 million under this alternative as well. In this case the rate at which the forward deposit is placed is the six-month (bid) interest rate expected to prevail in six months' time. Similar argument can be used to derive the offered interest rates expected to prevail in future.

Generalizing the above argument it is easy to derive forward rates of any tenor from the cash market interest rates. Chapter 5 develops a comprehensive approach to deriving zero coupon and forward rates from par yields. Here we will adopt a simpler approach. Suppose there exist zero-coupon money and debt market instruments for maturities of up to 10 periods. Suppose these cash market instruments have equally spaced maturities, say six months, twelve months, eighteen months and so on. We define the discount factor d_1 as

---

[3] Even if it were not possible to hedge the interest rate exposure under the last two alternatives, according to a version of Expectations Hypothesis of the term structure of interest rates, these investments would be expected substitutes for one another. Another version of pure Expectations Hypothesis postulates that the investor's expected holding period returns would be the same regardless of the alternative chosen. This return is postulated to be the current short-term return plus the forward yields over the residual term.

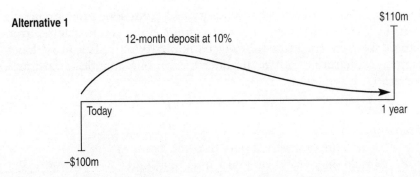

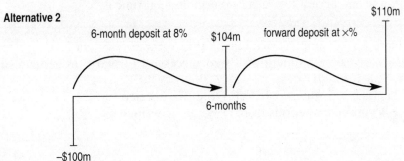

Fig 4.2 The law of one price

$$d_1 = \frac{1}{1 + r_1} \tag{4.3}$$

where r_1 is the one period zero coupon rate prevailing today and d_1 is, thus, the present value of \$1 received in one period's time. Similarly, we define d_2 to be the present value of \$1 received in two periods' time

$$d_2 = \frac{1}{(1 + r_1)(1 + R_{1,1})} \tag{4.4}$$

where $R_{1,1}$ is the one period rate expected to prevail in one period's time. $R_{1,1}$ is, therefore, the one-period forward rate applicable to a one-period investment. It can be obtained by dividing the one-period discount factor, d_1, by the two-period discount d_2

$$\frac{d_1}{d_2} = 1 + R_{1,1}$$

or

$$R_{1,1} = \frac{d_1}{d_2} - 1 = \frac{(1 + r_2)^2}{1 + r_1} - 1$$

In general, forward rates can be obtained from spot rates by noting that the yield-to-maturity of a zero-coupon bond is a geometric average of the forward rates through its maturity date. If a bond has n periods to maturity and we are interested in one-period forward rate, the yield is given by

$$r_n = [(1 + r_1)(1 + R_{1,1})(1 + R_{1,2}) \dots (1 + R_{1,n-1})]^{\frac{1}{n}} \qquad (4.5)$$

where

r_n = yield on an n-period pure discount bond
r_1 = yield on a one-period pure discount bond
$R_{1,i}$ = one period forward rate beginning at time i
  i = 1,2,....n-1

Equation (4.5) implies that, say, a three-year investment is equivalent to a one-year investment plus two successive forward investments at one-year forward rates.

The general formula for deriving the implied one-period forward rate beginning m periods from now can be written as

$$R_{1,m} = \frac{(1 + r_{m+1})^{m+1}}{(1 + r_m)^m} - 1 \qquad (4.6)$$

In general, the forward rate can be expressed in terms of the length of time between $m+j$ and m. For example for $j=1$, the implied forward rate would span one period, for $j=2$, the implied rate will relate to two periods and so on. The calculation of the j-period forward rate beginning at time m is

$$R_{j,m} = \sqrt[j]{\frac{(1 + r_{m+j})^{m+j}}{(1 + r_m)^m}} - 1 \qquad (4.7)$$

Example 1

Suppose we can invest for various terms at the following zero coupon rates:

Term	Zero-coupon yield (p.a.)
1 year	6%
2 years	6.25%
3 years	6.40%
4 years	6.55%
5 years	6.70%

From this information we wish to imply one year forward rates beginning in one, two, three and four years' time. Using Equation (4.6) we first compute the one-year forward rate in one year's time as under

$$R_{1,1} = R_{1 \text{ year, 1 year}} = \frac{(1 + r_{2 \text{ years}})^2}{(1 + r_{1 \text{ year}})} - 1$$

$$= \frac{(1 + 0.0625)^2}{(1 + 0.6)} - 1 = 0.065 = 6.50\%$$

Similarly the one-year forward rate beginning in two years' time can be calculated as

$$R_{1,2} = R_{1 \text{ year, 2 years}} = \frac{(1 + r_{3 \text{ years}})^3}{(1 + r_{2 \text{ years}})} - 1$$

$$= \frac{(1 + 0.064)^3}{(1 + 0.625)^2} - 1 = 0.067 = 6.70\%$$

One-year forward rates beginning in three and four years' time are similarly calculated to be 7.0 percent and 7.3 percent respectively.

Thus a 12×24 FRA would be priced to have a contract rate of 6.5 percent. It is worth noting that the actual contract rate may differ from that given by the implied forward rate on account of transaction costs.

Example 2

In the above example we had evenly spaced zero-coupon yields at annual intervals from which we were able to imply forward rates using formula (4.6). Suppose now we have the following zero coupon yields for various irregular maturities:

Term	Zero-coupon yield (p.a.)
1 month	5%
3 months	5.25%
6 months	5.45%
9 months	5.60%
1 year	5.70%
2 years	5.80%

In this example there is a gap of two months between the first two data points, followed by a gap of three months between the subsequent three data points, which is followed by a gap of twelve months. If we needed to find the forward two-month rate in one month's time we could obtain that simply by the yield data on 1-month and 3-month instruments since the gap between these two data points is exactly two months. However, since both these rates are money market rates which are quoted on simple interest basis we will use money market discount formula from Chapter 2 to compute the forward rate.

$$R_{2,\,1} = R_{2\,months,\,1\,month} = \frac{\left(1 + r_{3\,months} \times \frac{Days}{Basis}\right)}{\left(1 + r_{1\,month} \times \frac{Days}{Basis}\right)} - 1$$

$$= \frac{\left(1 + 0.0525 \times \frac{90}{360}\right)}{\left(1 + 0.5 \times \frac{30}{360}\right)} - 1 = 0.892\%$$

The computed rate of 0.892 percent is the per period rate which in this case is two months. To annualize this forward rate we use the following formula

$$R_{2,1} = R_{2\,months,\,1\,month} \text{ (annualized)} = [1 + R_{2\,months,\,1\,month}]^{\frac{Basis}{Days}}$$

$$= (1 + 0.00892)^{\frac{360}{60}} = 5.47\%$$

In order to imply, say, forward one month interest rate beginning in one month's time we will either need to know the two-month money market rate or we will have to interpolate between three-month and one-month yields to approximate two-month yields. Forward one-month rate in one month's time can then be imputed with reference to the discount factors for one and two month investments.

Table 4.3 summarizes forward rates for other terms based on the above example. It should be noted that while discount factors for money market instruments of up to one year's term are derived assuming simple interest payments, discount factors for longer term instruments are derived assuming periodic compounding (annual in our example for the two-year investment).

Table 4.3 Implied forward rates

Spot rates		Forward start date	Term of forward rate	Forward rate per period	Forward rate (p.a.)
Term	Yield p.a.				
1 month	5%	1 month	2 months	0.892%	5.47%
3 months	5.25%	3 months	3 months	1.394%	5.69%
6 months	5.45%	6 months	3 months	1.436%	5.87%
9 months	5.60%	9 months	3 months	1.44%	5.89%
1 year	5.70%	12 months	1 year	5.90%	5.90%
2 years	5.80%	–	–	–	–

Table 4.3 also provides contract rates for FRAs of various terms. For example, ignoring bid-offer spread, a 1 × 3 FRA should be priced today

to have a contract rate of 5.47 percent. Similarly, contract rates for FRAs of other maturities are summarized in Table 4.4. Notice that the FRA end-term is obtained simply by adding the forward start date to the term of the forward rate in Table 4.3. It is important to remember that actual contract rates will reflect transaction costs associated with the trade which may be approximately 4–7 basis points in major currencies.

Table 4.4 Forward rate agreement contract rates

FRA term (months)	Contract rate
1 × 3	5.47%
3 × 6	5.69%
6 × 9	5.87%
9 × 12	5.89%
12 × 24	5.90%

Marking-to-market

Table 4.4 gives contract rates for FRAs of various maturities. At the time a FRA is entered into these rates coincide with the implied forward rates for the term involved. At the outset, therefore, the value of an FRA should be zero to both parties (ignoring any bid-offer spread). If that were not the case, opportunities for riskless profit will arise that, when exploited, will drive the two rates in line.

However, at any time after the inception of the contract the implied forward rate can diverge from the contract rate resulting in a gain or loss on the FRA. Suppose you buy a 3 × 6 FRA at a contract rate of 10 percent with an NPA of $10 million in anticipation of a borrowing in three months' time. One month after entering into the contract your borrowing requirement falls to zero. You are left with an FRA that has two months to run. At this point it is effectively a 2 × 5 contract since one month has already elapsed. You now have a naked position from which you stand to gain if three-month reference rate, say LIBOR, fixes above 10 percent on the settlement date or lose if three-month LIBOR fixes below 10 percent. You can hedge your position either by cancelling the existing FRA or by selling a 2 × 5 contract at current market rates. Suppose the contract rate on a 2 × 5 FRA is 12 percent. You can sell this contract which will require that you make a payment to the buyer of the contract on the settlement date if three-month LIBOR fixes above 12 percent. If three-month LIBOR fixes below 12 percent we will receive a payment. Under your original position you will receive a payment if three-month LIBOR fixes above 10 percent and make a payment if it fixes below 10 percent. By selling a 2 × 5 contract at 12 percent you effectively lock-in a gain of 2 percent that will arise on settlement date irrespective of where three-month LIBOR fixes. The present value of this 2 percent gain on settlement date represents the value of the existing 3 × 6 FRA that you bought. Reverse would be true if current 2 × 5 contract rate was at, say, 8 percent, i.e. 2 percent below the contract rate on the existing FRA. It is possible to enter into a FRA with an off-market contract rate. Thus if the contract rate on a 2 × 5 FRA was 12 percent you could sell a 2 × 5 contract with an off-market contract rate of 10 percent to hedge your position under the existing FRA but you would also receive the discounted value of the 2 percent differential up front. Reverse would be the case if the contract rate on 2 × 5 FRAs were less than 10 percent. Needless to say, there would be no gain/no loss if 2 × 5 FRAs were being quoted at 10 percent.

FUTURES IMPLIED FORWARD RATES

Short-term interest rate futures contracts offer an alternative method of hedging interest rate exposure on future commitments. The main difference between FRAs and futures is that whereas the terms in the former case can be tailored to the requirements of the user, the terms in the latter case are fixed. Despite this inflexibility, futures contracts enjoy greater liquidity and are extensively used by FRA traders to hedge their positions. It is not surprising, therefore, that FRA contract rates are primarily driven by the futures market in the relevant currency where such markets exist. For example, Eurodollar futures contracts on the IMM are available on three-month LIBOR out to four years.

Table 4.5

Month	Price	Implied LIBOR
September	94.0	6.00%
December	93.8	6.20%
March	93.6	6.40%
June	93.2	6.80%
September	92.9	7.10%
December	92.7	7.30%
March	92.5	7.50%
June	92.3	7.70%

Consider the three-month Eurodollar futures prices given in Table 4.5.

Three month implied forward rates can be obtained directly from futures prices by deducting the futures price from 100. Thus, implied three-month LIBOR beginning on the settlement date of the September contract in year 1 is 6 percent. On the settlement date of the June (year 2) contract the implied forward three-month LIBOR is 6.80 percent. Thus, if we were to obtain a quote for an FRA that matched the IMM settlement date in September (third Wednesday of the contract month), the quote will be close to 6.0 percent, say 6.0 percent – 5.96 percent. If the FRA settlement date did not match the standard futures contract date, the quoted rate will be a linear interpolation between the two adjacent futures contract prices bracketing the FRA settlement date.

It is important to note the differences in terminology between the FRA and the futures markets. When you buy a FRA, you are seeking protection against future rises in interest rates. The buyer of an FRA can therefore be thought of as a borrower wishing to lock-in the cost of borrowing. On the other hand, when you sell a FRA you are seeking protection against falling interest rates. The seller of an FRA can therefore be thought of as an investor wishing to lock-in a return. The underlying expectation of an FRA buyer is that interest rates will rise in future, whereas the seller expects interest rates to fall in future. This terminology is the opposite of the futures market terminology; when you buy a futures contract, you expect interest rates to fall in future. Conversely, when you sell a futures contract you expect interest rates to rise in future. This difference in terminology arises because whereas the FRA market trades on the basis of quoted interest rates – you 'buy' or 'sell' the rate – the futures market trades on the basis of price – (100 – interest rate). Thus, as a borrower who expects interest rates to rise you will buy an FRA (or 'buy' the rate) or sell a futures contract. Conversely, as an investor who expects interest rates to fall you will sell an FRA (or 'sell' the rate) or buy a futures contract.

FORWARD FX CONTRACTS

For corporates and financial institutions foreign exchange exposure arises in various forms. A multinational company with business operations spread across continents is exposed to the effects of foreign exchange fluctuations on its balance sheet as much as a small company that merely engages in the import and export of goods. International banks and large companies regularly borrow and invest in foreign currencies again causing foreign currency exposure. A forward FX contract allows its user to hedge against future exchange rate movements.

An outright forward FX contract is simply an agreement to buy or sell currencies on a specified date in the future at an agreed exchange rate ('the forward rate') agreed at the time of executing the deal. For example, a US corporation expecting to receive an amount of £100 million in three months' time will be exposed to US$ appreciating against sterling. It can eliminate this risk by selling its sterling inflow forward, thereby locking-in the effective US$ amount in three months' time. By doing so, the corporation gives up the opportunity of receiving more dollars should sterling have appreciated against US$ in three months' time. To understand the mechanics of the forward FX contract and its variations it is important to set out the market terminology together with the dealing jargon at the outset.

Foreign exchange comprises both cash and forward transactions. In the context of foreign exchange markets the rate of exchange for one currency against another is referred to as the spot rate. The spot rate relates to deals transacted with a value date usually two business days after the dealing date. Same day and one day (or 'Tom Next') rates (i.e. transactions for value before the spot date) and forward rates (i.e transactions for value after the spot date) are a function of the spot rate and the interest differentials in the two currencies in question. While it is common to use such terms as 'buy' and 'sell' in the FX market, they can be confusing because each foreign exchange transaction involves purchase of one currency and simultaneous sale of another. For example when you buy US dollars against yen, you have simultaneously sold yen. The foreign exchange rate, as a ratio, reflects the value of one currency in terms of another currency. In foreign exchange markets most currencies are quoted in terms of one US$. The major exceptions, for historical reasons, are sterling, A$, NZ$, rand and IR£.

HOW IS THE FORWARD FX RATE DERIVED?

To calculate the outright forward rate on a forward FX contract the dealing bank will assume that it has to borrow funds in one currency (the currency it is selling) and invest funds in another currency (the currency it is buying) at the current market interest rates in these two currencies for the term of the forward contract. The cost or benefit of doing so will be used to adjust the spot exchange rate either upward or downward. This adjusted rate gives the forward rate for the term of the contract. More formally, the relationship between the spot and the forward exchange rate is described by the interest rate parity theorem. This theorem holds that the ratio of the forward and spot exchange rates will equal the ratio of interest rates in the two currencies in question for the forward term. That is

$$\frac{X_f}{X_s} = \frac{1 + r_f \left(\frac{n}{b}\right)}{1 + r_d \left(\frac{n}{b}\right)}$$

where

X_f = forward exchange rate expressed as units of foreign currency per unit of domestic currency

X_s = spot exchange rate expressed as units of foreign currency per unit of domestic currency

r_f = interest rate in foreign currency for the term of the forward contract

r_d = interest rate in domestic currency for the term of the forward contract

n = number of days in the forward period

b = interest basis

To explain the relationship between forward and spot exchange rates, consider the following information.

X_s = 1.5
r_f = 10%
r_d = 5%
n = 180 days
b = 360 days

Assuming that the two interest rates relate to the same period as the term of the forward contract, we have

$$X_f = \frac{1 + \left(0.10 \times \frac{180}{360}\right)}{1 + \left(0.05 \times \frac{180}{360}\right)} (1.5) = 1.5366$$

i.e., 1.5365 units of foreign currency equal one unit of domestic currency at the end of the forward period. Since a higher number in this case (from a spot rate of 1.5 to a forward rate of 1.5366) implies that the foreign currency has less value in future, it is said to be at a discount. Conversely, since the domestic currency is expected to appreciate, it is said to be at a premium. As a matter of a simple rule, if the foreign currency yields higher return than the domestic currency, it will be at a discount to the domestic currency and vice versa. It is important to note that for periods of longer than one year equation (4.8) must take into account any compounding effects as described in Chapter 2.

The forward rate given by equation (4.8) must be the market forward rate (ignoring bid-offer spread) if riskless arbitrage is to be avoided.

Example

Suppose the six-month interest rate for US dollars is quoted as 10 percent – 9.95 percent and the six-month yen rate is quoted as 5 percent – 4.94 percent. Also suppose the spot US$/yen is trading at 99.96-99.97. What is the six-month outright forward FX? To understand the principle behind formula (4.8) for the forward FX let us consider how a foreign exchange dealer would arrive at a quote for this contract.

The foreign exchange dealer can borrow, say, $1 million at 10 percent for six months. It can sell (exchange) these dollars to another foreign exchange dealer for yen at the bid side of the spot rate of 99.96. It will, therefore, receive yen 99.96 million which it can invest at 4.94 percent (bid interest rate in yen) for a six-month period. Its cash flows in six months time will be as under:

Yen Investment

Principal	Yen 99,960,000
Interest[4]	Yen 2,496,445
	Yen 102,456,445

US$ Borrowing

Principal	$ 1,000,000
Interest[5]	$ 50,556
	$ 1,050,556

The six-month outright forward rate is the ratio of the yen receipts to US$ payments. That is

$$\frac{Yen\ 102,456,445}{\$\ 1,050,556} = 97.5259$$

This is the bid rate for US$. Notice, since in this case yen is expected to appreciate in six months' time, the US$ is at a discount. The magnitude of the discount is the difference between the forward rate and the spot rate, i.e. $97.5259 - 99.9600 = -2.4341$.

To calculate the offer side of the outright forward rate the dealer would reverse the above hedging strategy. It would borrow, say, Y99.96 million for six months at the (offered) rate of 5 percent and sell the proceeds for yen at the current spot rate of 99.97. It could then

----

[4] $(99,960,000 \times \dfrac{4.94}{100} \times \dfrac{182}{360}$

[5] $(1,000,000 \times \dfrac{10}{100} \times \dfrac{182}{360}$

invest the US$ amount of $999,900 at 9.95 percent for a period of six months. The cash flows at maturity will be:

US$ investment

Principal	$ 999,900
Interest[6]	$ 50,298
	$ 1,050,198

Yen borrowing

Principal	Yen 99,960,000
Interest[7]	Yen 2,526,767
	Yen 102,486,767

The offered rate for forward US$ will be:

$$\frac{Yen\ 102,486,767}{\$\ 1,050,198} = 97.588$$

i.e. a discount of –2.382.

There is an active swap market in foreign exchange which is used by foreign exchange dealers to hedge positions arising on account of forward FX transactions. A foreign exchange swap transaction involves simultaneous sale and purchase of two currencies for spot delivery and an opposite sale and purchase of the same currencies for future delivery. For example, if a dealer sells a currency forward he will buy the equivalent of the currency spot and then swap the flows, i.e. sell the currency spot and buy it forward to the date corresponding with the forward contract being hedged. Swaps are a hedging tool for the interbank market which allows dealers to avoid deposit markets to cover outright forward contracts.

SUMMARY

Forward contracts comprise a number of agreements in which an underlying asset, commodity or currency is bought or sold at a future date. This chapter has dealt with forward contracts on interest rates and foreign currencies.

---

[6] $(999,900 \times \dfrac{9.95}{100} \times \dfrac{182}{360}$

[7] $(99,960,000 \times \dfrac{5}{100} \times \dfrac{182}{360}$

87

The forward rate agreement provides a mechanism to hedge against future interest rate changes. Borrowers and investors use forward rate agreements to lock in funding costs or investment returns at a future point in time. Forward FX contracts, on the other hand, allow borrowers and investors to hedge currency risk on forward commitments.

References

British Bankers' Association, *Forward Rate Agreements*, London, August 1985.
Stigum, M., *Money Market*, Homewood Illinois: Dow Jones-Irwin, 1983.

5

INTEREST RATE SWAPS

History of development

What is an interest rate swap?

Economic rationale for interest rate swaps

Features of a standard interest rate swap

Valuation of interest rate swaps – conceptual framework

Interest rate swaps pricing – market convention

Determinants of swaps pricing

Swap spreads

Factors affecting the level of swap spreads

Swaps pricing – basic concepts

Bond equivalent approach to swap valuation

Zero coupon approach to swap valuation

Summary

The past two decades have witnessed an explosion of financial innovations. Of the many extraordinary financial innovations of the past twenty years, however, none can rival the burgeoning of the global market for interest rate and currency swaps. The phenomenal growth of the swaps market in the 1980s and beyond has rendered what many considered a passing arbitrage product of the 1970s into one of the most durable tools of asset and liability management.

HISTORY OF DEVELOPMENT

The swaps market, as we know it today, has only existed since 1980 although some structured proprietary transactions were put together in the mid-1970s. The forerunner of the current swaps are generally considered to be parallel loans arranged mainly between American and British companies in the 1970s. However, a type of currency swap transaction involving foreign currencies and, initially gold, was undertaken between a number of key central banks and the Bank for International Settlement (BIS) long before parallel loans came to prominence. These transactions were similar to short-dated foreign exchange swaps combining a spot sale (purchase) of a currency with a simultaneous agreement to buy (sell) the currency at some future time. This swap network was designed to create additional international reserves to facilitate stabilization of the international monetary system.

With the introduction of exchange controls in the United Kingdom in the early 1970s parallel and back-to-back loans were developed as a vehicle by which companies in the United Kingdom could avoid the premium on investments outside the UK. These structured financing arrangements ultimately evolved into the first currency swap in 1976 between BOS Kalis Westminster of Holland and ICI Finance of the UK. The transaction was arranged by Continental Illinois Limited and Goldman Sachs. The swap was denominated in Dutch guilder and British pound. This important transaction was followed in April 1977 by a transaction involving Consolidated Goldfields and the government of Venezuela in connection with the construction of the Caracas Metro system. The currencies involved in this case were US dollars and French francs. Within two years of this transaction the first currency swap driven by a capital markets issue was transacted.

In 1979 Roy Lease, the leasing subsidiary of the Royal Bank of Canada, made a 60 million Deutschmark issue bearing a coupon of

6.75 percent which it swapped into Canadian dollars at a cost of 11 percent that was well below its target. The transaction was structured as a series of forward foreign exchange contracts which were used to hedge Deutschmark cash flows into Canadian dollars via US dollars.

Despite these transactions it was not until 1981 that currency swaps became an established feature of the international capital markets. In a landmark swap transaction completed in August 1981 the World Bank swapped a US$ 290 million bond issue into Deutschmarks and Swiss francs with IBM. The swap was arranged by Solomon Brothers.[1]

The first interest rate swaps were also transacted in 1981 on a proprietary basis by Citibank and Continental Illinois. However, the breakthrough for this segment of the swaps market came when in 1982 Deutsche Bank swapped a seven year US$300 million fixed rate bond into a synthetic US$ floating rate note. Ever since the completion of this landmark transaction, the interest rate swaps market has expanded at a phenomenal rate. So much so that it has outpaced its forerunner, the currency swaps market. Figure 5.1 graphically depicts the dramatic growth in the use of interest rate swaps since 1988.

WHAT IS AN INTEREST RATE SWAP?

An interest rate swap is an agreement between two parties to make to each other periodic payments calculated on the basis of specified interest rates and a notional principal amount. Typically the payments to be

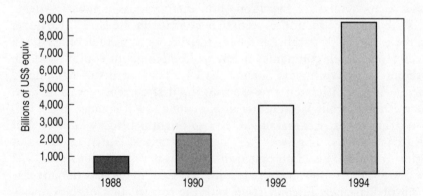

Fig 5.1 Growth in the interest rate swaps market (interest rate swaps outstanding: notional principal amount)

---

[1] David R. Boek, 'Fixed-to-fixed Currency Swap: the origins of the World Bank borrowing', in Antl, Boris ed. Swap Financing Techniques (1985) vol 2, Euromoney.

made by one party are calculated using a floating rate index (such as LIBOR) while the payments to be made by the other party are determined on the basis of a fixed rate of interest (coupon swap) or a different floating rate index (basis swap). The payments are made in the same currency and no exchange of principal takes place.[2]

While it is possible for the principals in a swap transaction to negotiate the swap directly with each other, in fact almost all swaps are transacted through an intermediary bank. An example of a typical interest rate swap is as depicted in Figure 5.2.

In this example, Party A enters into an interest rate swap with the intermediary bank under which it pays an annual fixed rate of 7 percent for the term of the swap against receiving six-month LIBOR bi-annually. By entering into this swap Party A effectively converts its floating rate liability into a fixed liability. Both payments are based on the same notional principal amount.

Another example of an interest rate swap involving an investor is depicted in Figure 5.3. In this example the investor uses an interest rate swap to create a synthetic FRN. The investor has an asset bearing annual fixed coupon of 7 percent. It is concerned about rising interest rates but does not want to sell the bond to buy an FRN. Instead it enters into an interest rate swap under which it pays annual fixed rate of 7 percent against receiving six-month LIBOR plus 20 basis points. The positive spread reflects the difference between the current fixed rate for the term of the swap and 7 percent, being the rate paid by the investor. A positive spread in this case means that the current swap rate is lower than 7 percent.

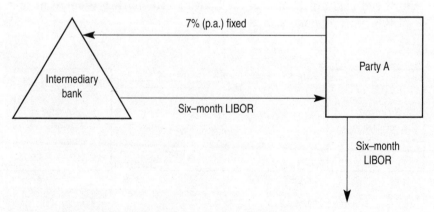

Fig 5.2 Interest rate swap (liability management application)

---

[2] Since both flows of the swap are denominated in the same currency the exchange of equal amounts of principal is unnecessary.

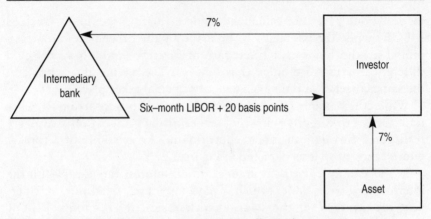

Fig 5.3 Interest rate swap (asset management application)

ECONOMIC RATIONALE FOR INTEREST RATE SWAPS

It is argued that the main motivation of end-users (mainly borrowers) in the early stages of the interest rate swaps market was to exploit differential credit spreads in the fixed and the floating rate debt markets. This can be best explained by way of an example: Consider the matched interest rate swap depicted in Figure 5.4. In this example a AAA-rated bank wishes to raise floating rate funds for a term of five years. It can do so at an all-in-cost of six-month LIBOR flat. It can also raise funds in the fixed rate market at an all-in-cost of 10 percent. An A-rated corporation, on the other hand, wishes to raise fixed rate funds for a term of five years. It can do so at an all-in cost of 11 percent. It can also raise funds in the floating rate market at an all-in cost of LIBOR plus 50 basis points.

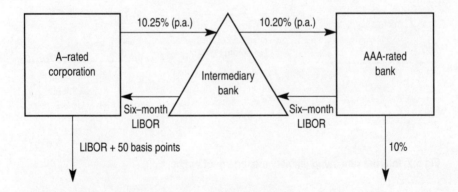

Fig 5.4 Credit arbitrage through an interest rate swap

Without the mechanism of an interest rate swap, the two unrelated borrowers have no alternative but to borrow directly in the markets of their funding requirement; floating rate in the case of the bank and fixed rate in the case of the corporation. We, however, notice that the differential in the cost of borrowing in the fixed and the floating rate markets for the two borrowers is unequal. In the fixed rate market the corporation is required to pay an additional 1 percent to compensate for its lower credit quality relative to the bank. In the floating rate market, however, the differential is only 0.5 percent. This difference in credit spreads in the two markets can be mutually exploited by the two parties by combining borrowings in markets where each has a relative advantage with an interest rate swap. In this example, the AAA-rated bank raises fixed rate funds at an annual cost of 10 percent whereas the A-rated corporation raises an equal amount of floating rate funds in the international banking market at a cost of LIBOR plus 50 basis points. The two parties then enter into an interest rate swap through an intermediary bank whereby they exchange their interest obligations.

Thus the bank pays six-month LIBOR and receives 10.20 percent annually under the swap. The corporation, on the other hand, receives six-month LIBOR and pays 10.25 percent annually. By combining its obligations under the swap with its obligations under the borrowing the bank achieves an effective cost of LIBOR − 20 basis points. That is 20 basis points less than it would have achieved had it borrowed directly in the floating rate market. The corporation, on the other hand, achieves an effective annual cost of 10.75 percent. That is 25 basis points lower than it would have achieved if it had borrowed directly in the fixed rate market. The intermediary bank, in this case, makes a bid-offer spread of 5 basis points p.a. Notice that the total saving from the swap is 50 basis points − 25 basis points for the corporation, 20 basis points for the bank and 5 basis points for the intermediary bank − which is equal to the net differential in the fixed and the floating rate markets for the two borrowers. Table 5.1 summarizes these computations.

Table 5.1

	Bank	Corporation
Fixed borrowing	−10.0%	−
Floating borrowing	−	−(LIBOR + 0.50%) −10.25%
Swap (pay)	−LIBOR	
Swap (receive)	10.20%	LIBOR
Net cost	LIBOR −0.20%	10.75%

The classic arbitrage opportunity described above is widely believed to have driven the interest rate swap market at least in its initial phase of development. Some of the early explanations put forth for the existence of this arbitrage were:

- greater risk aversion in fixed rate bond markets
- over-capacity in floating rate loan markets
- asymmetry of information across markets
- superior ability of banks to monitor credit
- banks' desire to diversify out of LDC debt

All these explanations, however, would suggest that greater use of swaps would, in a competitive market, lead to disappearance of the arbitrage opportunity arising from any of the above reasons and therefore take away the very reason for swapping. The reality, however, points in the other direction; not only has the market for swaps grown many fold over the years, it has also become an integral part of global financial markets. It was not until the middle of the 1980s that more plausible explanations for the existence of the swaps began to emerge, mainly from academics. We briefly outline the more important ones here.

The comparative advantage

This argument attempts to explain the economic gain that seems to arise from the use of an interest rate swap in terms of the comparative advantage principle in trade theory.[3] As in the case of international trade, market efficiency is regarded as the basis for the comparative advantage in capital markets. It is argued that the main motivation of end-users in the early stages of the interest rate swaps market was to exploit differential borrowing advantages to raise funds cheaply. Three major sources of the comparative advantage have been identified as:

1 Regulatory constraints causing distortions in the market that result in opportunities for arbitrage.
2 Informational inefficiencies that lead to differing risk (particularly credit risk) perceptions in various markets.
3 Lack of diversification in individual portfolios.

Completion of markets

An important alternative explanation for interest rate swaps is that it allows to create debt and investment structures that are not possible

---

[3] Bicksler et al.

with any combination of existing instruments beyond a few years. This argument claims that interest rate swaps market contributes to the integration of financial ·markets.[4] For example, the market for long-dated interest rate forward contracts has historically been illiquid beyond two to three years. However, since interest rate swaps can be viewed as combinations of forward interest rate contracts, long-term swaps are used to create synthetic long-term forward contracts. Additionally, combinations of interest rate swaps and the underlying debt can be used to create synthetic packages that cannot be replicated using existing securities. A reverse floater is a prime example of such a combination.

Agency theoretic argument

This explanation relies on differences in agency costs between long-and short-term debt.[5] It argues that once a lower rated borrower issues long-term debt, there is an incentive to make the firm riskier at the expense of the bond holders. Now even though the bond holders share in the loss should bankruptcy occur, they do not receive more than the promised yield. In view of this asymmetry in risk and return bondholders require a large premium on long-term debt issued by lower rated borrowers. It would seem that the premium required of higher rated issuers is lower because these borrowers have already established their reputation for long-term survival. Lower rated borrowers, however, can avoid agency costs by raising funds in the short-term floating rate market and swapping it into long-term fixed rate debt. Since borrowers in the short-term market are monitored in each interest period they are not required to pay the long-term premium for agency costs. Thus, interest rate swaps may reduce financing costs without resorting to the comparative advantage theory.

FEATURES OF A STANDARD INTEREST RATE SWAP

An interest rate swap is an agreement between two counterparties to make to each other periodic interest payments for the term of the swap. One series of these payments is based on a fixed rate of interest and is referred to as the 'fixed leg' of the swap. The other series is based on a floating rate index, primarily LIBOR, and is referred to as the 'floating leg' of the swap.

---

[4] Smith, Smithson and Wakeman (1986).
[5] Wall and Pringle (1987) and Wall (1989).

The fixed rate payments are usually made at annual or bi-annual intervals. At any moment in time the swaps dealers quote a bid and an offer fixed rate for various maturities; usually, one, two, three, four, five, seven and ten years in major currencies. The bid-rate is the fixed rate (annual or semi-annual) that the market-maker will pay for the term of the swap against receiving six-month LIBOR flat in the same currency for the same term. The offer-rate, on the other hand, is the fixed rate that the swaps trader wants to receive against paying six-month LIBOR flat for the term of the swap. The floating rate is set at the beginning of each interest period and paid at the end of this period i.e. six months after being set. Both payments are calculated on the basis of a notional principal amount.

A standard or 'vanila' interest rate swap refers to a swap that is transacted at the current market fixed rate against six-month LIBOR. Any swap in which the fixed rate is set above or below the current market fixed rate is by definition a non-standard or an off-market interest rate swap. A standard interest rate swap is completely defined by five factors:

1 Notional principal amount

2 The fixed rate

3 The floating rate index

4 Frequency of fixed and floating rate payments

5 The maturity date

Notional principal amount is the sum on which both the fixed and the floating interest payments are based. It is equivalent to the face value of a bond. However, since in the case of interest rate swaps no exchange of principal takes place, this sum is notional.

The fixed rate is the rate on which fixed interest payments are based. It is set at the outset for the term of the swap. As will be pointed out later, the market price for standard interest rate swaps is defined in terms of the fixed rate. Fixed rates are usually quoted as annual or semi-annual rates.

The floating rate is the interest rate index on which floating interest payments are based. In the case of major currencies the floating rate index is usually LIBOR. In Australian dollar swaps, fixed rates are quoted against the Bank Bill Rate (BBR) as the floating index. The fixed interest rate is usually quoted against six-month LIBOR flat. For each interest period, LIBOR is set at the beginning of the accrual period and paid in arrears.

Frequency of payments for the fixed rate payments in a standard inter-est rate swap is usually annual or semi-annual. The floating payments, on the other hand, are usually made at six-monthly intervals with six-month LIBOR being the underlying index.

The maturity date refers to the termination date of a swap on which final interest payments are exchanged.

VALUATION OF INTEREST RATE SWAPS – CONCEPTUAL FRAMEWORK

An interest rate swap can be viewed in two alternative ways; (i) a combination of a bond and an FRN and (ii) a strip of futures contracts or forward rate agreements. Understanding of this equivalence is important for the valuation of interest rate swaps.

Bond/FRN equivalence

An interest rate swap can be viewed as a simultaneous exchange of a fixed rate bond and a floating rate note of identical maturities. All we need to do is to assume that the two parties to the swap are going to exchange the (notional) principal amount at maturity. Since both the fixed and the floating interest payments in an interest rate swap are based on the same notional principal amount, the assumption of principal exchange at maturity does not alter the economics of the transaction. However, it greatly facilitates the valuation of interest rate swaps because it allows us to use traditional fixed income valuation techniques described in Chapter 2 to value interest rate swaps. This approach to pricing interest rate swaps is discussed in greater detail below.

Futures equivalence

Interest rate swaps can be replicated using LIBOR based interest rate futures. For example, a US dollar interest rate swap can be replicated using a strip of Eurodollar futures contracts. Eurodollar futures contracts on the IMM are available out to four years based on the three-month LIBOR. These contracts set rates on Eurodollar time deposits commencing on a future date – the third Wednesday of March, June, September or December, depending on the contract expiration month. The implied interest rate from a given futures contract is derived by subtracting the futures price from 100. Thus, a futures price of 90 implies a three-month interest rate of 10 percent commencing from the contract expiration date. Therefore, as interest rates fall, futures prices rise and as interest rates rise, futures prices fall.

Suppose you have an FRN with two years to run that pays three-month LIBOR. Let us assume that you are concerned about interest rates falling over the next two years. You can fix the return on your asset by entering into an interest rate swap under which you pay three-month LIBOR against receiving the current two-year fixed swap rate.[6] By entering into the swap your return is fixed at this rate. Alternatively, you can buy a series (strip) of Eurodollar futures contracts to achieve the same effect.[7] Suppose the current Eurodollar futures prices for the next seven contracts are as given in Table 5.2. The implied forward rates are given by subtracting the relevant futures contract price from 100.

Table 5.2

Contract Expiry	Price	Implied Forward Rate
June 19X1	95.00	5.00%
September 19X1	94.80	5.20%
December 19X1	94.55	5.45%
March 19X2	94.30	5.70%
June 19X2	94.00	6.00%
September 19X2	93.65	6.35%
December 19X2	93.30	6.70%

Given the implied forward three-month LIBOR rates we can compute the two-year strip rate as under:

$$\text{Strip Rate} = \left[\left(1 + r\frac{d}{360} \right) \prod_i \left(1 + r_{\text{fi}}\frac{DQ_i}{360} \right) \right]^{\frac{1}{n}} - 1 \tag{5.1}$$

where

r = current LIBOR to expiration of nearby futures contract
d = number of days to expiration of nearby futures contract
r_{fi} = forward LIBOR implied by contract i
DQ_i = actual number of days in quarter i beginning with the third Wednesday of the respective futures expiration month.
n = strip maturity (in years)

---

[6] This rate will differ from the rate quoted for payment against six-month LIBOR.

[7] A strip hedge involves buying or selling the same number of futures contracts of each maturity. Strips are very effective hedges for short-term assets and liabilities. Liquidity problems in longer dated futures contracts cause widening of bid-offer spreads. For longer term risk management a technique called a stack hedge is often used. It relies on near term contracts to hedge risk arising in distant periods. This technique is effective if the implied yield curve shifts in a parallel fashion.

Given the implied forward rates in Table 5.2 and assuming that the current LIBOR to the expiration of the nearby contract is 4.9 percent (in 90 days) we can calculate the two-year strip rate as under:

2 year Strip Rate =

$$\left[\left(1+0.049\frac{90}{360}\right)\times\left(1+0.05\frac{91}{360}\right)\times\left(1+0.052\frac{90}{360}\right)\times\left(1+0.0545\frac{90}{360}\right)\times\left(1+0.057\frac{91}{360}\right)\times\left(1+0.06\frac{90}{360}\right)\times\left(1+0.0635\frac{91}{360}\right)\times\left(1+0.07\frac{90}{360}\right)\right]^{\frac{1}{2}}$$

$= 0.0585 = 5.85\%$

To convert this strip rate into the equivalent money market yield we simply multiply it by 360/365 to give $5.85 \times 360/365 = 5.77\%$. To avoid any opportunities for arbitrage, therefore, the quoted three-year swap fixed rate should be close to 5.776 percent (on money market basis).

FRA equivalence

An interest rate swap can also be viewed as a series of forward rate agreements (FRAs). In Chapter 4 we noted that the contract rate of an FRA was chosen such that its present value is zero. It was also noted that on the settlement date of an FRA a discounted payment is made by one party to the other depending on interest rate movements.

Thus, for a normal strip of FRAs the contract or strike rate would usually be different for each FRA reflecting the shape of the yield curve. Now suppose we can purchase a strip of FRAs with a single strike rate such that the value of any single FRA may be higher or lower than zero but the present value of the strip is zero. By appropriate selection of the strike rate we can ensure that the value of the strip is zero. Also suppose that instead of making a discounted payment on the settlement date of an FRA we make an undiscounted payment on the maturity date of the underlying loan and deposit. That is, in the case of a 6×12 FRA, instead of making the discounted payment at the end of six months we make the undiscounted payment at the end of twelve months. Since the payment on the settlement date is discounted by the appropriate LIBOR for the period from the settlement date to the maturity date, the present value of the discounted payment equals the present value of the undiscounted payment. It is easy to show that such a strip of FRAs with a single strike rate and payment in arrears is a standard interest rate swap.

Consider purchasing the following series of FRAs.

FRA Term	Strike Rate
6 × 12	5.00%
12 × 18	5.20%
18 × 24	5.40%
24 × 36	5.50%
36 × 42	5.57%

When combined with the current six-month LIBOR of say 4.9 percent, purchasing the above combination of FRAs is an alternative to entering into a three-year swap under which you pay approximately 5.33 percent (annually) fixed for three years against receiving six-month LIBOR. Conversely, selling the above strip of FRAs would be equivalent to entering into a swap under which you receive fixed against paying LIBOR.

INTEREST RATE SWAPS PRICING – MARKET CONVENTION

Interest rate swaps are usually quoted as a fixed rate, payable on a notional principal amount. This rate is quoted for standard maturities against LIBOR flat (usually six-month LIBOR). At any point in time the market-maker quotes a bid rate – that is the fixed rate it is prepared to pay against receiving LIBOR flat – and an offer rate – that is the rate it wishes to receive against paying LIBOR flat. The difference between bid and offer rates reflects the cost of transacting a swap for the dealer including the costs of credit and regulatory capital.

As in the case of other financial instruments peculiar market conventions have evolved in the case of interest rates swaps in various currencies. Differences in convention mainly relate to payment frequency and day count basis for interest accrual. For example, fixed rate payments are usually paid either annually or semi-annually. To determine the fixed payment, any of the following day count conventions may be used:

- actual/360 day basis
- actual/365 day basis
- 30/360 day basis.

In the United States actual/360 day basis is referred to as the money-market basis, whereas in the United Kingdom actual/365 is the money market convention, while 30/360 day basis is also referred to as the bond basis.[8] Table 5.3 summarizes the day-count conventions used in various swaps markets.

---

[8] In the United States bond basis also refers to actual/365 day convention!

Table 5.3 Day count conventions for interest rate swaps

Currency	Standard fixed payment frequency	Fixed payment interest basis	Standard floating rate index	Floating payment interest basis
Australian dollar	semi-annual	act/365	A $ bank bills	act/365
Belgian franc	annual	act/365	BIBOR	act/365
British pound	semi-annual	act/365	£ LIBOR	act/365
Canadian dollar	semi-annual	act/365	Canadian BAs	act/365
Danish kroner	annual	30/360	CIBOR	act/360
Dutch guilder	annual	30/360	AIBOR	act/360
ECU	annual	30/360	ECU LIBOR	act/360
French franc	annual	30/360	FFr LIBOR, PIBOR, TAM	act/360 act/365
Hong Kong dollar	quarterly	act/365	HIBOR	act/365
Italian lira	annual	30/360	MIBOR	act/360
Japanese yen	semi-annual	act/365	Yen LIBOR	act/360
Spanish peseta	semi-annual	act/360	MIBOR	act/360
Swedish krona	annual	30/360	STIBOR	act/360
Swiss franc	annual	30/360	SFr LIBOR	act/360
Deutsche mark	annual	30/360	DM LIBOR	act/360
US dollar	annual	30/360	$ LIBOR	act/360

The actual/360 day convention assumes that there are 360 calendar days in a year and, therefore, the fixed interest payment between two dates, say, D_1 and D_2 on this basis is calculated as under:

$$Fixed\ Interest\ Payment = Notional\ Principal \times Fixed\ Rate \times \frac{(D_2 - D_1)}{360}$$

Similarly, the actual/365 day convention assumes a 365-day year irrespective of whether it is a leap year or not. The fixed interest payment in this case accruing between two dates, D_1 and D_2, can be computed as:

$$Fixed\ Interest\ Payment = Notional\ Principal \times Fixed\ Rate \times \frac{(D_2 - D_1)}{365}$$

The 30/360 day convention assumes that each month is of 30 days duration. To compute the fixed interest payment under this convention, therefore, we can no longer assume the actual difference between D_2 and D_1 but must take account of the number of complete calendar months plus any days in uncompleted months. That is;

Fixed Interest Payment = Notional Principal × Fixed Rate × 30 × number of complete months + max(30 – D_1, 0) + min(30, D_2)

Floating rate payments are usually based on the rate quoted in London for six-month deposits in major currencies (i.e. LIBOR). For other currencies a similar domestic benchmark rate is used. The floating rate is usually set two business days prior to the beginning of the interest accrual period. The payment is calculated using either actual/360 day or actual/365 day convention depending on the currency.

Example

Suppose you enter into a 5-year swap on 10 January 1995 in which you agree to pay a semi-annual fixed rate of 10 percent against receiving six-month LIBOR on a notional principal amount of 100,000,000. The value date, or the effective date of the swap is 12 January 1995 and, therefore, the interest on both the fixed and the floating legs will start to accrue on that day. Notice that the floating rate for the next interest period would have been set on 10 January 1995 (two days before the accrual begins). Suppose in this case six-month LIBOR was fixed at 8.50 percent. Since both the fixed and the floating interest payments are to be paid semi-annually, the first payment will become due on 12 July 1995. Using the above day-count conventions for fixed and floating rate payments, what will these payments be?

1 Actual/360 day

$$Fixed\ Interest\ Payment = Notional\ Principal \times Fixed\ Rate \times \frac{(D_2 - D_1)}{360}$$

$$= 100,000,000 \times 0.10 \times \frac{(12\ July\ 1995 - 12\ January\ 1995)}{360}$$

$$= 100,000,000 \times 0.10 \times \frac{181}{360} = 5,027,778$$

2 Actual/365 day

$$Fixed\ Interest\ Payment = Notional\ Principal \times Fixed\ Rate \times \frac{(D_2 - D_1)}{365}$$

$$= 100,000,000 \times \frac{181}{365} = 4,958,904$$

3 30/360 day

In this case we first need to determine the number of complete months and then take into account the number of days in incomplete months assuming 30 days per month. In our example there are five complete months – February through June – each assumed to have 30 calendar days. Thus we have

$$Number\ of\ Days = 30 \times number\ of\ complete\ months + \max(30 - D_1, 0) + \min(30, D_2)$$

$$= 30 \times 5\ months + \max(30-12,0) + \min(30,12)$$

$$= 150 + 18 + 12 = 180\ days$$

The fixed payment in this case will therefore be;

$$100,000,000 \times 0.10 \times \frac{180}{360} = 500,000,000$$

DETERMINANTS OF SWAPS PRICING

We noted above that an interest rate swap is quoted as a fixed rate payable on a notional amount against a floating index, such as six-month LIBOR, payable on the same notional amount. In this section we outline the primary factors that influence this rate.

The primary determinant of the fixed rate for an interest rate swap of a given maturity is the yield on a bench mark risk-free security of equivalent maturity such as a Treasury bond. Thus, the quoted fixed rate for a five-year swap depends on the yield quoted for the benchmark five-year government bond in the given currency. The difference between the underlying risk-free yield and the fixed swap rate is referred to as the swap spread. The swap rates are, therefore, subject to factors that affect both interest rates in general and swap spreads in particular.

The risk-free interest rates for various terms to maturity that may prevail in an economy at any point in time are determined by a complex interaction of supply and demand forces. For example, in a simple exchange economy the equilibrium rate or the market rate of interest is determined by the forces of supply and demand for current consumption claims vis-à-vis future claims. The rate of interest is simply a measure of the price of current consumption claims in relation to future consumption claims. As noted in Chapter 2, even when a bond is risk free in terms of default, various factors such as future inflation and liquidity will cause yield differences among risk-free bonds of various maturities and hence the term structure of risk-free interest rates. In Chapter 2 we described various theories that attempt to explain the existence of a term structure of risk-free interest rates.

Swap spread is the other key determinant of the fixed rate for an interest rate swap of a given maturity. The swap spread curve closely mirrors corporate spreads and as such is a surrogate for credit and other risks. It is therefore affected by all of the factors that affect corporate spreads. Moreover, since an interest rate swap is transacted through an intermediary bank, the swap spread must include the cost of intermediation. Intermediary banks assume the risk of default by each counterparty to a swap and must bear various costs associated with hedging and regulatory capital. These costs are reflected in the difference between the bid and the offer side of a quoted fixed rate.

It is important to note that the quoted fixed rate on an interest rate swap is against the floating index flat. What that means is that the market is assuming an average credit quality counterparty to the swap, say A or AA. For counterparties with a lower or a higher credit rating the fixed rate will be adjusted to reflect higher or lower credit risk, as the case may be. Moreover, BIS regulations treat swaps with corporates as a higher risk than swaps with the OECD banks. This results in a greater capital charge for corporates compared with the OECD banks.

SWAP SPREADS

Of all the determinants of a swap's price, swap spread is the most important element. It is the swap spread for a given maturity that determines whether a swap transaction is economically viable. Investors and borrowers use interest rate swaps to create synthetic assets and liabilities. Using swaps can be economically justified only if the return on a synthetic asset is higher and the cost of the synthetic borrowing is lower than straight assets and liabilities. It is therefore essential to understand the forces that drive swap spreads.

Short-dated swaps

For shorter maturities (up to three years) interest rate swaps in major currencies are priced relative to the implied yield on a strip of deposit futures for the same maturity. As we noted above, short-dated interest rate swaps can be replicated by a strip of futures contracts. Spreads on shorter dated swaps are, therefore, largely determined by hedging costs in the futures market. For example, spreads on short-term US dollar swaps are determined almost solely by the Eurodollar futures market.

When a market maker enters into an interest rate swap in which it either pays or receives a fixed rate of interest it assumes the risk of fluctuation in interest rates over the life of the swap. To hedge its position it can either enter into a matching interest rate swap with another counterparty or hedge its exposure by assuming an opposite position in a related instrument. Up to three years, futures market provides a convenient way of hedging interest rate exposure in some major currencies. Therefore, the fixed rate quoted on interest rate swaps of up to three years duration largely reflects the fixed rate that can be achieved by creating a strip of futures contracts for the same term as the underlying swap term. Any differences between the fixed swap rate and the strip rate will be small and arise on account of differences in timing between payment dates and contract expirations, the time value of money and margin requirements. Any significant difference between the two rates will create opportunities for arbitrage.

It is not surprising, therefore, that spreads for one, two and three year US dollar interest rate swaps are much influenced by changes in the prices of Eurodollar futures contracts as evidenced by Figure 5.5.

To prevent cash market futures arbitrage by market dealers, the swap market responds to price changes in these markets by adjusting the swap spreads. Consequently, spreads for short-dated swaps are extremely volatile.

Since short-term swap spreads closely mirror changes in futures prices, they are, in effect, reflecting changes in the spread between government and bank borrowing rates. For example, changes in the spread between T-bill futures and Eurodollar futures – the TED spread – are closely mirrored by changes in short-dated swap spreads. TED spreads represent risk premium associated with holding Eurodollar time deposits versus T-bills. Since Eurodollar time deposits are issued by unregulated banks that do not carry deposit insurance, their higher yields reflect the associated credit risk. Thus, events that threaten the credit worthiness of money centre banks tend to increase the TED spread resulting, in turn, in higher swap spreads. For example, when Continental Illinois Bank nearly became insolvent in 1984, TED spreads increased to around 200 basis points. However, as it became clear that the US government would not let the bank fail, the spread fell to under 100 basis points.[9]

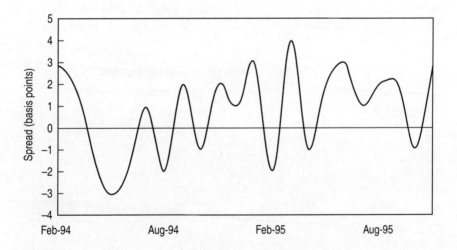

Fig. 5.5 2-year swap versus synthetic Euro-dollar strip rates

9 Slentz, J., 'The TED spread', *Market Perspectives* (Chicago Mercantile Exchange) 5 (1987): 1–4.

Long-term swaps

Longer-dated interest rate swaps, with maturities of over three years are priced relative to rates in fixed and floating rate corporate debt markets. While the short-dated interest rate swaps market is dominated by commercial banks – reflecting extensive exposure to LIBOR on their balance sheets – the longer term swaps market is driven by corporations, sovereigns and financial institutions wishing to raise medium to long term funds. The use of interest rate swaps has allowed these borrowers to achieve lower funding costs than would be possible otherwise. As we noted earlier, the source of this 'funding arbitrage' is the credit spread differential that exists between fixed and floating rate debt markets. Typically, fixed rate bond markets require a wider quality spread between higher and lower rated borrowers than does the floating rate market. By combining their borrowings with an interest rate swap, both the higher and the lower rated borrower achieves a reduction in funding costs.

It is hardly surprising, then, that nearly 80 percent of all euro-issues are swapped from floating to fixed or vice versa. As such, the fixed rate and, therefore, the swap spread is primarily driven by credit spreads in the fixed and the floating rate debt markets. Indeed, as can be seen in Figure 5.6, five-year swap spreads are roughly equivalent to corporate spreads over US Treasuries for investment grade borrowers. The swap spreads have consistently traded within 10-20 basis points of the corporate spread range defined by AAA- and AA-rated spreads.

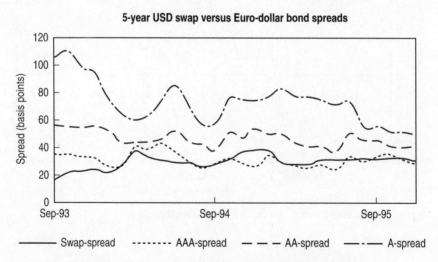

5-year USD swap versus Euro-dollar bond spreads

——— Swap-spread   ········ AAA-spread   – – – AA-spread   —·— A-spread

Fig 5.6 Five-year interest rate swap spreads vs. Eurodollar bond spreads over US Treasuries

Given that interest rate swaps provide a mechanism to convert floating rate debt into fixed rate debt and vice versa, we would expect swap spreads to trade within certain boundaries of credit spreads in the two markets for the swap to make economic sense. Suppose a AAA-rated borrower wishes to raise floating rate funds for a fixed term. It can do so at a cost of six-month LIBOR (L) minus a spread (M). It can also achieve the same objective by raising fixed rate funds and then swapping its liability into floating rate debt. Suppose it issues a fixed rate bond at Treasuries (T) plus a spread (C). It then enters into an interest rate swap in which it pays six-month LIBOR flat against receiving a fixed rate of Treasuries plus the swap spread (S). It therefore converts its fixed liability into a floating liability. It is easy to see that this swap makes economic sense for the AAA-rated borrower if the resultant floating cost is lower than that available in the floating rate market. That is

$$(T + C) = [(T + S) - LIBOR] \leq LIBOR - M$$

or

$$LIBOR - [(T + S) - (T + C)] \leq LIBOR - M$$

or

$$LIBOR - (S - C) \leq LIBOR - M$$

or

$$C + M \leq S \qquad\qquad (5.2)$$

That is, for a floating rate borrower, raising funds in the fixed rate market and converting it into a floating rate liability using an interest rate swap makes economic sense only if the spread in the fixed rate market plus the margin under LIBOR achievable in the floating rate market is lower than the swap spread.

Similarly, suppose an A-rated borrower wishes to raise term fixed rate funds. It can do so at a cost of Treasuries (T) plus a spread (c). Alternatively, it can borrow in the floating rate market at LIBOR (L) plus a margin (m) and convert it into a fixed rate liability by entering into an interest rate swap in which it receives LIBOR flat against paying Treasury yield plus the swap spread (S). Clearly the issuer will only consider the latter alternative if it results in a cheaper fixed rate than can be achieved by raising funds directly in the fixed rate market. That is

$$LIBOR + m - [LIBOR - (T + S)] \leq T + c$$

or

$$T + S \leq T + c$$

or

$$c - m \geq S \qquad (5.3)$$

That is the issuer will prefer synthetic fixed rate debt only if the difference between the spreads in the fixed and the floating markets for the borrower is greater than the swap spread.

Example

An AAA-rated bank can borrow for a given term at Treasuries plus 0.20 percent in the fixed rate market or at LIBOR – 0.10 percent in the floating rate market. An A-rated corporate, on the other hand, can borrow for the same term at Treasuries plus 0.90 percent in the fixed rate market and at LIBOR + 0.30 percent in the floating rate market. Suppose the term Treasury yield is 9.80 percent. Further suppose that the AAA-rated bank needs floating rate funds whereas the A-rated corporate requires fixed rate funds. Both of these borrowers can borrow directly in the market of their requirement or, alternatively, borrow in the market of other's requirement and combine it with an interest rate swap. If we assume the swap rate for the term of the borrowing to be 10.25 percent (ignoring bid-ask spread), the costs of borrowing directly or in combination with a swap for the two borrowers will be as under:

AAA-Rated Bank

Alternative 1 Borrow in the floating rate market LIBOR – 0.10%

Alternative 2	Borrow in the fixed rate market	9.80% + 0.20% = 10.0%
	Enter into a swap to receive fixed	10.25%
	and pay LIBOR	LIBOR
	Net floating cost with swap	LIBOR – 0.25%
	Cost saving through swap	0.15%

A-Rated Corporate

Alternative-1 Borrow in the fixed rate market 9.80% + 0.90% = 10.70%

Alternative-2	Borrow in the floating rate market	LIBOR + 0.30%
	Enter into a swap to pay fixed	10.25%
	and receive LIBOR	LIBOR
	Net fixed cost with swap	10.55%
	Cost saving through swap	0.15%

In this example both parties achieve a reduction of 15 basis points in their funding costs through the use of a swap.[10] The swap spread in

---

[10] The total saving of 30 basis points is simply the credit differential between the fixed and floating rate markets for the two borrowers. That is [10.70% – 10.00%] – [(LIBOR + 0.30%) – (LIBOR – 0.10%)] = (0.70% – 0.40%) = 0.30%

this case is 45 basis points (swap rate – Treasury rate i.e. 10.25% – 9.80% = 0.45%). We can now express the boundary conditions for the swap spread for each of the borowers. Referring to the funding cost calculations above, the AAA-rated bank will be economically better off with the swap alternative so long as the swap spread is greater than 30 basis points. If the swap spread is less than 30 basis points, it would be better off borrowing directly in the floating rate market. The A-rated company, on the other hand, will be economically better off with the swap alternative so long as the swap spread is less than 60 basis points. Therefore, the boundary conditions on the swap spread, in this case, are from 30 basis points to 60 basis points. If the swap spread were to trade outside this range then one of the borrowers would have no economic incentive to use the swap alternative. These boundary conditions can be directly established using Equations (5.2) and (5.3) as under:

For AAA-rated bank

$C + M \leq S$

$0.20\% + 0.10\% \leq S$

or $S \geq 0.30\%$

For A-rated corporate

$c - m \geq S$

$0.90\% - 0.30\% \geq S$

or $S \leq 0.60\%$

It needs to be emphasized that the boundary conditions for swap spreads of various maturities derived using the above approach will hold only if markets are efficient. Any imperfections, such as institutional restrictions or regulatory constraints may force borrowers to pay higher or receive lower swap spreads than dictated by Equations (5.2) and (5.3).

FACTORS AFFECTING THE LEVEL OF SWAP SPREADS

In general, as noted above, swap spreads reflect corporate credit spreads prevailing at any point in time. Therefore, all those factors that influence the shape and level of corporate credit spreads also influence the shape and level of swap spreads. Since credit spreads reflect the risk of default, both corporate and swap spreads tend to rise in times of greater credit sensitivity. It should be noted, however, that since swap spreads relate to average credit quality of, say, AA-rated borrowers, a general increase in corporate credit spreads may result in a less than proportionate increase in swap spreads.

Interest rate expectations also play an important role in determining the level of swap spreads. For example, toward the end of a recessionary period as industrial activity begins to pick up so does demand for capital. Such a period in an economic cycle is also characterized by expectations of rising interest rates to combat risks of inflation. As borrowers sense a rise in general level of interest rates they begin to raise funds to lock-in current low level of interest rates. As demand for capital increases investors demand higher corporate spreads and hence swap spreads tend to rise.

Interest rate expectations also result in variations in demand for and supply of fixed rate payers in the swaps market. This imbalance between fixed rate payers and receivers causes swap spreads to fluctuate constantly. Higher demand to receive fixed will tend to dampen swap spreads and vice versa. For example, as interest rates bottom out, floating rate borrowers' demand to fix interest costs increases. As more and more borrowers pay fixed, swap spreads widen as there are generally more fixed rate payers than receivers. On the other hand, as interest rates peak, fixed income investors tend to use asset swaps to lock-in fixed rates of return by receiving fixed in a swap. This tends to reduce swap spreads. Empirical studies also indicate that swap spreads are inversely related to yields on government bonds.[11]

The costs of hedging a swaps position also influences swap spreads. Hedging costs have assumed greater significance since swaps dealers no longer match each and every swap they enter into with an offsetting swap. Instead, every new swap is 'warehoused', that is, becomes part of the portfolio of swaps. Hedging is then carried out on a portfolio basis using, typically, government bonds and euro-deposit futures. Suppose a dealer enters into a ten-year US dollar swap in which it pays fixed against receiving floating payments. It can offset this position by immediately entering into a matching swap with another counterparty in which it receives fixed against making floating payments. Since it is not usually possible to find two counterparties with exactly the opposite requirements within a short period of time, swap dealers use other related instruments to hedge a swaps position until all or part of the swaps position is matched by an offsetting swap.[12] In our case the

---

[11] Evans, E. and Bales, G.P., 'What drives interest rate swap spreads', in *Interest Rate Swaps*, ed. Carl Beidleman (Homewood, Ill. Richard D. Irwin, 1991)

[12] This is almost a continuous operation. Every new swap that a swaps dealer transacts becomes part of its portfolio. The residual exposure is hedged using government bonds and futures. These hedges are liquidated as the dealer finds an opportunity to enter into an offsetting swap that fully or partly offsets the original swaps position. It may be necessary to maintain some hedging position.

dealer will use US Treasuries to temporarily hedge the swaps position. Since under this swap the dealer pays a fixed rate of interest, it is exposed to falling interest rates. Recall that US dollar swap yields are composed of the yield on an equivalent maturity on-the-run Treasury plus the swap spread. The dealer can, therefore, hedge against falling Treasury yields by purchasing a Treasury bond of equivalent maturity.[13] This position can be financed in the repurchase or Repo market. This hedging operation gives rise to a cost of carry being the difference between the LIBOR based payments received and repo payments made.[14] A higher repo rate relative to LIBOR results in higher hedging costs and vice versa. Consequently, as the cost of carry rises our dealer will aggressively seek to hedge the swaps position by being willing to receive a lower swap rate and vice versa. Swap spreads tend to vary directly with the spread between LIBOR and the repo rate.

SWAPS PRICING – BASIC CONCEPTS

Unlike other financial securities which trade in terms of price, interest rate swaps are quoted as a fixed rate that a swaps dealer is willing to pay (receive) against receiving (paying) a floating index, usually six-month LIBOR. Both rates are payable on a notional principal amount according to a predetermined frequency for the life of the swap. Since a swap involves future exchange of two sets of cash flows its value must, by definition, be zero at the outset. Otherwise, one party will stand to gain at the expense of the other party. Viewed from the point of view of the fixed rate receiver in a swap the current market value of the fixed coupons to be received must be at least equal to the current market value of the floating coupons to be paid. Reverse is true for the fixed rate payer. For both parties to be a willing counterparty in a swap, therefore, the market value of the two sets of cash flows in a swap must be equal, which in turn means that the value of the swap be zero.

At any point in time, the market makers quote a bid and an offer fixed rate for one, two, three, four, five, seven and ten years in all major currencies. The quoted fixed rates are either annual or semi-annual rates usually against six-month LIBOR flat. In this section we describe the basic concepts of swaps pricing. The objectives of a pricing methodology for swaps are to establish:

---

[13] Most dealers use duration to approximate the interest rate sensitivity of the swaps position being hedged with a Treasury bond. This leaves them exposed to second order or convexity risk.

[14] It should be noted that there exists a difference between the fixed swap payments made and the fixed Treasury yields received. The difference is the swap spread – which is being traded in this case.

1 Given the currently quoted rates for vanila swaps of standard maturities, the value of an existing swap. That is, how much should you expect to pay or receive to cancel or unwind an existing swap?

2 Given the currently quoted rates for vanila swaps of standard maturities, the fair price of a new but non-standard swap. That is, given a swap of non-standard structure what fixed rate should you pay or receive?

In Chapter 2 we described the basic methodology to value fixed income securities. Essentially, the methodology involves discounting future cash flows to recognize the time value of money. While the same underlying principles are necessary to price swaps, the exact methodology will differ according to which approach to pricing is used. Two broad approaches to pricing swaps are the bond equivalent approach and the zero coupon approach. The bond equivalent approach is a simple adaptation of bond pricing techniques for the valuation of swaps. This approach, however, requires a number of adjustments when used to value non-standard swaps. Zero-coupon approach, on the other hand, provides a consistent methodology to value all types of swaps, standard as well as non-standard. Before we discuss these approaches in detail, it is important to understand some of the basic concepts described below.

Standard interest rate swaps A standard or 'vanila' interest rate swap is characterized by the following features:

- The term of the swap is a whole number, commonly, one, two, three, five, seven and ten years.
- The fixed and floating coupon payments take place at regular intervals, for example every six months or every twelve months.
- The notional principal of the swap remains constant throughout the life of the swap.
- The fixed rate remains constant for the term of the swap.
- The floating rate is set at the beginning of each interest period and paid in arrears at the end of the interest period.

As will be noted later, extending the bond valuation techniques to value standard swaps is relatively easy. However, a large number of swaps that are transacted every day do not conform to the above description. Variations to the standard structure of a swap arise on account of payment frequency mismatches, day-count mismatches, reset frequency mismatches, irregular coupons, non-standard terms, variable notional principal, forward start dates, floating margins, short or long coupons etc.

114

Payment frequency mismatches   A payment frequency mismatch arises when the floating rate payment frequency differs from the term of the floating rate index. For example, a swap in which a counterparty receives three-month LIBOR reset quarterly but paid semi-annually results in a payment frequency mismatch.

Day-count mismatch   Day-count mismatch arises when the fixed or the floating payments of a swap are based on a convention that differs from the market convention for the currency involved. For example, if the market convention requires that the fixed coupons be calculated on 30/360-day basis, then a mismatch will arise if the fixed coupons are calculated on, say, actual/360-day basis.

Reset frequency mismatch   A reset frequency mismatch arises when the reset frequency differs from the term of the floating rate index. For example, a swap in which a counterparty receives six-month LIBOR reset every month but paid semi-annually results in a reset frequency mismatch.

Irregular coupons   Irregular coupon payments may arise because of a short or long a fixed or floating interest period (the 'stub') at the beginning or at the end of the swap. Zero-coupon swaps, in which no fixed coupons change hands, are another example of irregular coupons.

Non-standard terms   Non-standard terms refer to swaps with non-integer maturities. A swap with three and a half years to run is an example of a non-standard term.

Variable notional principal   A swap in which the underlying notional principal amount varies over the life of the swap. Rollercoaster swaps are an example of this type of swap.

Forward start   Forward start swaps refer to those swaps that are transacted now but in which the effective date is set at a future date.

Floating margins   A number of swaps are structured with floating-rate payments based on an index, such as six-month LIBOR, plus or minus a margin. Now while the market convention is based on flat LIBOR based payments, a margin causes a discrepancy if the payment frequency and day count conventions for fixed and floating payments differ.

Short coupons   A swap may involve a short coupon either at the front or at the back end. This is referred to as the stub.

Classifying swaps into standard and non-standard categories is akin to classifying bonds into conventional and structured categories. As in the case of bonds, standardization of swaps greatly helps trading of these instruments. Besides, as will be noted later, standard swaps can be easily valued using bond valuation techniques. However, to develop a more generalized valuation approach we need to borrow another concept from bond markets, that of par and non-par bonds.

Par or generic swaps

A bond is said to be valued at par when its price is equal to its face value. This can only happen when the coupon rate equals the market yield for the term of the bond. Thus, a bond that pays annual coupons at a rate of 10 percent will be valued at par if the current ten-year market yield equals 10 percent per year.

The concept of a par swap is akin to that of a par bond. On a bond equivalent basis that means that the value of the fixed and the floating legs of a par swap be equal to the swap's notional principal amount. As in the case of bonds, that can only be the case if both the fixed and floating payments are based on the current market rates. To elaborate, let us consider how a swap market is defined. As we noted above, interest rate swaps are quoted as a fixed rate payable on a notional principal amount. This rate is quoted against a floating rate index, such as six-month LIBOR flat. Both the fixed and the floating payments are calculated according to market convention in the case of standard swaps. The standard maturities quoted are, one, two, three, four, five, seven and ten years. A 'par swap' is defined as a standard swap with fixed coupon based on the current market rate for the term of the swap. For example, a par three-year swap in US dollars is defined as a swap starting at spot, maturing in three years from the spot date with a fixed coupon set at the current market rate payable annually on actual/360-day basis and a floating coupon based on six-month LIBOR payable semi-annually on actual/360-day basis.

Thus, the par-ness of a swap is determined by the fact that its fixed coupon is set at the current market rate for the term of the swap. An otherwise standard swap with an off-market fixed coupon is, by definition, a non-par or an off-market swap. Now since swaps dealers readily quote to pay or receive the current market fixed rate for maturities of one, two, three, four, five, seven and ten years there exist, by definition, par swaps for these maturities. That in turn means there exists a 'Par Yield Curve' for swaps spanning these maturities. As we will note later, the existence of this curve forms the basis of valuing both the off-market standard swaps as well as other non-standard swaps. This curve forms the benchmark for swaps valuation exactly as 'on-the-run' Treasury yield curve provides the benchmark for valuing 'off-the-run' Treasuries.[15]

---

[15] Effectively the 'on-the-run' Treasury yield curve is also used to value swaps since par swap yields are a spread over Treasuries.

BOND EQUIVALENT APPROACH
TO SWAP VALUATION

Several factors complicate the valuation of an interest rate swap within the confines of traditional bond pricing framework. Two such factors affect even the standard swap described above which is the most basic swap structure from the point of view of valuation. These are:

1 An interest rate swap involves exchange of two interest rate streams, one based on a fixed rate of interest and the other based on a floating rate index. While both these interest payments are calculated with reference to a notional principal amount, no principal actually changes hands and therefore, there is no investment involved.

2 While one series of coupon payments in an interest rate swap is fixed and, therefore, known in advance, the other is floating and cannot be determined in advance with any degree of certainty.

The first obstacle to pricing interest rate swaps in a bond valuation framework is overcome by viewing an interest rate swap as a simultaneous exchange of a fixed and a floating rate security rather than as an exchange of interest payments alone. This hypothetical construct allows us to value an interest rate swap as a combination of a fixed bond and a floating rate note. The fixed rate payer can be deemed to be selling a fixed rate bond and buying a floating rate note. The fixed rate receiver, on the other hand, can be deemed to be buying a fixed rate bond and selling an FRN. For standard swaps this can be done without loss of generality. By adding principal payments at the beginning and at the end of the swap we can use standard bond valuation techniques without affecting the actual cash flows. Addition of principals of equal amount will obviously cancel each other leaving the net cash flows equal to the underlying swap cash flows.

The second obstacle to pricing interest rate swaps in a bond valuation framework is overcome by assuming that the floating leg of the swap will be valued at par at the next payment date. For standard swaps this is a reasonable assumption since the interest rate swap involves exchange of payments based on a fixed rate of interest against a floating index flat. This feature allows the swap market to value the relative attractiveness of the floating leg of a swap by marking the fixed rate up or down. Consequently, the traditional techniques of valuing FRNs such as simple margin, total margin, adjusted total margin and the discounted margin are not required. The bond equivalent approach to valuing swaps, therefore, focuses on valuing the fixed leg of a swap.

Valuation of the fixed leg of an existing swap

To value the fixed leg of an existing interest rate swap as a hypothetical fixed rate bond, we will make use of the valuation tools developed in Chapter 2. Specifically we re-write Equation (2.10) to value the fixed leg of an interest rate swap as a fixed rate bond

$$V_{FIXED} = \sum_{i=1}^{N} \frac{\frac{C}{m}}{\left(1 + \frac{Y}{m}\right)^{T_i}} + \frac{100}{\left(1 + \frac{Y}{m}\right)^{T_N}} \tag{5.4}$$

where

V_{FIXED} = Value of the fixed leg of a swap
C = The fixed coupon rate (expressed as a percentage)
Y = Yield on a par swap converted to the same compounding frequency as the number of fixed rate payments per year.
N = Number of fixed coupon periods from the settlement date to the maturity date
m = Frequency of interest payments per year
T_i = Number of fixed coupon periods (whole and fractional) from the settlement date to the ith coupon payment date.

Notice that Equation (5.4) implicitly assumes that each coupon payment is equal in magnitude (i.e. on unadjusted bond basis). This assumption can be relaxed by simply replacing the coupon rate *(C)* with the actual coupon payments adjusted for day count and holidays. Equal coupon swaps are commonly traded in connection with eurobond issues.

Example

Consider an interest rate swap with three years to maturity in which you receive an annual fixed rate of 10 percent on 30/360-day basis. Suppose the current three-year swap rate is 11 percent (quoted on an annual basis). What is the value of the fixed leg of this swap? Using Equation (5.4) we have

$C = 10\%$
$Y = 0.11$
$N = 3$
$m = 1$

$$V_{FIXED} = \frac{10}{(1+0.11)} + \frac{10}{(1+0.11)^2} + \frac{100+10}{(1+0.11)^3}$$

= 99.556% of par or notional principal amount.

In the above example we assume that the swap had exactly three years to maturity. Now suppose we wish to value an interest rate swap with a short first fixed coupon. To value the fixed leg of such a swap consider the following example:

118

Example

Suppose the above swap had 2 years and 90 days to maturity with current two and a quarter year swap rate at 10.50 percent and assuming a day basis of 30/360, what would the value of the fixed leg be? Using Equation (5.4) we have

$$V_{FIXED} = \frac{10}{(1+0.105)^{\frac{90}{360}}} + \frac{10}{(1+0.105)^{1 + \frac{90}{360}}} + \frac{110}{(1+0.105)^{2 + \frac{90}{360}}}$$

$$= 106.447\% \text{ of par}$$

which includes accrued interest for nine months. The accrued interest can be calculated as follows:

$$\text{Accrued interest on fixed leg} = \frac{D}{B} \times C \qquad (5.5)$$

where D = the number of days from the last interest payment date (or the original effective date if first coupon payment) and the value date

C = fixed coupon rate expressed as a percentage

B = day basis

For our example swap that would be:

$$\frac{270}{360} \times 10 = 7.50\% \text{ of par}$$

Valuation of the floating leg of an existing swap

We noted above that under the bond equivalent framework for the valuation of interest rate swaps the floating leg is assumed to have a value of par at the next payment date. That means the only cash flow to be valued on the floating side is the next floating coupon payment (which is, by definition, known) plus par. The discount rate used to compute the present value of the floating leg should be the appropriate floating rate index for the period between the value date and the next payment date. Thus, if the period between these two dates is three months, we need to use the current three-month LIBOR to value the floating leg of the swap even though the floating payment may be based on six-month LIBOR. The valuation formula can be written as:

$$V_{FLOATING} = \frac{L\left(\frac{D_1}{B}\right) + 100}{1 + R\left(\frac{D_2}{B}\right)} \qquad (5.6)$$

where

$V_{FLOATING}$ = Value of the floating leg of a swap.

L =   Last LIBOR fixing (flat) as a percentage.

D_1 =   Actual number of days from the last floating payment date (or the original effective date if first floating payment) and the next floating payment date.

D_2 =   Actual number of days from the value date to the next floating payment date.

B =   Day basis – act/360 or act/365

R =   Current LIBOR for the period between the value date and the next payment date.

Example

Suppose in our base case swap described above you pay six-month LIBOR on actual/360 day basis. Suppose the LIBOR was set 91 days prior to the value date at 8.5 percent. Suppose the actual number of days between the value date and the next payment date is 92 and the current three-month LIBOR is 8.75 percent. Using Equation (5.6) we have:

$L = 8.50\%$
$D_1 = 91 + 92 = 183$
$D_2 = 92$
$R = 0.0875$
$B = 360$

$$V_{FLOATING} = \frac{8.50 \times \frac{183}{360} + 100}{1 + 0.0875 \times \frac{92}{360}}$$

$= 102.039\%$

The accrued interest portion can be computed using Equation (5.5) as under:

$$\text{Accrued interest} = \frac{D}{B} \times L$$

$$= \frac{91}{360} \times 8.50\% = 2.149\% \text{ of par}$$

Market value of the existing swap

The value of the swap is now simply the difference between the present value of the fixed leg of the swap less the present value of the floating leg of the swap. That is [16]

---

[16] From fixed rate payer's standpoint, the value of the swap is simply $V_{FLOATING} - V_{FIXED}$.

$$V_{SWAP} = V_{FIXED} - V_{FLOATING}$$
$$= 106.447\% - 102.039\% = 4.408 \% \text{ of par}$$

That is, if you were in this example to unwind or close out your swap under current market conditions you will receive a payment of 4.408 percent of the notional principal amount including accrued interest.

In our above analysis we assumed that the floating payments were based on LIBOR flat. If, however, the floating payments were based on a spread over or under the index we must incorporate the present value of such a margin in our calculation of the value of the fixed leg. In doing so we can always assume that floating payments are based on LIBOR flat. For example, if in the case of the above swap you paid six-month LIBOR plus a spread of 0.25 percent, the present value of this spread would effectively be deducted from (added to in the case of a negative margin) the present value of the fixed leg of the swap.

The present value of the floating spread can be computed as:

$$V_{SPREAD} = \sum_{i=1}^{N} \frac{S\left(\frac{D_i}{B}\right)}{\left(1 + \frac{Y}{m}\right)^{T_i}} \tag{5.7}$$

where

V_{SPREAD} = Present value of the floating spread payments
S = Spread (expressed as a percentage)
D_i = the actual number of days in the floating interest rate period i
B = Daycount basis (360 or 365)
Y = Yield on a par swap converted to the same compounding frequency (m) as the number of floating rate payments per year
T_i = Number of compounding periods (whole and fractional) from the settlement date to the ith coupon date

Assuming that our swap has two years and 90 days to maturity the value of the spread over LIBOR can be calculated using Equation (5.7) as under:

$$V_{SPREAD} = \frac{0.25 \times \frac{90}{360}}{\left(1+\frac{0.1024}{2}\right)^{\frac{90}{360}}} + \frac{0.25 \times \frac{181}{360}}{\left(1+\frac{0.1024}{2}\right)^{1+\frac{90}{360}}} + \frac{0.25 \times \frac{180}{360}}{\left(1+\frac{0.1024}{2}\right)^{2+\frac{90}{360}}}$$

$$+ \frac{0.25 \times \frac{182}{360}}{\left(1+\frac{0.1024}{2}\right)^{3+\frac{90}{360}}} + \frac{0.25 \times \frac{180}{360}}{\left(1+\frac{0.1024}{2}\right)^{4+\frac{90}{360}}}$$

$$= 0.50\% \text{ of par}$$

121

The net present value of the swap (including accrued interest) in this case would be:

$$V_{\text{FIXED}} - V_{\text{SPREAD}} - V_{\text{FLOATING}}$$

$$106.447\% - 0.50\% - 102.039\% = 3.908\% \text{ of par}$$

Notice that we used 10.24 percent as the discount rate to value the spread which is the semi-annual equivalent of 10.50 percent – the annual discount rate used to value the annual fixed cash flows. We need to use the semi-annual discount rate because the spread payments are made six monthly. The semi-annual rate can be computed from the annual rate using Equation (2.9) discussed in Chapter 2. That is

$$r_m = m \ [(1 + r_{ann})^{\frac{1}{m}} - 1]$$

where r_m is the m-period compounded rate and m is the frequency of compounding. In our case m is equal to 2 (two payments per year) and r_{ann} – the annual rate – is 10.50%. Applying (2.9) we have

$$r_2 = 2[(1 + 0.105)^{\frac{1}{2}} - 1]$$
$$\quad = 10.24\%$$

ZERO COUPON APPROACH TO SWAP VALUATION

For all its simplicity, the bond equivalent approach to interest rate swaps pricing is quite restrictive in application. While this approach is suitable for the pricing of 'vanilla' interest rate swaps, its application to non-standard swaps is fraught with problems. The main problem with the bond valuation approach is that it is suitable only if the security to be valued follows a certain cash flow structure: periodic (equally spaced) coupons and principal redemption at maturity. That is precisely the structure of cash flows for a bond or an FRN. The structure allows us to use an average discount rate – the yield-to-maturity – to value a security. While individual cash flows under this structure are generally mispriced (some over valued and some under valued) the value of the bond, in aggregate, is generally correct. The same cannot be said for swaps since swaps do not necessarily follow a fixed structure. In fact, a major reason for the growth of the swaps market is the product's ability to handle irregular payoffs or cash flows. Indeed, swaps can be simply viewed as streams of cash flows – both known and unknown. These cash flow streams do not have to follow any particular pattern. For example, the fixed coupon payments in an interest rate swap do not have to be constant. Similarly, the notional principal amount in an interest rate swap can vary over time. To handle these and a variety of other non-standard cash flows that may be involved in a swap what we need is a way to value individual cash flows accurately. The value of the swap would then simply be the sum of these individual values. The zero-coupon approach allows us to do precisely that. Essentially, each cash flow is treated as if it were a zero-coupon bond. A discount rate – the zero or spot rate – unique to the timing of the cash flow is then used to value the cash flow.

The application of the zero-coupon approach to the valuation of interest rate swaps essentially involves two steps:

- construction of the discount rates – the discount function – corresponding to various future points in times
- estimating the floating payments of the swap.

Constructing the discount function

A zero-coupon rate, or the spot rate, is simply the yield to maturity of a zero-coupon bond. If zero-coupon bonds of various maturities were traded in the market, pricing swaps or any set of arbitrary cash flows would be easy. However, in reality, there is no active market for zero-coupon bonds. We can, nevertheless, estimate spot rates (and hence discount factors or the discount function) for various terms to maturity from various money and capital market instruments that do trade. The process of constructing a zero-coupon curve from a par yield curve is known as 'stripping the curve'. The necessary inputs for this process are:

- a set of par money market rates; and
- a set of par swap rates.

Since the money market instruments, such as Eurodollar deposits, do not involve any intermediate interest payments, the yield on such instruments is, by definition, zero-coupon yield. In most currencies money market instruments are available from overnight to twelve month periods. Suppose the one-year swap is quoted at 9 percent on an annual basis: the zero-coupon yield for one year is therefore 9 percent. Now, at any point in time, par swap yields are quoted for two, three, four, five, seven and ten year terms. Suppose the two-year par swap yield is 9.3 percent. What is the two-year zero-coupon rate? Given the one-year zero yield and the two-year par yield we can infer the two-year zero yield using the following relationship:

$$1 = \frac{S_2}{1 + Z_1} + \frac{1 + S_2}{(1 + Z_2)^2} \tag{5.8}$$

where

S_2 = two-year par swap yield
Z_1 = one-year zero-coupon yield

Using Equation (5.8) we obtain

$$1 = \frac{0.093}{1 + 0.09} + \frac{1 + 0.093}{(1 + Z_2)^2}$$

$$= 9.316\%$$

Similarly, given the three-year par swap yield and one- and two-year zero-coupon yields, we can find the three-year zero yield using the following relationship,

$$1 = \frac{S_3}{1 + Z_1} + \frac{S_3}{(1 + Z_2)^2} + \frac{1 + S_3}{(1 + Z_3)^3} \tag{5.9}$$

where S_3 is the three-year par swap yield.

More generally, we can find the n-period zero-coupon yield using the following iterative formula:

$$Z_n = \left[\frac{1 + S_n}{1 - S_n \sum_{t=1}^{n-1} \left(\frac{1}{1 + Z_t} \right)} \right]^{\frac{1}{n}} - 1 \tag{5.10}$$

To continue with our example, let us assume a three-year swap yield of 9.5%. Given the zero-coupon yields of 9% and 9.316% for one and two years, we imply the three-year zero yield using Equation (5.10) as follows:

$$Z_3 = \left[\frac{1 + 0.095}{1 - 0.095 \left(\left(\frac{1}{1 + 0.9} \right) + \left(\frac{1}{1 + 0.9316} \right) \right)^2} \right]^{\frac{1}{3}} - 1$$

$$= 9.529\%$$

Table 5.4 provides the zero-coupon swap curve derived from par swap yields using Equation (5.10).

Table 5.4 Zero-coupon swap curve

Term (years)	Par yield	Zero-coupon yield
1	9%	9%
2	9.3%	9.316%
3	9.5%	9.529%
4	9.7%	9.75%
5	9.8%	9.865%

For the practical purposes of valuation, it is useful to generate a set of zero-coupon discount factors rather than absolute yields as we have done so far. We also need to be able to handle different day count conventions. We begin by defining the discount factor, F_0, for the start day (spot date) of the swap. This is, by definition, 1. The discount factor of a one-year point, F_1 is defined as:

$$F_1 = \frac{1}{1 + S_1\left(\frac{d_{1,0}}{B}\right)} \tag{5.11}$$

where

$S_1 =$ one-year par swap rate (assumed to be zero-coupon rate)
$d_{1,0} =$ actual number of days between spot date (d_0) and maturity date (d_1)
$B =$ interest basis (360 or 365)

Similarly, the discount factor for two years can be derived using the following formula:

$$F_2 = \frac{1 - S_2 F_1 \left(\frac{d_{1,0}}{B}\right)}{1 + S_2 \left(\frac{d_{2,1}}{B}\right)} \tag{5.12}$$

where

$S_2 =$ two-year par swap yield
$d_{2,1} =$ actual number of days between dates d_2 and d_1.

The relationships given by Equations (5.11) and (5.12) can be generalized to give the discount factor for an n-year point as under:

$$F_n = \frac{1 - S_n \sum_{t=1}^{n-1} F_t \frac{d_{t,t-1}}{B}}{1 + S_n \frac{d_{n,n-1}}{B}} \tag{5.13}$$

where index t runs from the first coupon to the last but one coupon.

Using Equation (5.13) we can generate a set of discount factors corresponding to the maturity dates of par swaps. Let us consider our base case example again. To make our example more realistic we will take account of the day count factor. Suppose the par yields for US dollar swaps of various maturity dates are as given in Table 5.5.

Table 5.5 Par swap yields

Term	Date	Actual no. of days	Par rate
O/N	13 Jan 1995	1	5.375%
1 week	19 Jan 1995	7	5.50%
1 month	13 Feb 1995	32	5.562%
2 months	13 Mar 1995	60	5.75%
3 months	12 Apr 1995	90	5.875%
6 months	12 Jul 1995	181	5.875%
1 year	12 Jan 1996	365	6.125%
2 years	13 Jan 1997	367	6.25%
3 years	12 Jan 1998	364	6.40%
4 years	12 Jan 1999	365	6.55%
5 years	12 Jan 2000	365	6.80%
7 years	14 Jan 2002	365	6.90%

Notice that in Table 5.5 the payment dates associated with par swaps, as well as with the money market instruments, are adjusted for weekends and business holidays.

Finding discount factors for dates up to twelve months is fairly easy, since these rates are by definition zero-coupon rates. For example, assuming the value date to be 12 January 1995, the discount factors from O/N to twelve months are calculated as follows:

$$F_{O/N} = \frac{1}{1 + r_{O/N}\left(\dfrac{d_{O/N,\,0}}{B}\right)}$$

$$= \frac{1}{1 + 0.05375\left(\dfrac{1}{360}\right)}$$

$$= 0.9998$$

$$F_{1W} = \frac{1}{1 + r_{1W}\left(\dfrac{d_{1W,\,0}}{B}\right)}$$

$$= \frac{1}{1 + 0.055\left(\dfrac{7}{360}\right)}$$

$$= 0.9989$$

$$F_{1M} = \frac{1}{1 + r_{1M}\left(\dfrac{d_{1M,\,0}}{B}\right)}$$

$$= \frac{1}{1 + 0.05562 \left(\frac{32}{360} \right)}$$

$$= 0.9951$$

$$F_{2M} = \frac{1}{1 + r_{2M} \left(\frac{d_{2M,0}}{B} \right)}$$

$$= \frac{1}{1 + 0.0575 \left(\frac{60}{360} \right)}$$

$$= 0.9905$$

$$F_{3M} = \frac{1}{1 + r_{3M} \left(\frac{d_{3M,0}}{B} \right)}$$

$$= \frac{1}{1 + 0.05875 \left(\frac{90}{360} \right)}$$

$$= 0.9855$$

$$F_{6M} = \frac{1}{1 + r_{6M} \left(\frac{d_{6M,0}}{B} \right)}$$

$$= \frac{1}{1 + 0.05875 \left(\frac{181}{360} \right)}$$

$$= 0.9713$$

$$F_1 = \frac{1}{1 + r_1 \left(\frac{d_{1,0}}{B} \right)}$$

$$= \frac{1}{1 + 0.06125 \left(\frac{365}{360} \right)}$$

$$= 0.9415$$

Given the discount factor for one year and the par swap rate for two years, we can compute the two-year discount factor using Equation (5.11):

$$F_2 = \frac{1 - 0.0625 \left[0.9415 \left(\frac{365}{360} \right) \right]}{1 + 0.0625 \left(\frac{367}{360} \right)}$$

$$= 0.8840$$

Similarly, the three-year discount factor is computed using the three-year par swap rate and the one- and two-year discount factors:

$$F_3 = \frac{1 - 0.064 \left[0.9415 \left(\frac{365}{360} \right) + 0.8840 \left(\frac{367}{360} \right) \right]}{1 + 0.064 \left(\frac{364}{360} \right)}$$

$$= 0.8276$$

Continuing with the iterative process, we find four- and five-year discount factors to be 0.7723 and 0.7143. Notice that in order to generate the discount factor for the five-year term we needed to know discount factors for one-, two-, three-year and four-year terms. Since the market does not quote six-year swaps, we cannot readily generate the seven-year discount factor since we need to have the discount factor for six years. We, therefore, need to generate the six-year par swap yield to be able to generate the seven-year discount factor. The easiest way to generate the six-year par swap yield is to assume that it lies on a straight line between five- and seven-year par yields. That is:

$$S_6 = \frac{1}{2} (S_5 + S_7)$$

$$= \frac{1}{2} (0.068 + 0.069) = 0.0685 \text{ or } 6.85\%$$

Equation (5.13) can now be used to generate discount factors for six- and seven-year terms. A similar need for interpolation arises when the observed par swap yields do not correspond with the frequency of interest payments. For instance, while sterling swap rates are quoted for one, two, three, four, five, seven and ten year maturities, the payment frequency is semi-annual. In this case, therefore, not only do we need to generate par yields for six, eight and nine years, we also need to generate par yields at each semi-annual point. For example, a two-year swap will involve coupon payments at six month, twelve month, eighteen month and two year points. In this case, we need to generate the par yield at the eighteen month point. As before, this can simply be done by linearly interpolating between one- and two-year points. When interpolating, it is important to ensure that the two par rates are expressed on the same basis. For example, when interpolating between one-year and two-year par sterling rates, it is important to express both rates on a semi-annual basis, since the one-year rate is quoted on an annual act/365 day basis whereas the two-year and beyond rates are quoted on a semi-annual basis. It should also be noted that while Equation (5.13) assumes that floating LIBOR payments accrue for the same period as the fixed payments, it makes no assumption about the frequency of such payments. Thus, whether a swap rate is quoted against the three-month or the six-month LIBOR does not alter the discount factor.

Interpolation

Having generated a set of discount factors at discrete points, we can value any arbitrary set of cash flows corresponding with the grid points for which the discount factors have been generated.

Thus, an arbitrary set of cash flows (C_i) with payment dates corresponding with the discount factors (F_i) has a present value (PV) given by:

$$PV = \sum_{i=1}^{n} C_i \, F_i \qquad (5.14)$$

In most cases, however, it is unlikely that the payment dates of a swap on your books will correspond exactly with the dates for quoted terms. For such cases we must specify a sensible interpolation procedure. As we noted above in the context of generating par yields for missing annual grid points, linear interpolation is the simplest way to estimate the discount factor for a specific date between two grid points for which discount factors are known. If d_t lies between grid points d_1 and d_2 with discount factors F_1 and F_2, then the discount factor, F_t, corresponding with d_t is:

$$F_t = \frac{(d_2 - d_t) \, F_1 + (d_t - d_1) \, F_2}{(d_2 - d_1)} \qquad (5.15)$$

Suppose the actual number of days between the two- and one-year grid points is 367 days with discount factors 0.8276 and 0.9415, respectively. What is the linearly interpolated discount factor for one year and 60 days? That is, we have

$$
\begin{aligned}
d_2 &= 365 + 367 = 732 \\
d_t &= 365 + 60 = 425 \\
d_1 &= 365 \\
F_2 &= 0.8840 \\
F_1 &= 0.9415
\end{aligned}
$$

Using Equation (5.15) we can obtain the discount factor for one year and 60 days as follows:

$$F_t = \frac{(732 - 425) \; 0.9415 \; + \; (425 - 365) \; 0.8840}{(732 - 365)}$$

$$= 0.9321$$

129

As can be seen from Figure 5.7, F_t lies on a straight line between F_2 and F_1. Clearly, linear interpolation imposes a linear shape on the curve between two grid points. Given that the shape of the yield curve is generally curved, this method may result in mispricing. A more sophisticated approach uses exponential interpolation which adds curvature to the line. Continuing with our above notation, the exponentially interpolated discount factor for time t, F_t, can be derived using the following formula:

$$F_t = F_1^{\,(d_t - d_0)\,K/(d_1 - d_0)}\, F_2^{\,(d_t - d_0)\,(1 - k)/(d_2 - d_0)} \tag{5.16}$$

where $K = \dfrac{d_2 - d_t}{d_2 - d_1}$ for $d_1, \leq d_t \leq d_2$

Applying Equation (5.16) to the above example we get:

$$K = \frac{732 - 425}{732 - 365} = 0.8365$$

$$F_t = \left[0.9415^{\,(425 - 0)\,(0.8365)/(365 - 0)} \right] \left[0.884^{\,(425 - 0)\,(1 - 0.8365)/(732 - 0)} \right]$$

$$= 0.9320$$

which is marginally different from the linearly interpolated discount factor of 0.9320. This difference is highlighted in Figure 5.7.

Incorporating futures in discount function generation

Thus far we, have used money market rates and par swap yields to generate the zero-coupon discount factors. There is, however, a third set of instruments that can be used to generate the spot yield curve. These are interest rate futures. In many cases, incorporating interest

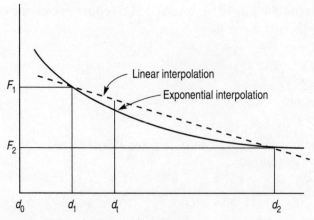

Fig 5.7 Linear versus exponential interpolation

rate futures in the stripping process is more useful than using money market rates. That is because futures, particularly the near-term futures, trade actively and therefore provide a better estimate of short-term interest rate expectations than is the case with money market instruments such as loans and deposits. Most swap traders, therefore, use futures contracts to generate the zero-coupon discount function. The number of contracts used is a function of liquidity. For example, while Eurodollar futures on three-month LIBOR extend to sixteen contracts, the liquidity beyond the first four contracts is thin.

To see how we can generate zero-coupon discount factors from futures, consider Eurodollar futures. Eurodollar futures are contracts for delivery of three-month LIBOR on the expiration date of the contracts. These contracts are essentially LIBOR forwards except for the fact that they are marked to market daily and therefore generate cash flows prior to their expiration date. With some adjustments, a series (or a strip) of futures contracts can be linked together to generate a swap equivalent discount function.

Consider the information in Table 5.6

Table 5.6 Eurodollar futures

Contract	Expiration date	Price (P)	No. of days between contracts
C1	15 Mar 1995	94.15	56 (from value date)
C2	21 Jun 1995	94.17	98
C3	20 Sep 1995	94.00	91
C4	20 Dec 1995	93.85	91
C5	20 Mar 1996	93.70	91
C6	19 Jun 1996	93.65	91
C7	18 Sep 1996	93.60	91
C8	18 Dec 1996	93.52	91

Let us assume the value date to be 18 January 1995. That means the number of days until the first contract is 56. In order to work out the futures strip we need to know the interest rate (LIBOR) applicable from the value date until the expiration of the first futures contract – that is the rate for 56 days. This rate can be worked out using one of the interpolation techniques described above. Let us call this rate the stub interest rate. Suppose the interest rate for the stub period is 5.72 percent. To work out the discount factors corresponding to the expiry dates of various futures contracts we use the following formula:

$$F_n = \frac{F_{n-1}}{1 + (100 - P_{n-1})\dfrac{D}{B \times 100}} \tag{5.17}$$

where

F_n = discount factor for the nth contract expiration date (1 in the case of the first contract expiry date)

P_n = price of the nth futures contract

D = actual number of days between the contract expiration dates (between the first contract expiration date and the value date in the case of the first contract expiry date)

Using Equation (5.17), the discount factor for the first contract expiry date, F_1, can be computed as under:

$$F_1 = \frac{1}{1 + 5.72 \left(\dfrac{56}{360 \times 100} \right)}$$

$$= 0.9911$$

Notice that, in the case of the first contract expiry date, we use the stub interest rate to compute the discount factor. To work out the discount factor corresponding with the second contract expiry date, we now make use of F_1:

$$F_2 = \frac{0.9911}{1 + (100 - 94.15) \left(\dfrac{98}{360 \times 100} \right)}$$

$$= 0.9756$$

Discount factors corresponding with other contract expiry dates are worked out in a similar fashion and are summarized in Table 5.7.

Table 5.7 Discount factors for futures dates

Date	Discount factor
15 Mar 95	0.9911
21 Jun 95	0.9756
20 Sep 95	0.9614
20 Dec 95	0.9470
20 Mar 96	0.9325
19 Jun 96	0.9179
18 Sep 96	0.9034
18 Dec 96	0.8890
19 Mar 97	0.8747

To work out discount factors corresponding with swap payment dates which may be different from the futures expiration dates, we simply use linear or exponential interpolation techniques described earlier.

Estimating the floating payments

Having established the discount factors for various payment dates, the only remaining task to value a swap is to specify its cash flows. On the fixed leg, it is fairly easy to determine the cash flows, given the fixed coupon rate, payment dates and day count convention. On the floating side, only the first coupon is known since it is set in advance. The subsequent interest payments will depend on the evolution of LIBOR over the term of the swap. To value a swap in the zero-coupon framework, however, we need to estimate all future floating payments. An unbiased estimate of future LIBOR settings is provided by currently implied forward rates. Thus, if the next LIBOR fixing is due in 60 days and the currently implied six-month LIBOR in 60 days' time is 10 percent, then we use 10 percent as an estimate of the next floating interest rate for the swap. Assuming that the zero-coupon discount factors are expressed at suitable intervals (six-monthly, quarterly etc) we can use the following formula to work out the implied forward rate for time t, $\tilde{r}_t$:

$$\tilde{r}_t = \left[\frac{Ft}{F_{t+1}} - 1 \right] \times \frac{B}{D} \tag{5.18}$$

where F_t = the discount factor for time t
D = actual number of days between t and $t+1$
B = day basis

From our base case example, we have

$$F_1 = 0.9415$$
$$\text{and } F_{6M} = 0.9713$$

Using Equation (5.18) we obtain the six-month forward rate in six months' time as under:

$$\tilde{r}_{6M} = \left[\frac{0.9713}{0.9415} - 1 \right] \times \frac{360}{184}$$

$$= 6.19\%$$

To work out the six-month forward rate in twelve months' time, we will need discount factors for 1 year and 1.5 years. The discount factor for 1.5 years can be interpolated between 1- and 2-year grid points using exponential interpolation. Assuming a discount factor of 0.884 for two years, the interpolated discount factor for 1.5 years (548 days) is found using Equation (5.16):

$$K = \frac{732 - 548}{732 - 365} = 0.5014$$

$F_{1.5} = [0.9415^{(548 - 0)(0.5014)/(365 - 0)} \ 0.884^{(365-0)}][0.884^{(548 - 0)(1 - 0.5014)/(732 - 0)}]$

$= 0.9127$

We can now work out the six-month LIBOR one year forward using Equation (5.18):

$$\tilde{r}_{1.5} = \left[\frac{0.9415}{0.9127} - 1 \right] \frac{360}{(548 - 365)}$$

$= 6.21\%$

Forward rates for the subsequent six-month periods are worked out in a similar fashion.

To value a swap using the zero-coupon methodology is now a straightforward matter. The value of a swap in which you receive fixed against paying floating is:

$$V_{SWAP} = \sum_{i=1}^{N} C_i F_i - \sum_{j=1}^{n} \bar{c}_j F_j$$

where

$C_i =$ ith fixed coupon payment
$\bar{c}_j =$ jth floating coupon payment
$N =$ number of fixed cash flows
$n =$ number of floating cash flows
$F_i =$ discount factor corresponding to the ith cash flow payment date

SUMMARY

Interest rate swaps were developed to allow borrowers to hedge against interest rate volatility. Interest rates became highly volatile following the fall of the Bretton Woods system of fixed exchange rates. Interest rate swaps allow users to shift interest rate risk. Interest rate swaps also allow borrowers and investors to access markets that may otherwise not be accessible. An early explanation for the existence and growth of interest rate swaps was the perceived arbitrage opportunity between fixed and floating rate debt markets: other theories including market completion and agency theories challenge this view.

Interest rate swaps can be viewed as packages of forward rate agreements. The two broad approaches to pricing these instruments are the bond equivalent and the zero-coupon approaches. It can be shown that the latter approach is superior and allows the pricing of a variety of interest rate swaps.

References

Arak, M., Esrella, A., Goodman, L. and Silver, A., 'Interest Rate Swaps: An Alternative Explanation', *Financial Management*, 1988, pp. 12–18.

Beidleman, C.R., *Interest Rate Swaps*, ed., Homewood Illinois: Richard D. Irwin, 1991.

Bicksler, J. and Chen, A., 'An Economic Analysis of Interest Rate Swaps', *Journal of Finance*, 41, 1986, pp. 645–55.

Giddy, I. and Hekman, C., *A Theory of Swaps*, unpublished manuscript, New York University, 1985.

Lipsky, J. and Elhalaski, S., *Swap-Driven Primary Issuance in the International Bond Market*, Solomon Brothers, 1986.

Marshall, J.F. and Kapner, K.R., *The Swaps Market*, 2nd edn, Miami: Kolb Publishing, 1993.

Miron, M., and Swannell, P., *Pricing and Hedging Swaps*, London: Euromoney, 1991.

Smith, C.W.Jr., Smithson, C.W. and Wakeman, L.M., 'The Evolving Market for Swaps', *Midland Corporate Finance Journal* 3, 1986, pp. 20–32.

Turnbull, S.M., 'Swaps: A Zero Sum Game?' *Financial Management* 15, 1987, pp. 15–21.

Wall, L.D. and Pringle J.J., 'Alternative Explanation of Interest Rate Swaps', *Working Paper No. 87–2*, Federal Reserve Bank of Atlanta.

Wall, L.D., 'Interest Rate Swaps in an Agency Theoretic Model with Uncertain Interest Rates', *Journal of Banking and Finance* 13, 1989, pp. 261–70.

6

CROSS CURRENCY SWAPS

Parallel loans

What is a cross currency swap?

Rationale for the use of cross currency swaps

Structure of cross currency swaps

Pricing cross currency swaps

Summary

In Chapter 5, when tracing the development of the interest rate swaps market, we noted that the currency swap was the forerunner of the interest rate swap. We also noted that currency swaps were preceded by parallel or back-to-back loans that were developed to circumvent the introduction of foreign exchange controls in the United Kingdom. The development of currency swaps greatly simplified the mechanism involved in parallel loans and led to a wider use of the concept in risk management. In this chapter we describe the structure of cross currency swaps, develop a pricing methodology and discuss its applications. To understand the nature of currency swaps fully, we begin this chapter with its forerunner, parallel loans.

PARALLEL LOANS

Parallel or back-to-back loans[1] were first developed as a financing vehicle through which the British companies were able to circumvent exchange control regulations. At the time of their development, the Bank of England regulations required British companies, interested in investing abroad, to purchase US dollars at a premium over the prevailing spot exchange rate. The objective was to reduce the selling pressure on the pound. Effectively, parallel loans helped these companies to avoid this investment premium.

A parallel loan involves two companies based in two different countries and having a subsidiary in each other's country lending equivalent amounts to each other in their respective currencies for the same term. Each loan is supported by a separate loan agreement that may involve more than two legal entities in each country, i.e. the two parent companies and their subsidiaries in each other's country. Figure 6.1 shows the example of a parallel loan involving a British and an American company and their subsidiaries in each other's country.

In this example we assume that a British company needs to inject US$150 million into its US subsidiary. Suppose the prevailing exchange rate is 1.5 US dollars per pound sterling, but exchange control regulations require the company to buy US dollars at a premium of, say 10 cents. The effective exchange rate for the company would, therefore, be 1.40. In order to purchase US$150 million, the company will have

---

[1] Parallel and back-to-back loans differ only in that the former agreement involves lending to subsidiaries whereas under the latter agreement two companies lend funds to each other directly.

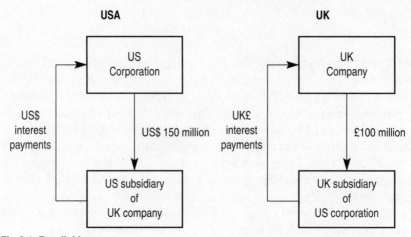

USA

UK

Fig 6.1 Parallel loan

to sell £107,142,857 costing it £7,142,857 in the form of the investment premium. Now, let us suppose a US corporation needs to transfer £100 million to its British subsidiary. It can do so by purchasing sterling at the spot exchange rate of £1.50. Alternatively, it can lend US$150 million to the US subsidiary of the UK company. The UK company, on the other hand, lends £100 million to the UK subsidiary of the US corporation. The financing requirements of both the subsidiaries are therefore met. In the process, however, the UK company was able to save the investment premium of £7,142,857. It can share a part of this with the US corporation by charging a lower rate of interest on the sterling loan than the commercial rates or using an exchange rate that is better than the spot rate for the US corporation.

It was not long before market participants realized that instead of arranging two parallel loans and documenting them as such, a simple swap agreement achieved the same objective with less documentation and the implied right of set-off against each other's obligations. This agreement came to be known as a cross currency swap.[2]

WHAT IS A CROSS CURRENCY SWAP?

A cross currency swap is an agreement between two parties to exchange periodic interest payments based on principal amounts denominated in two different currencies. Unlike an interest rate swap, in which interest

---

[2] A cross currency swap needs to be differentiated from the traditional FX swap that involves a spot FX transaction and a simultaneous forward sale/purchase of the currencies involved.

payments are denominated in a single currency, interest payments in a currency swap are denominated in two currencies. The principal amount in the case of currency swaps is, therefore, real rather than notional. Principal amounts are exchanged at the beginning and the maturity of the swap. In a standard cross currency swap, both the initial and the final exchanges of principal are based on the spot rate of exchange between the two currencies involved. Thus, unlike interest rate swaps cross currency swaps involve three sets of flows:

- initial exchange of principal
- periodic interest payments, and
- final exchange of principal at maturity.

It should be noted that the initial exchange of principal can be included in the swap contract or simply done as a spot foreign exchange transaction. The periodic interest payments in a cross currency swaps agreement can take three forms:

- fixed against fixed
- fixed against floating, or
- floating against floating.

RATIONALE FOR THE USE OF CROSS CURRENCY SWAPS

In Chapter 5 we discussed that a fixed-to-floating interest rate swap allowed borrowers to reduce their cost of funding by exploiting the difference in credit spreads in the fixed and the floating rate debt markets in a single currency. Cross currency swaps, on the other hand, allow borrowers to exploit credit spread differences between debt markets in different currencies. The markets in two currencies may be both fixed, both floating or floating in one and fixed in the other.

Suppose a UK based company needs US dollar funding for its American subsidiary for a period of five years. Let us assume it can raise five year US dollar funds at a fixed rate of 7 percent in the Eurobond market. Suppose it can also raise five year sterling funds in its domestic capital market at a fixed rate of 8 percent. Now suppose a US company needs fixed rate sterling funding for its UK subsidiary for a period of five years. Let us assume it can raise fixed rate US dollar funds at a rate of 6 percent in its domestic capital market. Suppose it can also raise five year sterling funds in the Eurobond market at a fixed rate of 7.4 percent. It is clear that the American company enjoys an absolute advantage in both the US dollar and the sterling markets. However, as we will note later, the British company has a comparative advantage in the sterling market. For comparative advantage to exist, we must show that each company can reduce its cost of funding by borrowing in a market where it has a comparative advantage and swapping it into the currency of requirement.

Table 6.1 summarizes the borrowing costs information for the two companies. Clearly, the American company is viewed as a better credit in both the dollar and the sterling markets relative to the British company. However, whereas the credit differential in the sterling market is 0.60 percent, the spread in the dollar market is 1.0 percent. Ignoring the fact that the differentials in US dollars and sterling are not directly comparable[3] there is a difference of 0.40 percent between the credit spreads in the US dollar and the sterling markets which can be exploited by combining the borrowing with a cross currency swap.

Table 6.1 Borrowing costs

	US dollar market	Sterling market
British company	7.0%	8.0%
American company	6.0%	7.4%
Absolute credit spread	1.0%	0.60%

Now, suppose each company borrows in its domestic market and both companies then enter into a cross currency swap for five years in which the US company pays 7.2 percent in sterling against receiving 6 percent in US dollars. The structure of the swap is shown in Figure 6.2. As we noted above, unlike interest rate swaps, cross currency swaps involve exchange of both principal and interest. However, here we just focus on the interest element of the swap.

Ignoring the currency effect, the interest cost, through the swap structure, for the British company will be as under:

---

[3] The difference of 0.4 percent is only approximate. To compare the interest rate differential in US dollars to the interest rate differential in sterling we need to take account of forward FX (or equivalently, the difference in spot interest rates in two currencies). Thus, if the US dollar is at a premium (expected to appreciate) to sterling, a credit spread of 0.60 percent in the sterling market will translate into a lower spread in dollar terms (because sterling is expected to depreciate in future).

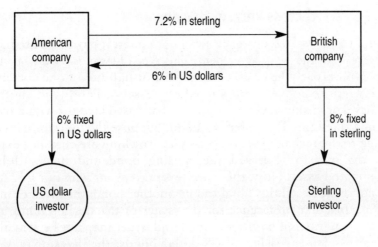

Fig 6.2 Exchange of interest payments

GBP interest on borrowing + USD swap interest payment – GBP swap interest receipt

= 8.0% GBP + 6.0% USD – 7.2% GBP
= 6.8%

which is 0.20 percent less than borrowing directly in the US market.

Similarly, the interest cost for the American company will be as under:

USD interest on borrowing + GBP swap interest payment – USD swap interest receipt

= 6.0% USD + 7.2% GBP – 6.0% USD
= 7.2%

which is 0.20 percent lower than borrowing directly in the sterling market. Note that, in the case of the British company, the saving of 0.20 percent through the swap needs to be adjusted by the forward currency differential between US dollars and sterling. It should also be noted that in practice nearly all swap transactions are executed through an intermediary bank.

STRUCTURE OF CROSS CURRENCY SWAPS

We noted above that a standard cross currency swap can involve three types of interest flows: fixed-to-fixed, fixed-to-floating and floating-to-floating.

Fixed-to-fixed cross currency swaps

Under a fixed-to-fixed currency swap both interest payments are fixed for the term of the swap agreement. This type of swap is used when the swap counterparty has a fixed rate asset or liability in one currency that it needs to convert into a fixed rate asset or liability in another currency. For example, consider a US dollar based investor with a position in a fixed rate Euro-sterling bond. Suppose the investor expects sterling to depreciate against US dollars. To eliminate currency exposure, the investor can sell the sterling bond and buy a dollar denominated asset. Now, there are several reasons why our investor may not want to sell this bond to buy another bond; the investor may have a particular preference for the issuer of the sterling bond; the credit spread offered by the sterling bond issuer may not be available from an equivalent issuer of US dollar bonds; the investor may be expecting a fall in the credit spread of the sterling issuer etc. Assuming that the investor still prefers a fixed rate asset, a fixed-to-fixed cross currency swap provides an alternative that hedges the currency exposure and allows the investor to take the credit risk of the sterling bond issuer. This is shown in Figure 6.3.

In the example we assume that the investor has a position of £10 million in a fixed-rate sterling bond paying a fixed coupon of 8 percent p.a.

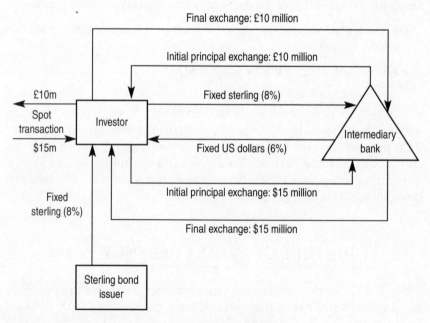

Fig 6.3 Example of fixed-to-fixed cross currency swap

144

and having a residual life of five years. The fixed-to-fixed cross currency swap allows the investor to convert this sterling asset into a dollar asset. The three sets of flows involved in the transaction are:

1 **Initial exchange of principals**   Assuming the spot exchange rate of 1.5, the investor makes a payment of £10 million to the intermediary bank against receiving $15 million. While most cross currency swaps involve initial exchange of principals, it is not necessary for swap counterparties to make the initial exchange because the same effect can be achieved by effecting a spot transaction. However, it should be remembered that the coupon payments are based on the principal amounts in each currency that are deemed to have been exchanged at the outset. Also, the market interest rates in two currencies are based on the assumption that the principal exchange is based on the spot FX. Any deviation from the spot FX will result in a change in the quoted rates.

2 **Periodic interest payments**   Under the swap the investor pays a fixed sterling amount calculated at the rate of 8 percent against receiving a fixed dollar payment calculated at the rate of 6 percent annually. Since the sterling bond pays an annual coupon of 8 percent, the fixed sterling swap rate can be based on this rate. Depending on how far away this rate is from the current five-year sterling swap rate quoted against US dollars, the US dollar fixed swap rate will be adjusted up or down relative to the current five-year US dollar swap rate quoted against sterling.

3 **Final exchange of principal**   On the maturity date of the swap the parties to the currency swap reverse the initial exchange of principals irrespective of whether the initial exchange was real or notional. In our example, the investor will make a payment of of £10 million to the intermediary bank and receive a payment of $15 million. Notice that £10 million payment to the intermediary bank will be matched by the redemption amount of the underlying sterling bond.

Fixed-to-fixed cross currency swaps are also widely used by borrowers to convert a fixed rate liability in one currency into a fixed rate liability in another currency. For example, a US based corporate borrower requiring fixed rate funding for a project in Indonesia may have little choice, both in terms of cost and availability, but to raise money in US dollars and then use a cross currency swap to convert the US dollar liability into a Rupiah based liability. Similarly, a British company making a long-term investment in the US may find it cheaper to raise sterling funds in the domestic market and then use a cross currency swap to convert the liability into US dollars. Fixed-to-fixed cross currency swaps also provide an effective vehicle for large fixed-rate funding requirements that are unlikely to be met through a single market. The borrower can access several markets to raise fixed-rate funds in different currencies and then use currency swaps to convert these liabilities into a single currency liability. Interestingly, it was this last reason that gave a big boost to the emergence of the market for currency swaps when IBM, in need of substantial funds, launched a global borrowing programme through which it raised funds in Swiss francs, Deutschmarks and yen. At that time all these currencies were low interest rate currencies. The funds thus raised were converted into US dollars. Clearly IBM was assuming exposure to DEM, CHF and yen. However, soon after raising these funds the US dollar began to appreciate significantly against the Swiss franc and the Deutschmark. IBM was approached by banks to explore if it was interested in locking-in the capital gain that accrued from the dollar's appreciation. At the same time the World Bank was approached to see if it would be interested in complementing its Swiss franc and Deutschmark borrowing programme by raising US dollars and converting them into Swiss francs and Deutschmarks through a fixed-to-fixed cross currency swap. The result was that the World Bank issued a two-tranch dollar fixed-rate Eurobond with maturities exactly matching IBM's Swiss franc and Deutschmark liabilities. A cross currency swap allowed the two parties to achieve exposure to desired currencies; US dollars in the case of IBM and Swiss francs and Deutschmarks in the case of the World Bank. The swap also allowed IBM to lock-in the capital gain arising from the dollar's appreciation following its foreign currency debt issuance.

Fixed-to-floating cross currency swaps

A fixed-to-floating cross currency swap involves exchange of fixed interest payments in one currency against floating interest payments in another currency. The motivation for this type of currency swap can be the need by one party to have floating-rate funding and the need by the other party to have fixed-rate funding. Also, even if the requirement of each party to the swap was to have fixed-rate funding, a fixed-to-floating cross currency swap may be used in combination with an interest rate swap if the credit differential for the two parties between the fixed rate market in one currency against the floating-rate market in another currency was higher than the credit differential between the fixed-rate markets in the two currencies.

Figure 6.4 provides an example of a fixed-to-floating cross currency swap. In this example, a US bank, in need of floating rate Deutschmarks, raises fixed rate US dollars in its domestic market and swaps fixed dollars for floating Deutschmarks. On the other hand, a German company in need of fixed rate US dollars raises floating Deutschmarks and swaps floating Deutschmarks for fixed US dollars. Both swaps are transacted through an intermediary bank.

146

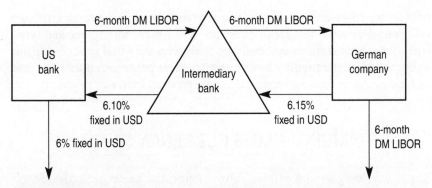

Fig 6.4 Periodic exchange of interest payments under fixed-to-floating cross currency swap

Suppose the US bank can raise floating rate Deutschmark funds at six-month LIBOR plus 0.10 percent, or fixed-rate US dollar funds at 6 percent. On the other hand, a German company can raise fixed-rate US dollar funds at 6.30 percent and floating rate DEM funds at six-month LIBOR flat. By borrowing in markets where each party enjoys a comparative advantage and combining it with a cross currency swap, each party reduces its cost of funding as shown in Table 6.2 (noting that the spreads in two currencies are not directly comparable).

Table 6.2 Borrowing costs

	Direct borrowing	Borrowing + swap	Saving
US Bank	DM LIBOR + 0.10%	6% USD+DM LIBOR–6.1% USD = DM LIBOR – 0.1%	0.20%
German Company	6.3% in USD	DM LIBOR+6.15% USD – DM LIBOR = 6.15%	0.15%

Floating-to-floating cross currency swaps

A floating-to-floating cross currency swap, also known as the cross currency basis swap, involves exchange of floating interest payments denominated in two different currencies. It allows borrowers and investors to swap floating rate liabilities or assets from one currency into another. For example, a floating-to-floating cross currency swap can be used to convert a Deutschmark LIBOR based asset into a US dollar

147

LIBOR based asset. Investors can use floating-to-floating cross currency swaps to diversify their credit exposure while maintaining market exposure in the desired currency. Similarly, borrowers may find it advantageous to combine the debt with a cross currency basis swap to reduce their cost of funding, as in the case of the other two types of currency swaps.

PRICING CROSS CURRENCY SWAPS

Cross currency swaps can be valued using the methodologies developed in Chapter 5 to value interest rate swaps. The difference, of course, is that while to value an interest rate swap we need to have a single currency discount function, to value cross currency swaps we need discount functions in two currencies.

To value a fixed-to-fixed cross currency swap we first need to generate discount curves for the two currencies in question. Since in the case of fixed-to-fixed cross currency swaps both interest rates are fixed for the term of the swap, we can readily establish the cash flows in the two currencies. We next value the fixed cash flows using the relevant discount curve, giving us present values in two different currencies. One of the present values is then converted into the other currency using the spot exchange rate.

In theory, the floating-to-floating cross currency swaps, or basis swaps, should trade at LIBOR flat in one currency against LIBOR flat in another currency. In reality, however, there is a bid offer spread at which such swaps trade. The spread is driven by a number of factors and differs among various currency pairs. For example, in the dollar–yen cross currency swaps market, a three-year basis swap may be quoted dollar LIBOR plus 10 basis points against yen LIBOR flat. In most other major currency pairs the spread is usually lower.

Under the assumption that cross currency basis swaps trade at LIBOR flat in one currency against LIBOR flat in another currency, valuing fixed-to-floating cross currency swaps is straightforward. For example, to value a DM/US$ cross currency swap involving fixed DM payments against floating US dollar payments, we would use the discount functions in each currency. All fixed coupon payments plus the principal amount in Deutschmarks would be valued using the Deutschmark discount curve. To value floating US dollar payments we will first need to generate the forward rates using the US dollar discount curve and then value the estimated floating payments plus the principal amount in US dollars using the dollar discount curve. If the associated basis swap in the currency pair in question is not quoted at LIBOR flat, we would need to make an adjustment by adding or deducting the spread to the fixed rate.

SUMMARY

Cross currency swaps are the forerunner of the interest rate swap. These instruments emerged as a refinement of parallel or back-to-back loans that were developed to circumvent the introduction of foreign exchange controls in the UK. The development of cross currency swaps greatly simplified the mechanism involved in parallel loans.

Cross currency swaps allow borrowers and investors to convert liabilities and assets from one currency into another, thereby hedging currency exposure on the underlying liabilities and assets. These instruments allow borrowers and investors to separate the underlying debt market and currency decisions. Borrowers can raise funds in a market where they have the greatest comparative advantage and then use a cross currency swap to transform the currency exposure. Investors can, likewise, invest in foreign currency debt and use cross currency swaps to hedge the resultant currency exposure. Like interest rate swaps, cross currency swaps are priced using either the bond equivalent or the zero-coupon pricing methodologies.

References

Batlin, C.A., 'Linkages Between Interest Rate Swaps and Cross Currency Swaps', in *Interest Rate Swaps*, Carl R. Beidleman ed., Homewood Illinois: Richard D. Irwin, 1991.

Park, Y.S., 'Currency Swaps as a Long Term International Financing Technique', *Journal of International Studies*, 15:3, Winter 1984, pp. 47–54.

Bock, D.R., 'Fixed-to-Fixed Currency Swaps: The Origins of the World Bank Borrowing', in *Swap Financing Techniques*, Boris Antl, ed., London: Euromoney, 1985.

7

EQUITY SWAPS

Basic structure of an equity swap

Rationale for the use of equity swaps

Pricing equity swaps

Variations on the basic structure

Strategies and applications in
investment management

Summary

Equity or equity-index swaps represent one of the most significant innovations in the global swaps market. Exactly as interest rate and currency swaps bridge the gap in national and global capital markets, equity swaps have the potential to bridge the gap between equity and debt markets. Like its interest rate and currency predecessors, equity swaps have opened significant new opportunities, particularly in the area of investment management. Equity swaps allow investors to achieve investment objectives more efficiently and, indeed, in many cases allow investors to pursue equity-related investment objectives that would otherwise not be possible. Equity swaps are increasingly being used to create synthetic equity structures to diversify risk, to bypass transfer and withholding taxes and to reduce transactions costs. In this chapter we review the basic structure of equity swaps, describe various variations and their applications and provide an overview of pricing.

Table 7.1 Outstanding equity swaps (notional principal in US$ millions)

Index by country	Interbank	End-users	Total
Index by country:			
Japan	3,000	3,000	6,000
USA	1,000	1,000	2,000
Other	–	1,000	1,000
Baskets	–	1,000	1,000
Total	4,000	6,000	10,000

Source: International Swap and Derivatives Association

BASIC STRUCTURE OF AN EQUITY SWAP

In its simplest form, an equity swap is an agreement between two parties to exchange periodic payments one of which is based on a stock index while the other is based on an agreed upon interest rate. Typically, the 'equity leg' of the swap is linked to total return on a stock index, i.e. including dividend and capital gain returns. The 'interest leg', on the other hand, is typically based on a floating-rate index such as LIBOR but may also be fixed for the term of the swap. Like its interest rate counterpart, the payments under an equity swap are based on a notional principal amount that does not change hands since both the equity and interest legs of the swap are denominated in the same currency. The popular stock indexes against which equity swaps are quoted include S&P 500, FT 100 and the Nikkei Index. Increasingly, dealers are willing to quote on equity swaps linked to minor stock indices. Investors use equity swaps both to hedge existing exposure and to assume exposure to new markets.

A typical use of equity swaps involves hedging an equity portfolio against downside risk. For example, an equity fund with a diversified portfolio that mimics the performance of the FT 100 may be concerned about a market fall over the next three years. It can enter into an equity swap with a notional principal amount (NPA) equal to the value of the FT Index-linked fund, say £100 million, under which it agrees to pay FT index return against receiving six-month sterling LIBOR. This structure is shown in Figure 7.1.

The equity swap allows the fund to hedge against equity risk by effectively converting the equity portfolio into a fixed income portfolio. Of course, the fund could achieve the same effect by liquidating the equity portfolio and purchasing fixed income securities. That would, however, entail incurring transactions and other costs such as capital gains tax. Moreover, should the fund's expectations change, it can easily reverse the equity swap to resume exposure to FT index without having to incur transaction costs.

A more typical use of equity swaps involves index funds receiving the equity leg against paying a fixed or a floating rate of interest. A strong reason for index funds to be a receiver of the index under the swap, in addition to the benefits described above, is that the swap allows it to track the index perfectly whereas a cash portfolio may not. Figure 7.2 shows the example of an index-fund receiving S&P 500 index against paying six-month USD LIBOR on agreed upon notional principal amount for the term of the swap.

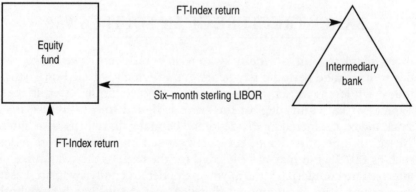

Fig 7.1 Basic structure of an equity swap

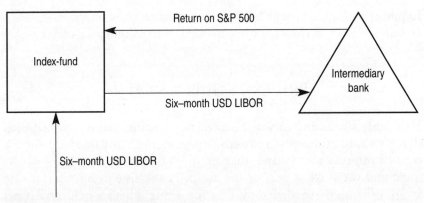

Fig 7.2 Use of equity swap by index funds

RATIONALE FOR THE USE OF EQUITY SWAPS

In its simplest form, an equity swap allows investors to convert an equities position into a synthetic fixed income position or vice versa for a given term. There are several reasons why investors may prefer to use equity swaps rather than cash market instruments to manage their equity or fixed income portfolios. In this section we briefly survey some of the important reasons that have led to the growth of equity swaps.

Transactions costs   An important reason for the use of equity swaps is that its use minimizes transactions and other costs. Whereas a cash position would entail buying and selling the underlying equities, an equity swap obviates the need for cash positions which results in avoiding the transactions costs. Besides the brokerage costs, investors can avoid or minimize costs associated with custody, portfolio restructuring, bid-offer spreads and stamp duties.

Regulatory and tax   Equity swaps provide a mechanism to assume exposure to stock markets that are either closed or restrictive for foreigners. For example, emerging stock markets such as South Korea and India do not provide full access to foreign investors. An equity swap provides an excellent mechanism to assume exposure to such markets.

Many countries impose withholding tax on dividends for foreign investors which reduces the effective return on stock investments. Equity swaps can be used to avoid withholding tax.

Tracking accuracy   Many equity funds' performance is judged by reference to a stock index. However, the underlying equity portfolio of such funds may not be totally correlated with the index. Equity swaps, on the other hand, are by definition perfectly correlated with the index.

155

Liquidity   Liquidity can be a serious issue in some markets or for a certain set of stocks. Swaps can provide a better liqidity in such cases.

PRICING EQUITY SWAPS

Like other swaps and forward contracts, an equity swap is priced such that its value at inception is zero. As was noted in Chapter 5, in the case of interest rate swaps, that involves equating the values of the fixed and the floating legs of the swap. In the case of an interest rate swap, pricing involved finding that fixed rate which would give a net present value of zero. In the case of equity swaps, pricing involves finding that interest rate (fixed or the spread over or under LIBOR) which would give a net present value of zero. However, whereas in the case of interest rate swaps we relied on the prevailing yield curve which in some cases goes out to 30 years, in the case of equity swaps, valuing the equity leg is fraught with practical difficulties. First, whereas in the case of interest rate swaps it is relatively easy to link short and long term interest rates, in the case of equity swaps it is by no means easy to define an arbitrage relationship between interest rate and equity returns. Second, even if the two markets were conceptually linked, lack of forward markets in most equity indices results in the lack of pricing benchmarks.

Despite these difficulties equity swaps are widely priced using implied forward returns on the index, which is akin to using implied forward rates in the pricing of interest rate swaps. The methodology involves calculating the theoretically fair value of stock-index futures contracts.[1] It can be shown that, in the absence of arbitrage, a stock-index futures price must be given by:

$$F_{T,t} = I_0[1 + r_T - D] \tag{7.1}$$

where

$F_{T,t}$ = price of the T-period index future at time t
I_0 = current value of the index
r_T = T-period interest rate or the cost of carry
D = dividend yield

Equation (7.1) states that the index futures price expiring at time T must be equal to the current value of the index compounded at the current rate of interest less the dividend yield.

---

[1] Where sufficient index-futures contracts are traded, the index returns can be imputed from Equation (7.1) in which r_T is the implied index return.

156

Example

Consider an equity swap that involves exchange of the return on the S&P 500 against a fixed interest rate. Suppose the swap involves two semi-annual payments based on a notional principal amount of $1,000,000. Suppose the current S&P 500 Index is 540 and the six-month futures price is 567. Assuming a dividend yield of 4 percent, we can impute the expected six-month index return $E(\tilde{r}_T)$ using the cost of carry model given by Equation (7.1). Thus we have

$$F_{6,0} = I_0 \left[1 + E\left(\tilde{r}_6\right) - D \right]$$

$$567 = 540 \left[1 + \frac{E\left(\tilde{r}_6\right)}{2} - \frac{0.04}{2} \right]$$

$$E\left(\tilde{r}_6\right) = 0.07 = 7\%$$

This is the annualized expected index return for a six-month period. Next, we need the expected index return for the twelve-month period. In the absence of a twelve month S&P 500 futures contract, we rely on the underlying arbitrage argument implicit in Equation (7.1) which states that the current index futures price is equal to the spot index level compounded at the cost of carry (i.e. the repo rate less the dividend yield). Assuming that the twelve-month cost of carry is the same as the (annualized) cost of carry for the six-month index futures, we have the twelve-month expected index return of 7 percent. In interest rate swaps pricing parlance, we now have the par yields for six and twelve months. Since the equity leg of the swap is assumed to make six-monthly payments we need, as in the case of the floating leg of an interest rate swap, to imply the six-month index return expected to prevail in six months' time. We can use the methodology developed in Chapter 5 to derive the implied six-month forward index return as under:

$$(1+r_{12}) = \left(1+\frac{r_6}{2}\right)\left(1+\frac{r_{6,6}}{2}\right)$$

$$(1+0.07) = \left(1+\frac{0.07}{2}\right)\left(1+\frac{r_{6,6}}{2}\right)$$

$$r_{6,6} = 0.06764 \text{ or } 6.764\%$$

To work out the fixed rate of interest (R) on the swap, recall from Chapter 5 that at inception the NPV of a swap contract must be zero. Assuming discount rates of 6.95 percent and 7.05 percent for six and twelve month periods we can calculate R as under:

$$\frac{NPA\left[\left(\frac{r_{6,0}}{2}\right) - \frac{R}{2}\right]}{\left(1 + \frac{0.0695}{2}\right)} + \frac{NPA\left[\left(\frac{r_{6,6}}{2}\right) - R\right]}{(1 + 0.0705)} = 0$$

$$\frac{\$1,000,000\left[\dfrac{0.07}{2}-\dfrac{R}{2}\right]}{\left(1+\dfrac{0.0695}{2}\right)}+\frac{\$1,000,000\left[\dfrac{0.0674}{2}-\dfrac{R}{2}\right]}{(1+0.0705)}=0$$

Solving for R we get R equal to 6.88%

VARIATIONS ON THE BASIC STRUCTURE

Like other derivatives, equity swaps market has witnessed a proliferation of variants on the basic structure described above. While most of the variants are the more structured versions of the basic swap, a number of other variants are quite different. The more important of these variations are described below.

Equity basis swap   Equity basis swap is similar in concept to interest rate or currency basis swaps. Under this structure, two parties agree to exchange periodic payments based on the performance of two stock indices. That is, unlike the 'vanilla' equity swap in which an equity index is swapped against a fixed or a floating interest rate, an equity basis swap involves exchange of payments based on, say, S&P 500 index against DAX index. An example of such a swap is depicted in Figure 7.3.

Non-index equity swap   While most of the equity swaps are linked to broad market indices such as S&P 500, Nikkei or DAX, there exists a market for equity swaps that are based on narrower indexes such as specific industry groups, arbitrary baskets of stocks and even single stocks.

Blended-index equity swaps   In a blended-index equity swap the equity leg is based on the returns of more than one stock index. For example, it may involve exchange of payments based on the performance of Nikkei and DAX as shown in Figure 7.4. In this example Party A receives the index return based on the average performance of the two indexes against paying six-month US$ LIBOR.

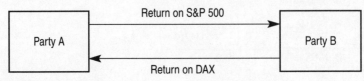

Fig 7.3 Equity basis swap

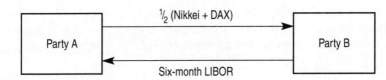

Fig 7.4 Blended equity swap

STRATEGIES AND APPLICATIONS IN INVESTMENT MANAGEMENT

Equity swaps are among the most fundamental innovations in financial markets over the past two decades. While its early acceptance in the market place has been relatively slow, no one doubts its profound implications for investment management. It is undoubtedly an extremely versatile tool for bridging the gap between equity and fixed income markets. It allows investors to assume exposure to markets that would otherwise be impossible and even where possible, equity swaps provide a cost effective mechanism to assume equity exposure. On the other hand, equity swaps also provide a tool for risk management.

The most important application of equity swaps in investment management is that it allows investors to assume equity exposure without having to buy a stock. As we noted earlier, investors can assume exposure to broad based equity indexes such as Nikkei or S&P 500, industry specific indexes, baskets of stocks or even individual stocks. Using equity swaps to assume equity exposure means no brokerage fees, no custody charges, no withholding taxes etc. We also noted earlier that foreign investors can use OTC equity swaps to assume exposure to stock markets where participation is restricted to domestic players.

Fund managers who track broad based stock indexes can use equity swaps with greater success because an equity swap with returns pegged to a particular index is by definition 100 percent correlated with that index. This can, in particular, obviate the need for costly rebalancings.

In some cases equity swaps can guarantee a better performance than the underlying index. For example, in Germany equity swaps have at times provided DAX plus 50 to 70 basis points against LIBOR flat. The reason for this pick-up is that the German investor who is long an equity position but wants to swap it against a LIBOR based return receives a tax credit that is not available to foreign investors. Thus, a foreign investor who wishes to assume exposure to DAX can achieve a better than DAX performance by entering into an equity swap rather than buying equities. Effectively, the German investor shares the benefit arising from the tax credit with the foreign investor. While the foreign investor can achieve a pick-up over DAX, the domestic investor is able to achieve a pick-up over LIBOR.

Equity swaps also allow investors to reduce their exposure to equity markets without having to liquidate their stock positions. This is particularly efficient if the desire to reduce exposure is of a short-term nature.

SUMMARY

Equity swaps represent a major innovation in the global swaps market. These swaps have the potential to bridge the gap between equity and debt markets. Equity swaps allow investors to achieve their objectives in a more efficient and cost effective way than would be possible in cash markets. Indeed, in some cases equity swaps are the only vehicle through which investors can assume exposure to an equity market that is otherwise closed.

Investors can use equity swaps to convert equity positions into synthetic fixed income positions and vice versa. The motivation for the switch may be transactions costs, tax and regulatory considerations, tracking accuracy and liquidity. Equity swaps are priced using the fixed income valuation framework.

References

Francis, J.C., Toy, W.W. and Whittaker, J.G., *The Handbook of Equity Derivatives*, New York: Irwin, 1995.

Marshall, J.F., Sorensen, E.H. and Tucker, A.L., 'Equity Derivatives: The Plain Vanilla Equity Swap and its Variants', *Journal of Financial Engineering*, 1(2), 1992, pp. 219–41.

8

INTEREST RATE OPTIONS

General features of interest rate options

Interest rate caps

Interest rate floors

Pricing caps and floors

Cap and floor applications and structured strategies

Swaptions

Pricing swaptions

Swaption applications

Bond options

Pricing bond options

Bond option applications

Summary

Interest rate options provide important new ways for managing the interest rate risk of asset and liability portfolios. In particular, interest rate options provide an effective means of managing the risk/return characteristics of a bond portfolio. For example, interest rate options can be used to create a floor on portfolio returns or to manage the convexity risk.

Compared with options on equities, commodities or currencies, interest rate options are more difficult to price and hedge. That is because, unlike options on other variables, interest rates are not traded variables. Moreover, while stock, currency and commodity options are based on the performance of a single underlying variable – the price of the underlying – interest rate options must take into account the behavior of the yield curve that is effectively composed of a number of distinct, though interrelated variables.

In this chapter we analyze a variety of interest rate options including caps, floors, swaptions and bond options. We will study, in detail, various pricing and hedging methodologies for these options.

GENERAL FEATURES OF INTEREST RATE OPTIONS

Interest rate options can broadly be classified into two categories:

1 short-term interest rate dependent options, and
2 long-term interest rate dependent options.

Short-term interest rates, or money market rates, extend up to twelve months and are quoted on a variety of instruments such as Treasury bills, Eurodollar deposits, etc. Most of the short-term interest rate dependent options are, however, based on the London Interbank Offered Rate (LIBOR) on deposits of various maturities up to one year. These options include caps, floors and collars.

Long-term interest rates extend up to thirty years in some currencies and constitute the market for corporate and sovereign debt. Long-term interest rate dependent options comprise bond options and swaptions.

The distinction between short-term and long-term interest rate dependent options is necessary both from the point of view of their applications as well as for pricing and hedging.

In general, interest rate options are more difficult to analyze and value than other types of options such as equity options. The primary reason for this is that while equity options depend on the price of an underlying equity (a single variable) the price of an interest rate option depends on the yield curve (multiple variables). When pricing an equity option we need to model the price behavior of a single variable – the underlying stock price. When pricing an interest rate option we must model the behavior of the yield curve consisting of interest rates for securities of various terms.

Second, while the underlying in the case of an equity option is a traded stock, the underlying in the case of interest rate options is an interest rate such as three-month LIBOR which is not a traded security. The hedging arguments described in Chapter 3 cannot, therefore, be applied to interest rate options without making further assumptions.

Finally, while it is relatively easy to model the stochastic behavior of a stock price, modeling of interest rate behavior is fraught with difficulties. For example, while the assumption of a random walk is plausible for stock prices, it does not provide a good fit for the behavior of interest rate changes which tend to follow mean reversion.

INTEREST RATE CAPS

A cap is an option contract in which the seller agrees to pay to the buyer the difference between an agreed upon interest rate index, such as three-month LIBOR, and a strike rate if the index sets above the strike rate for any interest period. In effect the contract allows borrowers to 'cap' the cost of borrowing at the strike rate while still being able to benefit from lower interest rates. A cap is essentially a series of European call options written on an interest rate index.

To understand a cap, let us first consider a single period interest rate call option. Suppose you have a loan of $100 million with one year to maturity on which you pay six-month US dollar LIBOR. The interest rate for the first six-month period is already set but you are concerned about interest rates rising over the next six months at the end of which interest for the second six-month interest period will be set. Suppose you buy a call option with the following terms:

Trade date: 4 January 1995
Settlement date: 4 January 1995
Expiration date: 4 July 1995 (181 days)
Notional amount: US$100 million
Strike rate: 10% or 0.10
Underlying index: six-month US dollar LIBOR

The settlement date refers to the date when the terms of the contract are set which in this example is the same as the trade date. The option term is six months (181 days) with the underlying interest rate index defined as six-month LIBOR. This call gives you the right to receive the difference between the six-month US dollar LIBOR prevailing in 181 days' time and the 10 percent strike rate, if LIBOR sets above 10 percent, on the notional amount of $100 million. The option is European style, i.e. it can be exercised only on the expiration date. Thus, if six-month LIBOR on the expiration date sets at or below 10 percent the option will expire worthless. However, should six-month LIBOR on the expiration date set above 10 percent you will receive a payment computed as under:

$$Cap\ Payoff = (LIBOR - Strike) \times \frac{Actual\ number\ of\ Days}{Day\ Basis} \times Notional\ Amount$$

$$(8.1)$$

That is, the payoff is determined by the difference between the actual six-month LIBOR on the expiration date and the strike rate of 10 percent. This difference is multiplied by the actual number of days in the subsequent six-month period as a proportion of day basis – 360 days in the USD money market – and the notional amount of the option. Note that this payoff is received six months after the option expiry date to coincide with the interest payment on the underlying liability to be hedged. It is important to note the three dates that are relevant to the definition of the call as shown in Figure 8.1. The trade date is when the option contract is bought or sold. The expiration date, 181 days from the trade date, relates to the term of the option. The payment date is the maturity date of the underlying interest payment, 184 days from the expiration date.

Suppose on the expiration date six-month LIBOR fixes at 12 percent. What payoff should you receive? Using formula (8.1) we have

$$Call\ Payoff = (0.12 - 0.10) \times \frac{184}{360} \times \$100,000,000$$
$$= \$1,022,222$$

The payoff of $1,022,222 is received 184 days after the option expiration date. Alternatively, the discounted value of this amount can be received on the expiration date. In either case, ignoring the call premium, the interest rate on the underlying liability would be 'capped' at 10 percent.

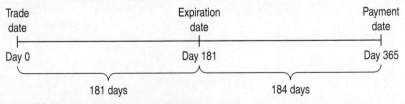

Fig 8.1 Key dates in the life of a call option

The payoff diagram for this call is presented in Figure 8.2. Notice that unlike call options on securities or commodities, the slope of the payoff line is not equal to one. That is because in the case of an interest rate call the x-axis represents the interest rate whereas the y-axis represents the dollar payoff. For normal calls both the axes are expressed in dollar terms.

An interest rate cap is a strip or a series of (sequentially maturing) European style interest rate call options, also called caplets, such as the one described above. As such, it is a portfolio of call options written on interest rates in successive interest periods. Interest rate caps allow borrowers to create a ceiling (or a 'cap') on their cost of borrowing while being able to benefit from interest rates below the cap strike rate. For example, an interest rate cap purchased with a strike rate of 10 percent guarantees that the borrower's cost of funding will never exceed 10 percent. However, should rates for any interest period set below 10 percent, the borrower benefits directly by paying the lower rate of interest for that period. This is shown graphically in Figure 8.3 for a cap over six semi-annual interest periods. Since LIBOR for the first interest period is usually known, the effective start date of the cap is from the beginning of the second interest period.

INTEREST RATE FLOORS

An interest rate floor is a strip of European put options, also called floorlets, written on an interest rate index such as three-month LIBOR. Each floorlet gives its holder the right to receive the difference between an agreed upon strike rate and an interest rate index such as three-month LIBOR. A floor allows its holder to hedge against a fall in short-term interest rates. For example, an investor with a floating-rate portfolio can

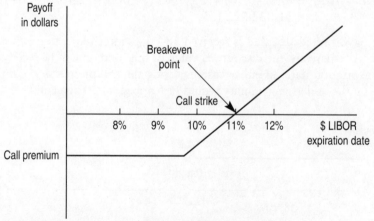

Fig 8.2 Profit/loss diagram for a single period interest rate call option

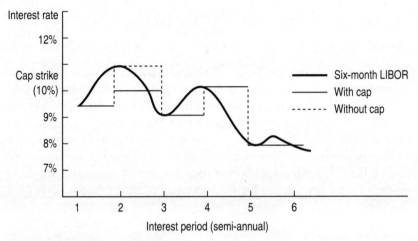

Fig 8.3 Capped interest rate

purchase a floor to ensure that the return on his portfolio does not fall below a certain level should short-term interest rates drop, while at the same time being able to benefit from higher short-term interest rates. For example, suppose the current six-month LIBOR is 8 percent. If the investor is concerned about six-month LIBOR falling significantly below this level, he can buy a floor with a strike rate of, say, 7 percent. During the term of the floor, should six-month LIBOR fall below 7 percent, the investor will be entitled to receive the difference between 7 percent – the strike rate – and the actual six-month LIBOR. That means, the investor's return will never be less than 7 percent irrespective of how far the interest rates fall. Should interest rates settle above 7 percent for any interest period during the term of the floor, the investor will benefit directly by earning a higher rate of return (the floor for that period expires worthless). On each floorlet expiration date the floor holder will receive a payoff computed as under:

$$Floor\ Payoff = (Strike - LIBOR) \times \frac{Actual\ number\ of\ Days}{Day\ Basis} \times Notional\ Amount$$

$$(8.2)$$

That is, the payoff is determined by the difference between the strike rate and the actual six-month LIBOR on the expiration date. As in the case of a cap, this difference is multiplied by the actual number of days in the subsequent six-month period as a proportion of day basis – 360 or 365 – and the notional principal amount of the option. Suppose in our example, the six-month LIBOR fixes at 6 percent at the expiration of the first floorlet. Assuming 180 days for the interest period, and a notional amount of $100 million, what will be the payoff to the floor holder? Using Equation (8.2) we have

$$Floor\ Payoff = (0.07 - 0.06) \times \frac{180}{360} \times \$100{,}000{,}000$$
$$= \$500{,}000$$

Thus, the purchaser of the floor will receive $500,000 at the end of 180 days which will have the effect of increasing the return on his portfolio to 7 percent even though the actual six-month LIBOR fixes at 6 percent for the interest period. If we suppose that the investor purchased the floor for a period of three years, i.e. for six semi-annual interest periods his effective interest receipts will be as shown in Figure 8.4. Notice that since the LIBOR setting for the first interest period is known, the floor provides effective protection for the subsequent five interest periods.

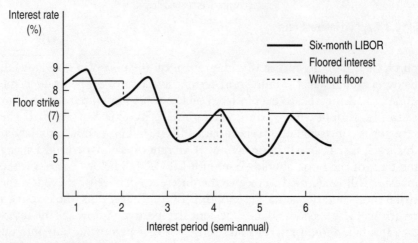

Fig 8.4 Floored returns

The payoff for a floorlet is shown in Figure 8.5.

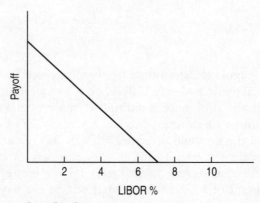

Fig 8.5 Payoff diagram for a floorlet

It should be emphasized that the interest rate index for caps and floors is not limited to LIBOR. Caps and floors can be arranged on commercial paper (CP) rate, Fed Funds rate, Constant Maturity Treasury (CMT) and the prime rate.

PRICING CAPS AND FLOORS

We noted above that a cap is essentially a portfolio of European calls (caplets) written on an interest rate index such as LIBOR. Its price is simply the sum of prices of its individual caplets. Pricing a cap, therefore, involves pricing the caplets. Similarly, we noted that a floor is a portfolio of European puts (floorlets) written on an interest rate index. To value a floor we must value the individual floorlets and sum them up.

We noted at the outset of this chapter that valuation of interest rate options is fraught with difficulties. The Black and Scholes model when used to value interest rate options can result in serious inconsistencies. The first source of inconsistency relates to assumptions about the behavior of short-term interest rates. The model assumes that interest rates are constant throughout the term of the option. Yet, when valuing interest rate options such as caps and floors, it is precisely the stochastic behavior of interest rates that we must capture. The second problem arises on account of the probability distribution assumed for the underlying variable. The Black and Scholes model assumes that the underlying stock price follows a lognormal distribution. However, short-term interest rates tend to follow a mean-reverting process.

It turns out that both these problems can be tackled to a fair degree of accuracy if we use forward rather than spot interest rates in the Black and Scholes framework. A forward interest rate, for example, should incorporate market expectation on any mean reversion in the short-term rate. It is for this reason that a modified Black and Scholes model, developed by Black (1976) to value options on futures, is the most widely used model to value caps and floors.

Pricing a cap

The basic idea is simple. Let us consider a two-year cap written on six-month LIBOR. Given the current yields (or equivalently current prices) on various instruments such as Eurodollar deposit futures, LIBOR, Treasuries and swap rates, we compute the forward rates for six-month LIBOR expected to prevail on each reset date using the methodology developed in Chapters 2 and 5.

These rates are unbiased estimates of the six-month LIBOR on reset dates. However, the actual LIBORs on reset dates are stochastic in nature and do not have to correspond with the currently implied forward LIBORs. If we assume that forward interest rates are lognormally distributed, then the actual reset rates will have a distribution with a mean equal to the implied forward LIBOR for that reset date and a standard deviation given by the volatility of the underlying LIBOR. The current value of each caplet is its expected payoff given by the weighted average value in the shaded area of Figure 8.6 less the cap strike rate. The weighted average can be found by means of integration. That is precisely what the model developed by Black (1976) does.

Black's (1976) model is the most widely used model for valuing interest rate options. It is an extension of the Black and Scholes (1973) model and is given by

$$C = [R_f N (d1) - EN(d2)]e^{-rT} \qquad (8.3)$$

where

C = price of an interest rate call
R_f = forward rate or implied LIBOR
E = strike rate of the cap
e = 2.7183
r = risk free interest rate
T = time to expiration of the call

$$d1 = \frac{ln\left(\frac{R_f}{E}\right) + 0.5\sigma^2 T}{\sigma\sqrt{T}}$$

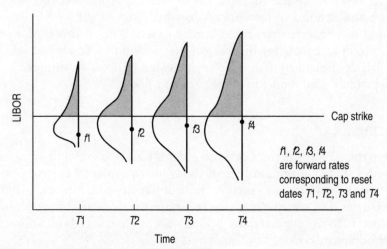

Fig 8.6 Cap pricing from a lognormal distribution

$$d2 = d1 - \sigma\sqrt{T}$$

Example

Let us price a call option written on six-month LIBOR with the following parameters:

$R_f = 7\%$
$E = 6\%$
$T = 180$ days $= 0.5$ years
$\sigma = 15\% = 0.15$
$r = 5\%$

In this example we assume that the implied six-month forward LIBOR has been worked out at 7 percent using the methodology described in Chapter 2. Using Equation (8.3) to value the interest rate call is now a simple matter. We begin by working out the values of $d1$ and $d2$.

$$d1 = \frac{\ln\left(\frac{R_f}{E}\right) + 0.5\sigma^2 T}{\sigma\sqrt{T}}$$

$$= \frac{\ln\left(\frac{0.07}{0.06}\right) + 0.5(0.15)^2 0.5}{0.15\sqrt{0.5}}$$

$$= 1.506$$

$$d2 = d1 - \sigma\sqrt{T}$$

$$d2 = 1.56 - 0.15\sqrt{0.5}$$

$$= 1.40$$

Substituting these values into formula (8.3) we get

$$C = [R_f N(d1) - EN(d2)] e^{-rT}$$

$$= [0.07N(1.506) - 0.06N(1.40)]\, 2.7183^{-(0.05)(0.5)}$$

Recall from Chapter 3 that $N(d1)$ and $N(d2)$ are cumulative probabilities of observing $d1$ and $d2$ values. These probabilities can be approximated using the model given at the end of Chapter 3 or can be read directly off a table of cumulative normal probabilities given in Appendix 1. From the table we get the values of $N(d1)$ and $N(d2)$ as under:

$$N(d1) = N(1.506) = 0.934$$

$$N(d2) = N(1.40) = 0.9192$$

Substituting these values in the call pricing equation we get

$$C = [\, 0.07(0.934) - 0.06(0.9192)\,]\, 2.7183^{-(0.05)(0.5)}$$

$$= 0.998\%$$

171

Notice that, in terms of the implied forward LIBOR versus the strike rate of the option, this call is in-the-money and hence is quite expensive given that it is a six-month option. It is also worth remembering that the volatility greatly influences the value of options.

We used Equation (8.3) to value a call option written on six-month LIBOR that expires and settles in six months' time. However, we noted earlier, that unlike a call option on, say, stock in which the payoff is paid on expiration, a cap payoff is received in arrears to correspond with the payment of interest on the underlying liability being hedged. This is an important point and needs re-emphasizing. Consider the time line showing various events in the life of a cap as shown in Figure 8.7.

Since each caplet payoff is paid in arrears (say six months after expiration in the case of a cap on six-month LIBOR) it should cost less today because of the time value of money. Thus, to convert the call value derived above into the cap value we need to discount the call price as under

$$Cap\ Price = \frac{Call\ Price}{1 + R_f} \tag{8.4}$$

where R_f is the forward rate relevant to the interest period. The cap price in our example assuming that the cap payoff will be paid 180 days in arrears is

$$Cap\ Price = \frac{0.998}{1 + \left(0.07 \times \frac{180}{360}\right)}$$

$$= 0.964\%$$

To value a cap involving more than one interest rate call (caplet), we simply value each caplet and sum the resulting values. That is

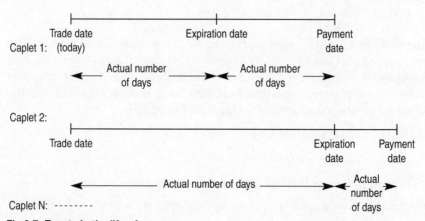

Fig 8.7 Events in the life of a cap

$$Cap\ Price = \sum_{i=1}^{n} q_i$$

where q_i is the price of caplet i.

As in the case of caps, to value floors we need to value each floorlet and sum the resulting values. To derive a pricing formula for interest rate puts, we invoke the put/call/forward parity relationship described below.

Put/call/forward parity

In Chapter 10, we will show that the put-call parity for European stock options is given by

$$P = C - S + PV\ (E) \tag{8.5}$$

where P is the price of a European put, C is the price of a European call both written on the same stock that is currently trading at a price of S with similar exercise and maturity terms and E is the exercise price of the put and the call. Equation (8.5) states that a long position in a put can be replicated by purchasing a call, selling the underlying stock and investing the present value of the exercise price. We note that, in general, the current price of an asset can be viewed as the present value of its forward price, F. That is

$$S = PV\ (F) \tag{8.6}$$

substituting (8.6) into (8.5) we get

$$P = C - PV(F) + PV(E)$$

$$P = C - PV\ (F - E) \tag{8.7}$$

Some useful implications from Equation (8.7) follow. First, it suggests that European calls and puts struck at the forward price, F, will have the same price since $PV(F - E)$ in this case will be zero. Secondly, it implies that buying a call and selling a put struck at the forward price is equivalent to having a long position in the underlying forward. Hence, its price should be zero.

Pricing a floor

We can use the put/call/forward parity relationship given by Equation (8.7) to value each floorlet in a floor. We replace forward price F with the implied forward interest rate in Equation (8.7). Let us value a floor with the following parameters:

$R_f = 7\%$
$E = 6\%$
$\sigma = 15\%$
$T = 0.5$
$r = 0.05$

Since these variables are the same as were assumed for our earlier example of a cap, except that we now have a put option written on six-month LIBOR at a strike rate of 6 percent, we already know the value of the call option to be 0.998 percent. We can use this information to compute the value of the put using Equation (8.7) as under.

$P = C - PV (F - E)$

$= C - (F - E)\, e^{-rT}$

$= 0.00998 - (0.07 - 0.06)\, 2.7183^{-(0.05)(0.5)}$

$= 0.023\%$

Notice that we used e^{-rT} to compute the present value of $(F - E)$ because the Black and Scholes model is derived in a continuous time framework. A discrete time compounding would be inconsistent with the pricing model.

As in the case of a cap, we need to discount the value of the put to account for the settlement of its payoff in arrears, say, 180 days after its expiration date. That is

$$Floor\ Price = \frac{Put\ Price}{(1 + r)}$$

$$= \frac{0.00023}{1 + 0.07 \times \frac{180}{360}}$$

$= 0.022\%$

We can also use the put/call/forward parity relationship to value put options on short-term interest rates using the following formula.

$$P = [EN(-d2) - R_f N(-d1)]\, e^{-rT} \tag{8.8}$$

where all variables are defined as before. Using Equation (8.8) for our example we have

$P = [\, 0.06\, N(-1.40) - 0.07\, N(-1.506)]2.7183^{-(0.05)(0.5)}$

and, from Appendix I we have

$N(-1.506) = 0.0659$
and $N(-1.40) = 0.0808$

Substituting these values into the put pricing equation we obtain

$$P = [\ 0.06\ (0.0808) - 0.07\ (0.0659)]2.7183^{-(0.05)(0.5)}$$

$$= 0.023\%$$

which is the same as given by Equation (8.7). To get the value of the floor we need to discount the put price to obtain the floor price as before.

As in the case of caps, if a floor consists of multiple puts, i.e. involves more than one interest period, we would simply use Equation (8.8) to value each put or floorlet, discount their value using the appropriate forward rate for discounting and sum the values of each floorlet to obtain the price of the floor.

CAP AND FLOOR APPLICATIONS AND STRUCTURED STRATEGIES

The most important application of a cap is in the area of liability management. A cap allows borrowers to insure against rising interest rates while at the same time being able to benefit directly if short-term interest rates do not rise or indeed fall below the prevailing levels.

For investors, caps provide one of many option based strategies to enhance yield on assets by taking a view on (i) the direction of short-term interest, and (ii) any likely changes in volatility. We consider each in turn. Suppose the current interest rate environment is characterized by a steep yield curve. That is, the market is expecting the short-term interest rates to rise. If, as an investor in floating rate assets, you believe that the forward interest rates implied by the current steep yield curve are an overkill, you can take a short position in an interest rate cap (i.e. sell a cap) and receive up-front premium that enhances the yield on your assets. By selling a cap you effectively create a ceiling on your floating returns. In a steep yield curve environment it is possible to write caps at a strike that is significantly above the prevailing short-term interest rate (known as out-of-the-money caps) and still command reasonable premium which will also be a function of the prevailing volatility. If, as you expected, interest rate sentiment changes and the curve begins to flatten, you can buy a corresponding cap to match your short position at a lower premium or continue to assume exposure to rising rates for the residual life of the cap. This strategy is akin to writing covered calls on a portfolio of stock in which the investor gives up potential for gain beyond the strike price but benefits from the premium income received up front. Capped floaters are an example of an FRN with an embedded short cap. The higher spread on LIBOR in the case of capped floaters is on account of the cap that the investor is effectively selling as part of the floater. The impact of writing a cap on a floating asset is shown in Figure 8.8.

175

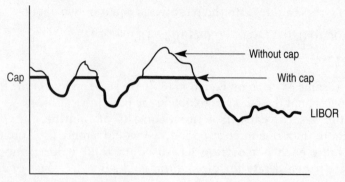

Fig 8.8 Return on a floating asset

In its simplest form the floor provides insurance against falling short-term interest rates. Liability managers are generally sellers of floors to reduce the cost of purchasing caps.

For investors, floors provide a mechanism to guarantee a minimum return on floating rate assets. Investors, in this case, are buyers of floor contracts. In interest rate environments that are characterized by steep or flat yield curves, floors tend to be cheaper than caps because interest rates are either expected to rise or remain unchanged. If, as an investor, you take a contrary view and believe that short-term interest rates are going to fall, you can buy a floor before the shape of the curve changes in line with your expectations, i.e. becomes inverted. In an inverted yield curve environment floors will tend to be expensive. In such an environment you can sell a corresponding floor to match your long position at a higher premium.

Caps and floors can be used to structure a variety of strategies individually or in combination to achieve complex hedging requirements or to reflect a particular market view. While we will discuss their applications in investment management in Chapter 12, here we summarize some of the more popular structures.

Interest rate collar

An interest rate collar is a contract that is created by combining a cap and a floor. It involves buying a cap and simultaneously selling a floor to fully or partly offset the cost of the cap. For borrowers, a collar provides protection against a rise in short-term interest rates as in the case of a cap but limits the benefits of falling interest rates to the floor level. A collar with strike rates of 10 percent –5 percent means that the holder is long a cap with a strike of 10 percent and short a floor with a strike of 5 percent. It is possible to structure a collar such that the premium payable on the cap is equal to the premium received from the floor which makes it a zero cost structure.

Interest rate corridors

A corridor involves simultaneous purchase and sale of two caps written at different strike rates. The difference between the two strike rates creates a corridor. For example, a borrower may purchase a cap with a strike rate of 10 percent giving protection against short-term rates rising above the strike level. To offset the premium for this cap, the borrower sells a cap with a strike rate of, say, 12 percent. The corridor is, thus, established between 10 percent and 12 percent. Thus the borrower is protected against a rise in interest rates above 10 percent but only up to 12 percent. If interest rates rise above 12 percent, the benefit from the corridor will be restricted to 2 percent as shown in Figure 8.9.

Investors can be sellers of corridors to pick-up yield with limited risk – restricted to the corridor.

Reverse collar

A reverse collar involves selling a cap and buying a floor. This strategy is attractive for investors who believe that short-term interest rates are going to fall. The strategy provides greatest value when undertaken just before the interest rate environment changes from a positively sloped yield curve to a flat or a negatively sloped yield curve. The payoff to an investor selling a call at 10 percent and buying a floor at 6 percent is shown in Figure 8.10. We assume that this position is established at zero cost.

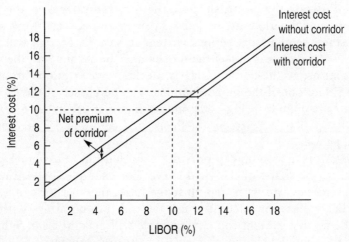

Fig 8.9 Interest rate corridor

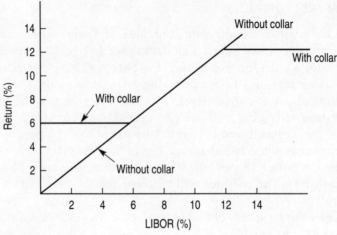

Fig 8.10 Reverse collar

Step-up caps

A step-up cap is a variable strike cap. Specifically, the strike rate for each subsequent caplet is higher than the previous caplet. Step-up caps allow borrowers to reduce the cost of purchasing the protection while investors can pick-up higher premium by selling step-up caps. We noted earlier that the price of a cap is the sum of the price of individual caplets that comprise the cap. We also noted that the value of a caplet is determined, among other things, by the implied forward interest rate corresponding to the term of the underlying option. Since an ordinary cap is struck at a fixed rate – meaning that each caplet has the same strike – it is possible that some of the caplets may be in-the-money which makes them expensive. To illustrate the point, suppose the forward rates over the next three semi-annual periods are 6, 7 and 8 percent respectively. Now, a cap covering three semi-annual periods written at, say, 6.5 percent will have the first caplet that is is out-of-the-money and the second and the third caplets that are in-the-money. Clearly, in-the-money options are more expensive than out-of-the-money options. The purchaser of the cap can reduce the premium by using a step-up cap that is struck at say 6 percent for the first period, 6.5 percent for the second period and 7 percent for the third period.

For investors, a step-up cap provides a mechanism to assume a position against the shape of the yield curve. For example, by writing an out-of-the-money cap with step-up strike rates, the investor can generate higher premium income than would be possible with an out-of-the-money straight cap. An example will make it clear. Suppose the currently implied six-month forward rates are as under:

- 6 months forward: 5%
- 12 months forward: 6%
- 18 months forward: 6.5%

Now if the investor were to write an out-of-the-money cap, given the forward rates, the strike of such a cap would have to be above 6.5 percent. However, by using a step-up structure, it would be possible to lower the strike of the first two caplets such that the strikes are closer to the implied forward at that point but still above it (i.e. the caplet will still be out-of-the-money). Figure 8.11 shows the forward rates for six-months, 12-months and 18-months from today. If the investor's view was that actual six-month rates will turn out to be as implied by the forward rates and he wanted to benefit by taking an aggressive position on this view he could write a cap with strike rates of 5.5, 6.5 and 7 percent. All these strikes lie above the implied forward rates and are, thus, out-of-the-money. A straight cap at, say 7.5 all percent, (thus, out-of-the-money) would pay significantly less premium because all caplets would be more out-of-the-money than in the case of the step-up cap.

SWAPTIONS

We began this chapter by classifying interest rate options into two categories: those written on short-term interest rates and those written on long-term interest rates. Under that classification, swaptions belong to the latter category. Of the many risk management products that have emerged over the last decade, swaptions are one of the most innovative with wide capital markets applications. Swaptions are used extensively in fixed income portfolio management.

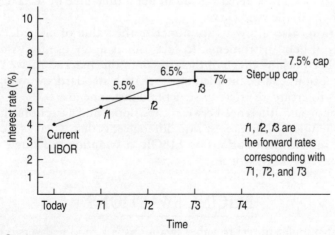

Fig 8.11 Step-up cap

As its name suggests, swaptions or swap options are options on swaps. A swaption gives the buyer the right to enter into an interest rate swap of a specified maturity and fixed rate at or during a specified time period. An American swaption gives its holder the right to enter into an interest rate swap at any time during the life of the swaption, whereas a European style swaption can be exercised only at its maturity date. A third category of swaptions known as Bermuden swaptions, can be exercised on any coupon payment date. As in the case of other options, swaptions can also be categorized into calls and puts. However, in the case of swaptions this terminology can be extremely confusing. Accordingly, most market practitioners use the terms 'payer swaption' and 'receiver swaption.'

Payer swaption   A payer swaption gives its buyer the right, but not the obligation, to enter into an interest rate swap of a specified term in which the buyer pays a specified fixed interest rate against receiving a floating interest rate such as LIBOR. A payer swaption is equivalent to a call option on interest rates.

Receiver swaption   A receiver swaption gives its buyer the right, but not the obligation, to enter into an interest rate swap of a specified term in which the buyer receives a specified fixed interest rate against paying a floating interest rate such as LIBOR. A receiver swaption is equivalent to a put option on interest rates.

Swaptions allow issuers and investors to take opportunistic hedging or investment positions. For example, a payer swaption allows a corporate to benefit from low current short-term interest rates while providing protection against rising interest rates in the future. Unlike a cap which creates a ceiling on floating interest payments allowing borrowers to take a view on short-term interest rates over the term of the borrowing, a swaption is essentially a view on term interest rates. It can, therefore, be used to lock in the fixed rate at an opportune time or to take a view on the shape of the yield curve.

Swaptions also allow us to monetize the value of embedded calls and puts in debt instruments. In fact, this is a key use for swaptions and has been behind much of the growth in this market. As we will see later, swaptions can be bundled together with standard swaps and debt securities to create a variety of structured instruments.

An important difference between caps/floors and swaptions, in addition to the underlying interest rate difference, is that whereas a cap is a series of independent options on LIBOR, a swaption is a single option that is exercisable only once.

PRICING SWAPTIONS

The most popular model to value swaptions is a modified version of the Black and Scholes model. Let us first consider a European style payer swaption. As noted above, a European payer swaption gives its buyer the right to enter into an interest rate swap of a designated maturity at option expiry in which it pays a specified fixed rate, the strike rate, against receiving LIBOR. The payoff from this option can be written as:

$$\max (V_L - V_F, 0)$$

where

V_L = value of the floating leg
V_F = value of the fixed leg with fixed rate equal to the exercise rate, E

V_L and V_F can be obtained directly from zero-coupon discount factors for relevant option expiry and swap interest payment dates[1] using the following:

$$V_L = F_t - F_n \qquad (8.9)$$

$$V_F = E \sum_{i=1}^{n} Fi \left(\frac{d_{i-1,i}}{B} \right) \qquad (8.10)$$

where

F_t = discount factor corresponding with option expiry date, t
F_n = discount factor corresponding with the maturity date of the swap, n
F_i = discount factor for the ith swap interest payment date
$d_{i,j}$ = actual number of days between payment dates i and j
B = day basis (360 or 365)

Using the above expressions for V_L and V_F, the value of the European call option (payer swaption) on an interest rate swap is given by:

$$\text{Payer swaption} = V_L N(d_1) - V_F N(d_2) \qquad (8.11)$$

where

$$d_1 = \frac{1}{\sigma\sqrt{t}} \left[\ln \left(\frac{V_L}{V_F} \right) + \frac{1}{2} \sigma^2 t \right]$$

$d_2 = d_1 - \sigma \sqrt{t}$
t = time to expiration of the option
σ^2 = instantaneous variance of the underlying interest rate

The terms $N(d_1)$ and $N(d_2)$ are the cumulative probability for a unit normal variable.

Using the put-call parity argument gives the value of the put (receiver swaption) as:

$$\text{Receiver swaption} = \text{Payer swaption} - \left[(F_s - E) \sum_{i=1}^{n} F_i \left(\frac{d_{i-1,i}}{B} \right) \right] \quad (8.12)$$

---

[1] The methodology to derive zero-coupon discount factors is described in Chapter 5.

where F_s is the implied forward swap rate gives by;

$$F_s = \frac{F_t - F_n}{\sum\limits_{i=1}^{n} F_i \left(\frac{d_{i-1,i}}{B}\right)} \qquad (8.13)$$

The terms being as defined before.

Example

Consider a one-year payer swaption that gives its holder the right to enter into a two-year interest rate swap at a strike rate of 6 percent semi-annually on an actual/360 day basis. Suppose the current one year volatility is 15 percent and the par swap yields and zero-coupon discount factors[2] are as detailed in Table 8.1.

Table 8.1 Par swap yields and zero discount factors

Term	Date	Par yield	Discount factor
6 months	12 Jul 1995	5.875%	0.9713
12 months	12 Jan 1996	6.125%	0.9415
18 months	12 Jul 1996	–	0.913 (interpolated)
2 years	13 Jan 1997	6.25%	0.8840
2.5 years	12 Jul 1997	–	0.8555 (interpolated)
3 years	12 Jan 1998	6.40%	0.8276

Using the information from Table 8.1 and assuming the value and expiration dates to be 12 Jan 1995 and 12 Jan 1996, respectively, we have:

$$V_L = 0.9415 - 0.8276$$
$$= 0.1139$$

$$V_F = 0.06 \left[0.913\left(\frac{182}{360}\right) + 0.884\left(\frac{185}{360}\right) + 0.8555\left(\frac{180}{360}\right) + 0.8276\left(\frac{184}{360}\right) \right]$$
$$= 0.1060$$

$$d_1 = \frac{1}{0.15\sqrt{\frac{365}{360}}} \left[\ln\left(\frac{0.1139}{0.106}\right) + \frac{1}{2}(0.15)^2\left(\frac{365}{360}\right) \right]$$
$$= 0.55$$

$$d_2 = 0.551 - 0.15\left(\frac{365}{360}\right)$$
$$= 0.398$$

From Appendix 1 we obtain the values for $N(0.551)$ and $N(0.398)$ as 0.7088 and 0.6551, respectively. Plugging these numbers into Equation (8.11) gives us the value of the payer swaption as:

---

[2] The zero-coupon methodology is described in Chapter 5.

Payer swaption = $V_L N(d_i) - V_F N(d_2)$

$\qquad = 0.1139 \, (0.7088) - 0.106 \, (0.655)$

$\qquad = 1.13\%$

To work out the value of a receiver swaption we first need to compute the implied forward swap rate using Equation (8.13). Assuming the same parameters as for the payer swaption example given above, we have:

$$F_s = \frac{0.9415 - 0.8276}{0.913 \left(\frac{182}{360}\right) + 0.884 \left(\frac{185}{360}\right) + 0.8555 \left(\frac{180}{360}\right) + 08276 \left(\frac{184}{360}\right)}$$

$\qquad = 6.45\%$

and

$$\text{Receiver swaption} = 0.0113\% - (0.0645 - 0.06) \left[0.913 \left(\frac{182}{360}\right) + 0.884 \left(\frac{185}{360}\right) + 0.8555 \left(\frac{180}{360}\right) + 0.8276 \left(\frac{184}{360}\right) \right]$$

$\qquad = 0.34\%$

SWAPTION APPLICATIONS

When combined with vanilla swaps or debt instruments, swaptions result in a variety of innovative structures. For example, when combined with a plain vanilla interest rate swap, swaptions allow us to create callable, puttable, reversible and extendable interest rate swaps. Swaptions also allow issuers and investors to monetize the value of an embedded debt option.

Callable swap

A callable swap is a combination of an interest rate swap and a receiver swaption. A callable swap allows the user to benefit from a fall in term interest rates. To illustrate, suppose a corporate treasurer enters into a five-year interest rate swap in which he pays a fixed rate of 10 percent against receiving LIBOR flat. Simultaneously, he buys a receiver swaption expiring in two years' time that gives him the right to receive a fixed rate of 10 percent against paying LIBOR flat for a period of three years. Now, in two years' time if the prevailing three-year swap rate is below 10 percent, the treasurer can exercise the option to enter into a three-year swap. This new swap effectively cancels the existing swap since the cash flows of one are offset by the other. This strategy allows the treasurer to lock-in a lower swap rate at a future point in time.

Puttable swap

A puttable swap is a combination of a swap in which you receive fixed against paying floating and a payer swaption. A puttable swap allows the user to benefit from a rise in term interest rates. To illustrate, suppose an investor enters into a five-year interest rate swap in which he receives 7 percent fixed against paying LIBOR. Simultaneously, the investor purchases a payer swaption, giving him the right to enter into a three-year swap in which he pays 7 percent fixed against receiving LIBOR at the end of two years. If in two years' time the three-year swap rate rises above 7 percent, say 8 percent, the investor will exercise the swaption and enter into a three-year swap in which he pays 7 percent fixed against receiving LIBOR. This swap offsets the existing swap that has three years to run. The investor can now enter into a new three-year swap in which he receives the prevailing three-year swap rate of 8 percent against paying LIBOR. The structure thus allows the investor to benefit from a rise in term interest rates. Should term interest rates remain below the strike rate of 7 percent, the investor will allow the option to lapse.

Reversible swap

A reversible swap allows the user to switch from being a floating rate payer in a swap to becoming a fixed rate payer. A reversible swap is synthesized by combining an interest rate swap with a receiver swaption with a notional principal that is twice the notional principal of the underlying swap. Half the swaption, when exercised, allows the user to cancel the existing swap (as in the case of callable and puttable swaps), whereas the other half results in a new swaps position with opposite interest obligations than the existing swap.

Extendible swap

An extendible swap allows the user to extend the maturity of an interest rate swap at the original swap rate. This is achieved by simply buying a swaption (payer or receiver) with the expiry date coinciding with the maturity date of the existing interest rate swap.

Monetizing embedded debt options

One of the most popular uses of swaptions involves monetizing embedded options in corporate debt. For example, swaptions allow issuers to monetize the value of an embedded call option in a bond issue. A call option allows the issuer to refinance fixed rate debt at potentially lower cost if interest rates fall before the maturity date of the bond. The issuer can monetize the value of this option by selling a receiver swaption granting its purchaser the right to enter into an interest rate swap in which the issuer pays fixed against receiving LIBOR. From the issuers' standpoint, the callable bond would now become synthetic non-callable or straight bond. One of the primary reasons why issuers use synthetic non-callable bonds is the difference in valuation of the embedded option *vis-a-vis* the value of the swaption. The premise is that investors undervalue the call allowing issuers to reduce the cost of their borrowing by effectively buying a cheap call (from investors) and selling a fairly priced receiver swaption in the swaps market.

In a similar fashion, investors can use payer swaptions to synthesize non-puttable bonds from a puttable bond. Investors can improve the yield on a fixed rate bond by buying a puttable bond with an undervalued put and simultaneously selling a fairly priced payer swaption to coincide with the put date. By 'stripping' the put option, the investor creates a synthetic non-puttable bond.

BOND OPTIONS

A bond (or debt) option gives its holder the right to buy (call option) or sell (put option) a specific bond at a specified price (strike price) at (European style) or any time (American style) before the expiry date. Like swaptions, bond options are essentially options on term interest rates. The underlying bonds are almost always government bonds such as US treasuries.

Bond options allow investors to repackage and reallocate interest rate risk not otherwise possible. Debt options allow investors to alter the interest rate exposure of a portfolio without having to liquidate the bonds. For example, call options can be used if the investor expects a fall in interest rate. Put options can be used to express an opposite view. Put options, therefore, provide insurance against interest rate rises. Debt options can also be used to tailor risk/return preferences that may otherwise be impossible to achieve. Finally, like all options, debt options allow investors to assume geared positions in interest rate markets.

PRICING BOND OPTIONS

Three factors complicate the pricing of bond options within the Black and Scholes option pricing framework. These are:

- The price of a bond cannot be assumed to be lognormally distributed since it is forced to par at maturity.
- Since the bond must trade at par at maturity, the volatility of its price must fall as it nears the maturity date.
- Short-term interest rates cannot be assumed to be constant when valuing interest rate dependent options.

These considerations render both the Black and Scholes (1973) model to value stock options and the Black (1976) model to value options on forward contracts less useful for the pricing of bond options. As a result, a number of new models have been developed to value interest rate options in general and bond options in particular. These include the Rendleman and Barter (1979) binomial bond option valuation model; Cox, Ross and Rubinstein (1979) model to value stocks, bonds and other assets, and the Ho and Lee (1986) model based on the entire term structure of interest rates.

We will employ a simple binomial approach to value bond options. Instead of modelling the movement of bond prices, we will model the movement in the underlying bond yield. Suppose the current yield on the bond is Y_0. At the end of an arbitrary time interval, Δt, the yield can either go up to uY_0 or down to dY_0. If T is the time to expiration of an option and n is the number of time steps chosen between now and T, then $\Delta t = T/n$ and we have $n + 1$ yield nodes until the option expiration date.

Suppose we wish to price a one year call option on a five year bond. Further suppose that we divide the time until option expiration into four steps of three-month periods ($\Delta t = 0.25$). The binomial lattice for possible yields at three-month intervals is shown in Figure 8.12. The factors u and d are defined as:

$$u = e^{\sigma \sqrt{\Delta t}}$$
where $e = 2.718$ \hfill (8.14)

$$d = \frac{1}{u} \hfill (8.15)$$

and the risk-neutral probabilities of up and down movement in yields are:

$$p = \frac{1 - d}{u - d} \hfill (8.16)$$

and

$$q = 1 - p \hfill (8.17)$$

respectively.

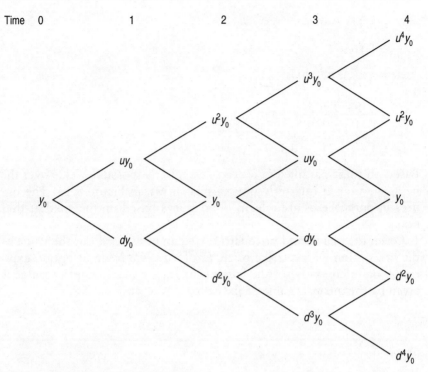

Fig 8.12 Binomial lattice of bond yield

The valuation of bond options using the binomial approach involves three steps:

1 Generate the yield lattice.
2 Compute the bond price at each node corresponding with the yield at that node.
3 Recursively work out the option price.

Example
Consider a one-year European call option with an exercise price of 100 on a five-year bond currently trading at 100 with an annual coupon of 10 percent. Suppose the current one-year risk-free rate is 9 percent and the yield volatility, σ, is 20 percent. The time to expiration of the option, T, is one year and we assume the number of binomial steps, n, to be 4. The time increment, Δt, is, therefore, 0.25 years.

We first need to work out factors u and d and probabilities p and q using Equations (8.14) to (8.17):

$$u = 2.718^{\,0.20\sqrt{0.25}}$$

$$= 1.105$$

$$d = \frac{1}{1.105} = 0.905$$

$$p = \frac{1 - 0.905}{1.105 - 0.905} = 0.475$$

$$q = 1 - 0.474 = 0.525$$

Based on these parameters we can generate the possible yields over the next one year at quarterly intervals as shown in Figure 8.13. The figures in parentheses are (clean) bond prices based on the yield at that node.

Given the yield/bond price lattice we can now work out the value of the call option with a strike price, E, of 100. We begin at option expiration date (column 4 of the lattice). At each node, the option value is given by the intrinsic value of the call.

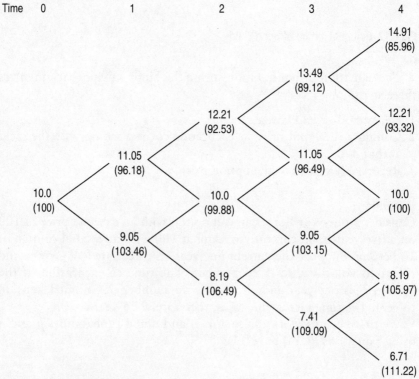

Fig 8.13 Yield/bond price lattice

That is:

$$C_{n,i} = \max (0, B_{n,i} - E) \tag{8.18}$$

The option values one step before expiration (column 3) are calculated by discounting the expected future value of the option. Now, at any node i in column $n - 1$, the yield can move up with probability p or down with probability q. If the call values associated with up and down states are C_u and C_d, respectively, then the call value at node i in column $n - 1$ is given by[3]:

$$C_{n-1} = \frac{C_u\, p + C_d\, q}{e^{r\sqrt{\Delta t}}} \tag{8.19}$$

where r = short-term risk-free interest rate

Figure 8.14 gives the call values associated with each node. To illustrate the computations involved, consider node 1 (the top node) in column 3. To work out the call value at this node we need to know the call values for up (C_u) and down (C_d) nodes one period forward. These are 14.04 and 6.68, respectively. Using Equation (8.19) we have:

$$C_{n-1} = \frac{14.04\,(0.475) + 6.68\,(0.525)}{1.046}$$

$$= 9.73$$

Similarly, to work out the option price at node 2 in column 3 we use up (C_u) and down (C_d) call values one period forward, which are 6.68 and zero, respectively. Again using Equation (8.19) we obtain the call value at this node as 3.03. Call values at other nodes are worked similarly until we obtain the call value in column 0 of 1.86 percent which is the current value of the European call.

To compute the value of a European put option, P, we would employ the same procedure except that the put values in column 4 are derived using the terminal boundary condition for put options. That is:

$$P_{n,i} = \max (B_{n,i} - E, 0) \tag{8.20}$$

We would then work backwards as in the case of the European call option.

The binomial approach described in this section can also be used to value American style calls and puts. In this case we will need to compare the option value derived at each node with the early exercise value given the bond price at that node.[4] The early exercise value for a call is:

---

[3] For put options, C_u and C_d are replaced with P_u and P_d.

[4] Notice that when working out the call values for European options we did not need the bond prices at nodes other than in column 4, the last column.

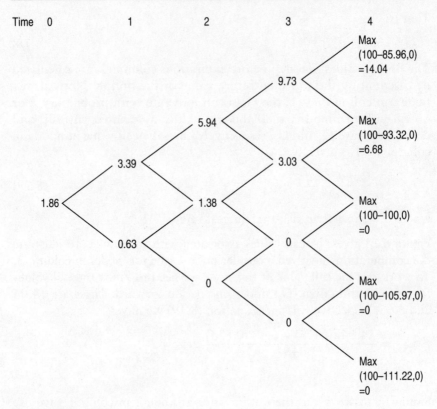

Fig 8.14 Call values

$$C_{i,j} = \max (B_{i,j} - E, 0) \tag{8.21}$$

and for the put it is

$$P_{i,j} = \max (E - B_{i,j}, 0) \tag{8.22}$$

At each node j in column i (starting with column $n-1$) we need to work out the early exercise value, using Equations (8.21) and (8.22), as well as the call and put values, using Equation (8.19). If the early exercise value is higher than the call or the put value derived using Equations (8.19) or (8.20), then the computed call or put value is replaced with the early exercise value. We continue with this procedure until we obtain the option value in column 0.

BOND OPTION APPLICATIONS

The most important application of debt options is to hedge a fixed income portfolio. Two common portfolio hedging strategies against a rise in interest rates involve buying protective puts and selling covered calls. A long position in the put establishes a minimum value for the portfolio while at the same time allowing the investor to benefit from any interest rate declines.

Covered calls involve an investor selling call options against an existing portfolio. The strategy usually involves selling out-of-the-money calls to generate premium income, the view being that interest rates will not rise significantly above current levels. The premium received provides some protection against a rate rise.

Debt options can also be used to protect against falling interest rates. Investors can purchase call options to protect against a fall in reinvestment rates. Selling put options can provide limited protection, as in the case of covered call writing. In both cases, however, the investor is exposed to rates changing more than expected.

Duration of bond options

As noted above, on of the common applications of debt options is to hedge a portfolio against interest rate risk. Since one of the common measures of interest rate exposure is modified duration, it is important for investors wishing to use options as a hedging tool to measure correctly the duration of options bought or sold.

Since the value of a bond option crucially depends on the value of the underlying bond, the duration of the option is also linked to the duration of the underlying bond. The modified duration of an option is given by:

$$D_{OPTION} = D_{BOND} \times Delta \times \frac{P_{BOND}}{P_{OPTION}} \qquad (8.23)$$

where

D_{OPTION} = modified duration of the option
D_{BOND} = modified duration of the underlying bond
Delta   = Delta of the option
P_{BOND} = price of the underlying bond
P_{OPTION} = price of the option.

Notice that the last ratio in Equation (8.23) suggests that the higher the price of the underlying bond relative to the price of the option, the greater the interest rate sensitivity for the option (the leverage effect). The implication is that deep-out-of-the-money options offer a greater leverage effect than do deep-in-of-money options.

SUMMARY

Interest rate options can be categorized into those that are linked to short-term interest rates and those that are linked to long-term interest rates. The former include caps, floors and other variations based on them, whereas the latter include swaptions and bond options. Caps, floors and variations based on these allow users to create a ceiling or a floor for funding costs or investment returns. Swaptions and bond options allow users to take a view on or hedge exposure against term interest rates.

Interest rate options valuation is complicated by the fact that there is more than one state variable that needs to be modelled. Restrictive assumptions regarding the behavior of the term structure of interest rates allows us to use the Black and Scholes options pricing framework as well as the binomial lattice to price interest rate options.

References

Ball, C.A. and Torous, W., 'Bond Price Dynamics and Options', *Journal of Financial and Quantitative Analysis*, 18, (4) 1983, pp. 517–30.

Black, F., 'The Pricing of Commodity Contracts', *Journal of Financial Economics*, 3, 1976, pp. 167–79.

Black, F. and Scholes, M., 'The Pricing of Options and Corporate Liabilities', *Journal of Political Economy*, 81 May/June 1973, pp. 637–59.

Courtadon, G., 'The Pricing of Options on Default Free Bonds', *Journal of Financial and Quantitative Analysis*, 17, September 1982, pp. 75–100.

Cox, J.C., Ross, S.A. and Rubinstein, M., 'Option Pricing: A Simplified Approach', *Journal of Financial Economics*, 7, September 1979, pp. 229–63.

Cox, J.C., Ingersoll, J.E. and Ross, S.A., 'A Theory of the Term Structure of Interest Rates', *Econometrica*, 53, March 1985, pp. 385–407.

Cox, J.C. and Ross, S.A., 'The Valuation of Options for Alternative Stochastic Processes', *Journal of Financial Economics*, 3, 1976, pp 145–66.

Cox, J.C., Ingersoll, J.E. and Ross, S.A., 'The Relation Between Forward and Futures Prices', *Journal of Financial Economics*, 9 December 1981, pp. 321–46.

Fama, E.F., 'The Information in the Term Structure', *Journal of Financial Economics*, December 1984, pp. 509–28.

Figlewski, S., Silber, W. and Subramanyam, M., *Financial Options*, New York: Irwin, 1990.

Gemill, G., *Options Pricing: An International Perspective*, Maidenhead: McGraw-Hill, 1993.

Ho, T.S.Y. and Lee, S.B., 'Term Structure Movements and Pricing Interest Rate Contingent Claims', *Journal of Finance*, 41, December 1986, pp. 1011–1029.

Malkiel, B.G., 'Expectations, Bond Prices and the Term Structure of Interest Rates', *Quarterly Journal of Economics*, May 1962, pp. 197–218.

Merton, R.C., 'Pm the Pricing of Corporate Debt: The Risk Structure of Interest Rates', *Journal of Finance*, 29, March 1975, pp. 449–70.

Merton, R.C., 'Rational Theory of Option Pricing', *Bell Journal of Economics and Management Science*, 4, 1973, pp. 141–83.

Schaefer, S.M. and Schwartz, E.S., 'Time Dependent Variance and the Pricing of Bond Options', *Journal of Finance*, 42, 5, 1987, pp. 1113–1128.

Vasicek, O.A., 'An Equilibrium Characterization of the Term Structure', *Journal of Financial Economics*, 5 November 1977, pp. 177–88.

9

CURRENCY OPTIONS

Foreign trade accounts for a significant proportion of the GNP for many economies. In Britain, for example, foreign trade accounts for nearly 25 percent of the GNP. In many emerging economies, exports account for between 10 percent to 25 percent of the GNP. International trade inevitably exposes importers and exporters to fluctuations in foreign exchange rates. The problem of currency or foreign exchange risk assumed importance following the break down in early 1970s (see Chapter 1) of the Bretton Woods system of fixed foreign exchange rates. As exchange rates became floating, the need for hedging instruments became critical. The financial industry's response was swift. A huge interbank market for spot and forward foreign exchange developed.[1] Organized markets soon emerged in foreign currency futures, options on foreign currencies and options on foreign currency futures.

In 1972 the International Monetary Market (IMM) of the Chicago Mercantile Exchange (CME) began trading currency futures. Unlike forward foreign exchange contracts which can only be used by large companies that are able to secure credit from banks, the futures market opened the way to hedge currency exposure for small and medium sized companies. In 1982 the Philadelphia Stock Exchange began trading options on Deutschmarks, French francs, Swiss francs, Japanese yen, British sterling and Canadian dollars. In 1984 the IMM began trading options on foreign currency futures.

The OTC market for currency options developed in response to the growing need for tailored hedging instruments which could not be met by the standardized futures contracts traded on various exchanges. While the first OTC currency options were transacted in the 1970s, the market began to grow at a phenomenal rate in the early 1980s particularly following the introduction of exchange traded currency options contracts in 1982 by the Philadelphia Stock Exchange. The availability of exchange traded contracts provided additional liquidity in the dealer market. The OTC market continues to dominate the exchange traded market for currency options and is estimated to account for around $20 billion in daily volume. In this chapter we analyze the nature of OTC currency options, discuss their pricing and describe various applications and strategies in investment management. In order to understand the nature of the product and its role in currency exposure management, however, we begin by considering the nature of the spot and forward markets for foreign exchange.

---

[1] The interbank market for spot and forward foreign exchange markets dwarfs in turnover all other financial markets. An estimated $500 billion of currency trades are transacted every day in the main FX centres of London, New York and Tokyo.

SPOT AND FORWARD MARKETS FOR FX

The spot market for foreign exchange allows us to buy or sell one currency against the other for spot delivery, usually two days from the trade date. For example, a British importer who needs to remit US dollars to its American supplier can buy dollars and sell sterling at today's FX rate of, say, 1.5 for delivery in two business days. In two days time its USD bank account will be credited with $150 million and its sterling account will be debited by £100 million.

While a lot of commercial and industrial establishments buy and sell foreign currencies on spot delivery basis as described above, a great proportion of them buy and sell currencies for forward, instead of spot, delivery. The forward market in foreign currencies allows its users to buy and sell foreign exchange for delivery at a future point in time. In some currencies, the forward period can extend beyond ten years. Most forward contracts, particularly those used to manage international trade, are of a shorter duration, usually up to twelve months. Long term asset and liability management, on the other hand, calls for longer dated forward contracts. It is estimated that up to 30 percent of the foreign exchange market consists of forward contracts.

Consider a German exporter who is expecting a US dollar payment for his exports to the US in 180 days from today. Suppose he is expecting $10 million. He has a choice of waiting until the 178th day, at which point he can sell US$10 million to buy Deutschmarks at the then prevailing spot DM/USD FX rate for delivery in two days or, alternatively, he can enter into a 180-day forward contract to sell US$ 10 million for Deutschmarks at the forward FX rate of, say, 1.485 prevailing today. Let us first analyze the economic implications of the decision of not to hedge. Figure 9.1 shows the exposure to the German exporter who will own $10 million in 180 days time.

Clearly, relative to the forward FX of 1.485, the exporter stands to make a profit (i.e. receive more Deutschmarks for every dollar) if DM trades above 1.485 in 178 days and he stands to make a loss if DM trades below 1.485, i.e. if DM appreciates against the dollar. By leaving the position open the exporter is clearly assuming the risk of DM appreciating against the dollar. If the exporter's view was that DM was more likely to depreciate over the next six months, it would obviously be beneficial to leave the position open. In so doing, he would be taking a bet on the currency. Now suppose our exporter believes that he is not in the business of taking bets on exchange rates and decides to enter into a 180-day forward contract in which he agrees to sell $ 10 million for Deutschmarks at the currently prevailing forward

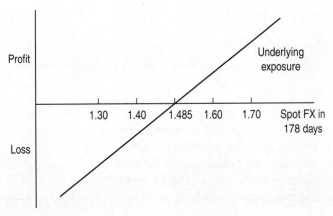

Fig 9.1 Foreign exchange exposure

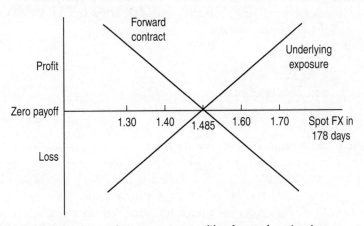

Fig 9.2 Hedging foreign exchange exposure with a forward contract

FX rate of 1.485. As shown in Figure 9.2, the forward contract provides a perfect hedge since it locks in the forward FX rate of 1.485.

By combining the underlying exposure with a forward contract the exporter is able to guarantee that the US dollars he receives in six months' time will have a fixed DM value as established through the forward contract. The combination of the underlying exposure and the forward contract will therefore have a zero payoff under all exchange rate scenarios as shown in Figure 9.2. We next turn to the derivation of the forward FX rate.

Recall from Chapter 2 that forward foreign exchange rates are derived using the interest rate parity theorem which holds that the ratio of the forward and spot exchange rates will equal the ratio of foreign and domestic interest rates. From Equation (2.14) we have

$$X_t = X_0 \left[\frac{1 + \left(\frac{n}{N}\right) r_{ft}}{1 + \left(\frac{n}{N}\right) r_{dt}} \right] \qquad (9.1)$$

where

X_t = forward exchange rate for time t expressed as units of foreign currency per unit of domestic currency

r_{ft} = foreign spot interest rate for time t

r_{dt} = domestic spot interest rate for time t

n = number of days up to the forward date

N = number of days in a year

If we assume that six month German and US interest rates are 4 percent and 6 percent respectively and the spot USD/DM is 1.5, we can use Equation (9.1) to give us the 180-day forward USD/DM FX. Assuming DM to be the foreign currency we have

$$X_6 = 1.5 \left[\frac{1 + \left(\frac{180}{360}\right) 0.04}{1 + \left(\frac{180}{360}\right) 0.06} \right]$$

$$= 1.485$$

In order to understand the rationale for currency options, let us consider the currency hedge provided by the forward contract. The first important feature of the forward contract is that it represents an obligation to buy or sell the currency at a future point in time. In the absence of an underlying position, a forward contract is a speculative position in the currency. However, when there is an underlying position in a currency – as in the case of the German exporter – the forward contract locks-in the exchange rate for future. The second important feature of a forward contract is that it does not result in a cash inflow or outflow at the outset since, by definition, its value at that point is zero to both parties.

WHAT IS A CURRENCY OPTION?

A currency option is a contract between a buyer and a seller in which the buyer has the right but not the obligation to buy one currency against another at or any time up to the expiration of the option contract. Unlike options on other financial variables which entail either a right to buy or a right to sell, a currency option entails both the right to buy and the right to sell in a single contract. That is because a currency option is written on foreign exchange which, by definition, involves exchange of one currency against another currency. Thus, a call on US dollars against Japanese yen inherently involves a put on Japanese yen. For example, if you buy a US dollar call (right to buy US dollars) against yen, you are also buying a yen put (right to sell yen against dollars). An American style currency option gives the purchaser the right to buy or sell a currency any time during the life of the option, whereas a European option can be exercised at expiration only.

To illustrate the use of a simple currency option and to highlight its relationship with a forward FX contract, let us consider our earlier example involving a German exporter. Recall that the exporter in that example expects to receive US$ 10 million in 180 days' time. Using a forward FX contract, our exporter can lock-in the forward USD/DM FX rate of 1.485. The payoff for the forward FX position *vis-a-vis* the underlying exposure is shown in Figure 9.2. If the exporter does nothing, then he would need to sell the dollar proceeds in 178 days' time (for delivery on day 180) at the then prevailing USD/DM exchange rate. In this case, the exporter would be exposed to a DM appreciation against US dollars.

Now, very often, the reason for not hedging through a forward contract hinges on the expectation that the future FX rate will be favorable. In our example, that would mean that the exporter expects a depreciation in Deutschmarks against US dollars. Expressing this view – however strong it may be – through the strategy of not hedging is clearly risky. That is because although it allows the exporter to benefit from a depreciation in Deutschmarks against US dollars, it also exposes him to an appreciation in DM. Currency options provide a mechanism to capture the upside associated with a view (depreciation of DM in one example) while at the same time eliminating the risk of being caught with the wrong view. Thus, our exporter can purchase a European style DM call/USD put to benefit from a depreciation in the DM exchange rate while at the same time hedging against an appreciation in DM value against US dollars.

For example, our exporter could purchase a DM call/USD put expiring in 178 days with a strike rate of 1.485. If, on the expiration date, the spot DM trades above 1.485, the exporter will allow the option to lapse and sell dollars at the prevailing spot rate which is better than the strike rate of 1.485. If, on the other hand, the spot DM trades below 1.485 on the expiration date, the exporter will exercise the option and sell dollars at the exercise rate of 1.485.[2] The payoff on the expiration date from the exporter's standpoint is depicted in Figure 9.3. The payoffs shown in Figure 9.3 ignore the initial cost of purchasing the option, which represents the maximum downsize from the option purchaser's standpoint.

---

[2] In the case of cash settled options, a similar result is achieved by selling dollars at the prevailing spot FX and receiving the difference between the strike rate and the prevailing spot FX from the option seller.

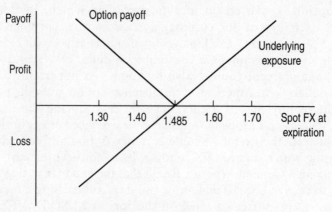

Fig 9.3 Hedging foreign currency exposure with an option

PRICING CURRENCY OPTIONS

A currency option can be viewed as an option on a stock that pays a continuous dividend. A model to value such options was developed by Merton (1973) as an extension of the Black and Scholes (1973) model to value puts and calls on non-dividend paying stock. To derive the valuation model for currency options we begin with the Black and Scholes model to value a European call on a non-dividend paying stock. It is given by:

$$C = SN(d_1) - Ee^{-rt} N(d_2) \qquad (9.2)$$

where

S = the spot price
E = the exercise price
t = the time to expiration
r = risk-free interest rate
e = 2.7183

$$d_1 = \frac{ln\ (S/E) + (r + \sigma^2/2)t}{\sigma\sqrt{t}}$$

$$d_2 = d_1 - \sigma\sqrt{t}$$

σ = the volatility of the stock

and $N\ [\ ]$ = the normal cumulative probability function.

Equation (9.2) assumes that the stock price will rise at the investor's required rate of return. The forward price of the stock is, therefore, given by:

$$F = Se^{rt} \qquad (9.3)$$

In the case of an option on a dividend paying stock, the stock price cannot be assumed to rise at the investor's required rate of return anymore because this return will be reduced by the amount of dividend rate. That is because, unlike the stock holder who gets dividends and, therefore is not affected by a fall in the stock price because of a dividend payment, the option holder is affected by the fall in the stock price due to dividend payment since he does not get any dividends. To value an option on a dividend paying stock, the stock price needs to be discounted at the dividend rate, D. Assuming that the stock pays a continuous dividend, D, the adjusted price, S' is given by:

$$S' = Se^{-Dt} \tag{9.4}$$

The value of a call on a dividend paying stock is now obtained by replacing S in Equation (9.2) with Equation (9.4). That is:

$$C = Se^{-Dt} N(d1) - Ee^{-rt} N(d2) \tag{9.5}$$

Equation (9.5) is due to Merton (1973). Notice that a dividend rate of zero reduces formula (9.5) to formula (9.2) for the value of an option on a non-divided paying stock.

Now, for a currency, as we noted above, the forward price is a function of the differential between foreign and domestic interest rates. If we assume that the domestic interest rate, r_d, and the foreign interest rate, r_f, are continuously compounded, the forward currency price is given by:

$$F = Se^{(r_d t - r_f t)} \tag{9.6}$$

where S = spot exchange rate [replacing the stock price in Equations (9.2) and (9.5)]

Equation (9.6) is a continuous time version of formula (9.1) for forward currency prices.

To obtain the correct forward price in the Black and Scholes model we need to adjust the spot price, S, in Equation (9.2). If we let S^* be the adjusted spot price and let r_d replace r in Equation (9.2) we have the relationship:

$$S^* e^{r_d t} = F = Se^{(r_d t - r_f t)} \tag{9.7}$$

or

$$S^* = Se^{-r_f t} \tag{9.8}$$

Replacing the adjusted spot price in Equation (9.2) we have:

$$C = Se^{-r_f t} N(d_1) - Ee^{-r_d t} N(d_2) \tag{9.9}$$

where $d_1 = \dfrac{ln\left(\frac{S}{E}\right) + \left(r_d - r_f + \frac{1}{2}\sigma^2\right)t}{\sigma\sqrt{t}}$ (9.10)

and $d_2 = d1 - \sigma\sqrt{t}$ (9.11)

Equation (9.9) is the valuation formula for a European-style call option on a currency. Formula (9.9) is usually attributed to Garman and Kohlhagen (1983) but as we noted it is merely an extension of Merton's model for options on dividend paying stock.

To illustrate the use of Equation (9.9) consider a European-style DM call/USD put option. Suppose the parameters are as under:

r_d = DM interest rate = 4%
r_f = USD interest rate = 6%

E = 1.485
S = 1.5
t = 178/365 = 0.488
σ = 10%

Using Equations (9.10 and 9.11) we have:

$$d1 = \dfrac{ln\left(\frac{1.5}{1.485}\right) + (0.04 - 0.06 + 0.5\,(0.10)^2)\ 0.488}{0.10\sqrt{0.488}}$$

$\quad = \quad 0.039$
$d2 = -0.039 - 0.10\sqrt{0.488}$
$\quad = -0.031$

and $N(0.039)$ and $N(-0.031)$ are 0.516 and 0.488, respectively, as given in Appendix 1. Replacing the values of $N(d1)$ and $N(d2)$ in Equation (9.9) we have:

$C = [1.50\,(2.7183)^{-0.06(0.488)}\,(0.516)] - [1.485(2.7183)^{-0.04(0.488)}\,(0.488)]$

$= DM\ 0.04$

We noted above that a call on one currency is a put on the other. Hence, the value of a call on DM against US dollars is also the value of the put on US dollars with premium translated at the spot rate from one currency to another.

To value American-style currency options, where there is a chance of early exercise, we need to use one of the numerical methods. The simplest way to value American-style currency options is to use the binomial method described in Chapter 3.

EXOTIC CURRENCY OPTIONS

A number of variations on the simple currency call/put structure have been developed over the years that allow users to create different risk/return combinations. The most popular among these 'exotic' structures, are average rate or 'Asian' currency options, look-back currency options, barrier currency options and binary or 'digital' currency options.

Average rate currency options

Average rate or 'Asian' currency options are widely used for currency exposure hedging. The primary reasons for their popularity are that they are cheaper than regular options and, in many cases, they reflect the underlying positions more accurately. As its name suggests, an average rate option allows its holder to buy (call option) or sell (put option) an underlying currency at an average price over a given period. For example, one can purchase a dollar call/yen put with a strike price of 100 whose payoff depends on an average of $/yen rates over a given period. The averaging is done at specified intervals. For example, a one-year option may be based on an average of twelve month-end currency prices. Thus, a dollar call/yen put will have a positive payoff if the average of twelve month-end spot rates is above 100.

In general, the payoff of a European average rate call option at expiry will be given by:

$$C = \max (A - E, 0) \qquad (9.12)$$

where A is the average price over the term of the option. The average price can be established in a number of ways. The most popular method is based on the arithmetic average given by:

$$A = (S_1 + S_2 + ...Sn)/n \qquad (9.13)$$

where S_i is the ith currency price.

An important variation of the basic average rate option is the average-strike rate option. In this case, the payoff for a call at maturity is given by:

$$C = \max (S - A, 0) \qquad (9.14)$$

Valuation of average rate options
The value of an average rate option is path dependent because the terminal payoff is based on an average of prices observed at discrete intervals over the life of the option. An important effect of the averaging process is the reduction in price volatility due to the smoothing of

the underlying price. William Margrabe suggests that average rate options can be valued using the appropriate version of the Black and Scholes model, but with a volatility input that is $1/\sqrt{3}$ (or 57.73 percent) of the actual price volatility. A more explicit model to value average rate currency options is given by:

$$C_A = S_A\, N(d_1) - e^{-rd\tau}\, EN\,(d_2) \qquad\qquad (9.15)$$

where

$$S_A = \frac{S}{(^r_d - ^r_f)T}$$

$$d_1 = \frac{1}{\sqrt{V}}\left(\frac{1}{2}\,\log_e D - \log_e X\right)$$

$$d_2 = d_1 - \sqrt{V}$$

$$V = \log_e D - 2\,(r_d\tau + \log S_A)$$

$$X = E - \frac{t}{T}\,S^* \quad D = \frac{Y}{T^2}$$

$$Y = \frac{2\sigma^2}{(r_d - r_f + \sigma^2)}\left[\frac{(e^{\,2(r_d - r_f)\,+\,\sigma^2} - 1)}{2(r_d - r_f + \sigma^2)} - \frac{e^{\,(r_d - r_f)\tau} - 1}{(r_d - r_f)}\right]$$

S = spot rate at time T
r_d = domestic interest rate
r_f = foreign interest rate
σ = volatility
T = original term
τ = remaining time to expiration = $(T - t)$
S^* = arithmetic average of known spot rate fixings

Look-back currency options

A look-back currency option gives its holder the right to buy or sell an underlying currency at the best price observed during the life of the option. For example, a look-back call on yen against US dollars gives the holder the right to buy at the highest observed spot rate during the term of the option. For this reason look-back options are sometimes called 'no regret' options.

Investors can use look-back options to translate foreign currency dividends or interest income into domestic currency at the best FX rate attained during the term of the option. Look-back options are particularly suitable for fund managers with foreign currency assets.

Like an average rate option, a look-back option is an example of a path-dependent option. However, unlike an average rate option that, because of the smoothing effect, tends to be cheaper than a standard option, a look-back option tends to be significantly more expensive than a normal option because it guarantees the highest possible payoff. This difference is highlighted in Figure 9.4 for a yen call/$ put.

The payoff of a look-back call at maturity is given by

$$C_{LB} = \max (H{-}E,0) \tag{9.16}$$

where H = highest price achieved during the term of the option.

Valuation of look-back options

Since a look-back option gives its holder the highest possible payoff with the benefit of hindsight, it must be worth more than an ordinary option. The value of a look-back call can be derived as the sum of an ordinary call with the same strike as the look-back call and a 'strike-bonus' option. The value of a European look-back call is given by.[3]

$$C_{LB} = C + \frac{S}{M}\left[e^{-r_d t}\left(\frac{S}{L}\right)^{-M} N\left(d_3 + 2\,(r_d - r_f)\sqrt{\frac{t}{\sigma}}\right) - e^{-r_f t}\,N\,(d_3)\right] \tag{9.17}$$

where

$$M = \frac{2(r_d - r_f)}{\sigma^2}$$

L = lowest price achieved so far

$$d_3 = \frac{-\ln\left(\frac{S}{L}\right) - (r_d - r_f + \frac{1}{2}\sigma^2)t}{\sigma\sqrt{t}}$$

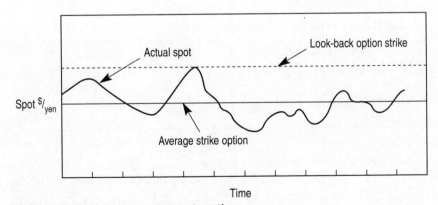

Fig 9.4 **Look-back versus average rate options**

---

[3] See Garman (1989).

C = value of an ordinary European call with strike price equal to the current minimum value and other terms are the same as before.

Barrier currency options

Barrier currency options are options whose existence depends on the price of the underlying currency. A down-and-out call, for example, is a call that expires if the price of the underlying falls below a specified barrier. An up-and-out call is a call that expires if the underlying price rises above a specified barrier. These options are also referred to as knock-out options. Down-and-in calls and up-and-in puts are examples of knock-in options.

Barrier options allow the users to reduce the cost of hedging by taking a view both on the speed and magnitude of the underlying price movement during the term of the option. For example, an up-and-out call is based on the view that the underlying will increase over the term of the call, but will not move fast enough to hit the 'out' barrier. Barrier options tend to be cheaper than regular options.

Valuation of barrier currency options

If we buy a down-and-out call and a down-and-in call with the same barrier price, H, exercise price, E, and time to expiration, t, the portfolio has the same payoff as the payoff of a standard call option. For this reason, knowing the value of one automatically provides us the value of the other. The value of a European down-and-in call is given by:

$$C_{DI} = Se^{-r_f t}\left(\frac{H}{S}\right) N\,(d_3) - Ee^{-rd\,t}\left(\frac{H}{S}\right)^{2\lambda-2} N\,(d_4) \qquad (9.18)$$

where

H = barrier price

$$d_3 = \frac{\ln\,[H^2/(SE)]}{\sigma\sqrt{t}} + \lambda\,\sigma\sqrt{t}$$

$$d_4 = d_3 - \sigma\sqrt{t}$$

$$\lambda = \frac{r_d - r_f + \tfrac{1}{2}\sigma^2}{\sigma^2}$$

and other terms are the same as before.

To figure out the value of a down-and-out call we would simply deduct the value of a down-and-in call given by Equation (9.18) from the value of a standard call with the same parameters as the down-and-in call.

Binary currency options

Binary or 'digital' currency options are so called because their payoffs are either positive or zero. In other words, the payoff for binary options is discontinuous. This is unlike standard options where the payoff is continuous. The important characteristic of binary options, therefore, is that the magnitude of their payoff is pre-specified while the likelihood of that payoff being achieved is uncertain. The fixed payoff is conditional on the underlying price reaching the strike or trigger level. For example, a digital call on yen may require the seller to make a fixed payment, P, if the $/yen trades at or below a certain trigger level, T. The payoff for the purchaser of this option is shown in Figure 9.5.

Valuation of binary currency options
Valuing binary options is relatively complex because the payoff is not a continuous function of the underlying price. Indeed, since the payoff is fixed in advance, the only relevant parameter is the likelihood or the probability of that payoff being realized. Since the payoff is conditional on the underlying price reaching a specified exercise or trigger level, we can still use the Black and Scholes framework to work out the risk neutral probability of reaching the trigger level. Recall that this probability is given by $N(d_2)$ in Equation 9.9. Thus, if the fixed payoff is P, the value of the binary option is given by:

$$Pe^{-r_d t} N(d_2) \tag{9.19}$$

where

$$d_2 = \frac{\ln\left(\frac{S}{E}\right) + (r_d - r_f - \frac{1}{2}\sigma^2)\,t}{\sigma\sqrt{t}}$$

and other terms are the same as before. Since we need to work out the probability of the terminal price exceeding P we are interested in $1-$ prob $(z < d_1)$.

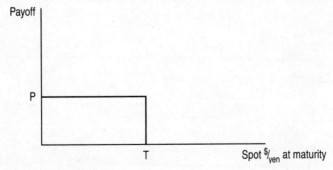

Fig 9.5 Payoff for a digital call

SUMMARY

Currency options provide an important new way of managing currency exposure. These options allow users to manage currency exposure in a way that is consistent with their views. Using forward contracts, on the other hand, means hedging on the basis of market consensus views. Unlike other options, a currency option involves a simultaneous use of calls and puts. That is because the underlying involves two currencies – a call on one involves a simultaneous put on the other.

A number of exotic currency options allow users to tailor currency exposure management to their specific requirements. Average rate, look-back, barrier and binary currency options are some of the more important variations on the basic currency option.

References

Black, F., 'The Pricing of Commodity Contracts', *Journal of Financial Economics*, 3, 1976, pp. 167–79.

Black, F. and Scholes, M., 'The Pricing of Options and Corporate Liabilities', *Journal of Political Economy*, 81, May/June 1973, pp. 637–59.

Cox, J.C., Ingersoll, J. and Ross, S., 'The Relationship Between Forward Prices and Future Prices', *Journal of Financial Economics*, 9, December 1981, pp. 321–46.

Feiger, G. and Jacquillat, B., 'Currency Option Bonds Puts and Calls on Spot Exchange and Contingent Foreign Earnings', *Journal of Finance*, 33, December 1979, pp. 1129–1139.

Garman, M. and Kohlhagen, S., 'Foreign Currency Option Values, *Journal of International Money and Finance*, December 1983.

Gemill, G., *Options Pricing: An International Perspective*, Maidenhead: McGraw-Hill, 1993.

Geske, R., 'The Valuation of Compound Options', *Journal of Financial Economics*, 7, March 1979, pp. 63–81.

Goldman, B., Sosin, H. and Gatto, M., 'Path Dependent Options: Buy at the Low and Sell at the High', *Journal of Finance*, 34, December 1979, pp. 1111–1127.

10

EQUITY OPTIONS

What is a stock option?

Pricing stock options – basic analysis

Valuation of stock options

A one-period option pricing model

Multi period binomial option pricing

Stock index options

Exotic stock options

Summary

Equity or common stock option contracts have been traded in the over-the-counter market for more than fifty years. In April 1973, the Chicago Board Options Exchange (CBOE) became the first organized secondary market in call options on sixteen common stocks traded on the New York Stock Exchange (NYSE). The opening of the first organized exchange for trading listed stock options almost coincided with the publication of a path-breaking paper by Fisher Black and Myron Scholes which presented the first general equilibrium solution to pricing stock options. The growth in both the market for stock options and the academic literature devoted to their study has been phenomenal since.[1] In 1975, the American Stock Exchange (AMEX) and the Philadelphia Stock Exchange (PHILEX) began to trade stock options following the early success of CBOE initiative. In 1977, the Securities and Exchange Commission (SEC) authorized the trading of put options, allowing each exchange to list up to five put option series. In 1983, several exchanges introduced options on stock indices, thus broadening the appeal of equity options to a wider universe of end users.

This chapter focuses on over-the-counter (OTC) equity options. Unlike listed stock options, the OTC equity options can be customized to end user requirements. OTC equity options are very well established in Europe. In the United States, where exchange traded options are available on a wide range of individual stocks and stock indexes, OTC equity options are gaining wider acceptance by institutional investors with ever growing requirements for structured products. In the US, call and put options trade on over 1,000 individual stocks on five exchanges. In Asia, where exchange traded equity derivatives are mainly restricted to futures contracts on major stock indexes, OTC equity options market provides the only feasible way to buy and sell options on Asian stock and stock indexes.

In general, demand for OTC stock options has grown significantly across various financial centres. The demand for structured equity options has been driven by:

- investors seeking to create risk management strategies that better reflect the composition of their underlying portfolios

- investors seeking to alter the risk/return characteristics of their portfolios in line with their market views

- retail demand for equity-linked investment products such as Nikkei-linked deposits

---

[1] For example, CBOE is now the second largest securities exchange in the world, second only to the New York Stock Exchange.

211

- corporate borrowers seeking to reduce cost of their funding, for example, by issuing convertible bonds
- corporate borrowers looking for alternative financing vehicles, for example, by issuing warrants.

While OTC equity options provide a flexible way of managing equity risk and return and enjoys a higher profile, it should be noted that many of the complex OTC equity options were made possible by the availability of liquid listed equity derivatives for hedging.

WHAT IS A STOCK OPTION?

A stock option is a contract between a buyer and a seller (writer) that gives the buyer the right to buy (a call option) or sell (a put option) an underlying stock at a pre-specified price (exercise or strike price) at or during a pre-specified period of time. Options that can be exercised at any time prior to maturity are called American options, whereas options that can be exercised only at maturity are referred to as European options.

Call options

A European style call option gives the buyer the right to buy a specified number of shares of a given common stock at a pre-specified exercise price on the maturity (or expiry) date. The buyer of a call option is betting on a rise in the price of the underlying stock. For a call buyer to make a profit, the price of the underlying stock must rise sufficiently above the strike price. Call buyers are, therefore, bullish on the underlying stock. For example, a European call option written on a share of IBM stock at an exercise price of $50 gives its purchaser the right, but not the obligation, to buy one share of IBM stock on the expiry date at a fixed price of $50. For this privilege, the purchaser of this option pays a premium (the option premium) to the seller of the option, say $1.0. If, on the expiry date, IBM stock trades above $50, the holder of the call option will exercise the option to make an immediate profit. On the other hand, should IBM stock trade below $50 the holder of the call option can let the option expire unexercised. Thus, the payoff to the call buyer is

$$\max (S - E, 0) \tag{10.1}$$

where S is the price of the underlying stock at expiry and E is the exercise price of the option, i.e. $50 in our example. The net payoff (taking premium paid into account) at expiry for our example is shown in Figure 10.1.

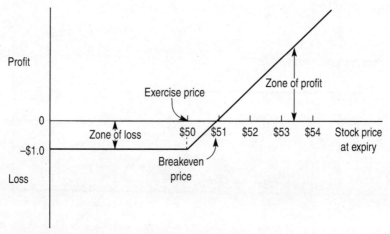

Fig 10.1 Payoff diagram for the buyer of a call option

For the seller (writer) of this call option, the payoff at expiry will be the mirror image of the payoff of the buyer of the call option. That is because the seller of the call option is paid to assume the obligation to sell underlying shares to the call holder at the option exercise price. Any gain to the call holder must, by definition, be a loss to the call writer. In this sense, options are a zero sum game. The seller of a call option is betting on no rise in the price of the underlying stock. The payoff to the call writer is given by

$$\min (E - S, 0) \tag{10.2}$$

That is, the call option seller faces a loss should the stock price rise sufficiently above the strike price. The call seller's gain is limited to the option premium received. The payoff to the call seller in our example is shown in Figure 10.2.

The call seller in our example stands to incur a loss if the price of the IBM stock at expiry rises above $51. The call seller's gain, on the other hand, is limited to $1.0 if the stock price does not exceed the strike price of $50 at expiry.

Put options

A European style put option gives the buyer the right to sell a specified number of shares of a given common stock at a pre-specified exercise price on the expiry date. The buyer of a put option is expecting a fall in the price of the underlying stock. That is, the holder is bearish on the stock. For the put holder to make a gain, the price of the underlying stock must fall sufficiently below the exercise price. Should the underlying stock trade above the strike price at the maturity of the

213

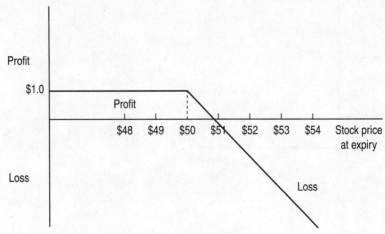

Fig 10.2 Payoff diagram for the seller of a call option

option, the put will expire worthless since, from the put holder's standpoint, selling the underlying stock at a price lower than the market price will result in an economic loss.

For example, a European put option written on a share of Microsoft stock at an exercise price of $10 gives its holder the right, but not the obligation, to sell one share of Microsoft stock at expiration at a fixed price of $10. Suppose the cost of purchasing this option is $0.50. If, on the expiry date, the price of Microsoft stock is below $10, the put holder will exercise the option and make a profit. Suppose the Microsoft stock on the expiry date of the option trades at $8. The put holder will exercise the option under which it will sell a share of Microsoft stock to the put seller at the exercise price of $10. To deliver the stock the put holder can buy it at the current market price of $8 giving him an instant payoff of $2. Since the purchaser paid an option premium of $0.50 at the outset, his profit will be $1.50. Now, if the put holder had purchased a put that gave him the right to sell one million shares of Microsoft stock, his profit would simply be $1.50 million and the initial cost would have been $0.50 million. In either case, the investor would end up with a return on investment of 300 percent from a price move in the underlying stock of 20 percent which shows the leverage effect of investment in option contracts. If the Microsoft stock trades at or above the exercise price of $10 at the expiration date, the put holder will allow the option to lapse unexercised. Thus, the payoff to the put buyer is

$$\max (E - S, 0) \tag{10.3}$$

The possible gains and losses for the put holder in our example are shown in Figure 10.3.

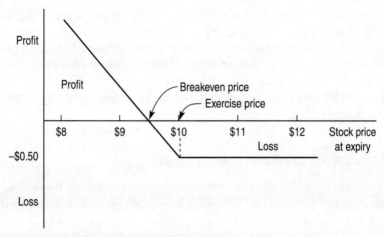

Fig 10.3 Payoff diagram for the buyer of a put option

As in the case of the call option, the payoff for the seller of a put option is the mirror image of the payoff for the buyer of the put option. That is because the gain to one party is an exact loss for the other party in all states. The payoff to put writers at maturity is given by:

$$\min (S - E, 0) \tag{10.4}$$

The possible profit and loss for the put writer in our example is shown in Figure 10.4.

The put seller stands to make a gain equal to the initial premium of $0.50 if the Microsoft stock does not trade below the exercise price of $10. However, should the underlying stock trade below $10 at the expiration date, the put seller will be required to buy the stock at a

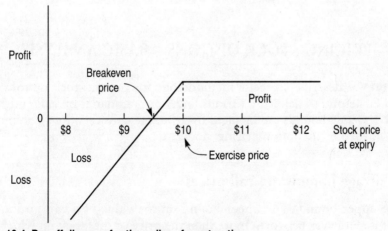

Fig 10.4 Payoff diagram for the seller of a put option

price that is above its current market price. If the underlying stock trades at $9.50, both the put buyer and the put seller will break even since the put seller will lose $0.50 on account of being obligated to buy the underlying stock at the exercise price of $10 and having to sell it at the current market price of $9.50. If the price of Microsoft stock trades below $9.50, the put seller will stand to lose more than the premium amount received up-front.

European versus American options

A European style option can only be exercised at maturity. An American style option, on the other hand, can be exercised anytime up to its expiration date. Most of the options exchanges trade American style stock options. The possibility of early exercise gives rise to differences in the price of American versus European options. These differences will be discussed in greater detail in the section on pricing, here we will summarize some of the general conclusions:

- it is never optimal to exercise an American call option on a non-dividend paying stock early
- it may be optimal to exercise an American put option on a non-dividend paying stock early
- under certain circumstances, it may be optimal to exercise an American call option on a dividend paying stock just prior to the dividend payment because the stock price falls following a dividend payment
- it is sub-optimal to exercise an American put option on a dividend paying stock during the period just prior to the ex-dividend date. Early exercise may, however, become optimal again immediately after the dividend is paid.

PRICING STOCK OPTIONS – BASIC ANALYSIS

Before we describe a precise methodology for pricing stock options, it will be helpful to delineate various limits or boundaries on call and put prices. These bounds are dictated by arbitrage considerations and must be satisfied by an option pricing model.

Arbitrage bounds, on call prices

The upper bound The upper bound on the value of a call option is that it can never be worth more than the price of the stock on which it is written. The reason is that the right to buy the underlying security cannot be worth more than the value of the security itself. For example, the most that an investor would pay for a call option with an exercise price of zero and a time to expiration of infinity would be the price of the stock. That is because, holding such a call is equivalent to having a long position in the underlying stock. Hence, the upper bound on the value of the call is

$$C \leq S \tag{10.5}$$

where S is the stock price. The upper bound on the value of the call is shown in Figure 10.5. Notice that the upper bound is represented by a 45-degree line. The shaded area is excluded by the bound.

The lower bound The lower bound for American call options, i.e. those options that can be exercised at any time up to expiration is given by their intrinsic value. Intrinsic value is the difference between the current stock price (S) and the exercise price (E) of the option. To avoid arbitrage, the minimum value for an American call is given by the difference between the stock price and the exercise price of the option. That is:

$$C \geq \max (S - E, 0) \tag{10.6}$$

where S − E is the intrinsic value. Otherwise the purchaser of the call makes an instant risk free profit. Suppose the current price of a stock is $100. An American call option written on this stock with an exercise price of $90 gives an intrinsic value of $10 and, therefore, the option must sell for at least $10. If the call price is less than $10, say $8, the holder of the call will make an instant risk free profit of $2 by purchasing the option at $8 and exercising it immediately. Since the call allows the holder to purchase the underlying stock at $90 which it can sell

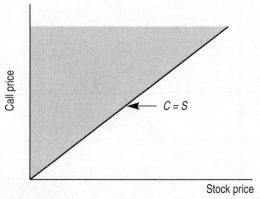

Fig 10.5 Upper bound on the value of a call

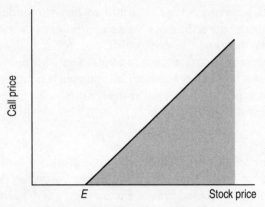

Fig 10.6 Lower bound on the value of an American call

immediately at the current market price of $100, the option provides an instant payoff of $10. Since the option cost $8 in premium, its holder makes an instant risk free gain of $2. To avoid arbitrage, therefore, an American call must be at least worth its intrinsic value. The lower bound for an American call is shown in Figure 10.6.

Unlike an American call, a European call can only be exercised at maturity. The lower bound of a European call at maturity is given by its exercise value (the intrinsic value at maturity). That is

$$C = \max{(S - E, 0)} \qquad (10.6)$$

Before maturity, however, a European call should sell for at least the present value (PV) of its exercise value at maturity. That is

$$C \geq \max{(S - PV(E), 0)} \qquad (10.7)$$

Comparing condition (10.7) with condition (10.6) derived for an American call we note that the intrinsic value $S - E$ in (10.6) has been

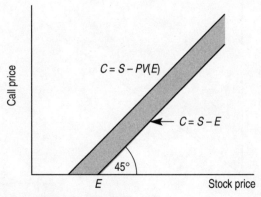

Fig 10.7 Lower bound on the value of a call

218

replaced by $S - PV(E)$ in (10.7). As illustrated in Figure 10.7, Equation (10.7) provides a stronger condition for the price range of a call option. It is easy to show that condition (10.7) also applies to American options. Since an American call has all the characteristics of a European option and also gives its holder the right of early exercise, it follows that an American option must be at least worth as much as a corresponding European option with similar exercise price and time to expiration. Thus, condition (10.7) provides the lower bound for American as well as European call options.

The upper and lower bounds for the price of call options are shown in Figure 10.8.

In between the upper and the lower boundaries for the price of a call, more arbitrage arguments can be used to restrict the range of possible call prices. Some of the important limits are summarized as under:

- the value of an option can never be less than zero because, on exercise, an option is worth the intrinsic value or zero, whichever is greater
- an option with a longer time to maturity will be worth at least as much as an option with a shorter time to expiration but the same exercise price
- a call option with a lower exercise price will be worth at least as much as an option with a higher exercise price but the same time to expiration
- in percentage terms, the call price will change by at least as much as the change in the stock price
- a call option written on a worthless stock ($S = 0$) will be worth zero
- if the stock price, S, is very high relative to the exercise price, E, then the call price will approach its lower bound of max $[S - PV(E), 0]$. That is because, as the probability of exercise approaches 100 percent, the option has no extra uncertainty value.

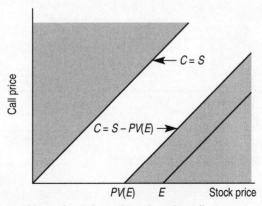

Fig 10.8 Upper and lower bounds on the value of a call

These last two limits on the price of a call option can be used to show the relationship between movements in the price of the underlying stock and the value of a call. Figure 10.9 depicts this relationship. When the underlying stock price is infinitesimally below the exercise price, i.e. the option is deep out-of-the-money, the call price will tend to be zero. If, on the other hand, the underlying stock price is infinitesimally large relative to the exercise price, i.e. the call is deep in-the-money, changes in the call price will approach changes in the stock price, S.

Figure 10.9 demonstrates graphically the sensitivity of call prices to changes in the underlying stock price. Prior to expiration, the value of a call changes smoothly, as the price of the underlying stock changes, as shown by the call price line in Figure 10.9. It increases with the stock price at a rate that varies from almost zero, when the call is deep out-of-the-money, to almost 1, when the call is deep in-the-money. This rate of change in the value of the option, known as delta (Δ), is given by the slope of the price curve, i.e. the curve that relates the option price to the price of the underlying stock.[2] For example, if the delta of a call option is 0.5, it means that when the stock price changes by a small amount, the call price changes by about 50 percent of that amount. We will have more to say about delta in a later section. Here it may be noted that delta, as a measure of price sensitivity, is an important risk parameter for market makers in options.

Arbitrage bounds on put prices

The upper bound A European put gives its holder the right to sell an underlying stock at a pre-specified exercise price, E. Hence, a

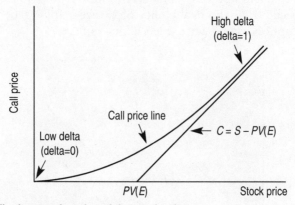

Fig 10.9 Call price as a function of the stock price

---

[2] Formally, $\Delta = \dfrac{\partial C}{\partial S}$

European put will have a maximum payoff of E at its expiration (if $S = 0$) or may expire worthless. The current value of a European put will thus be no more than the present value of its exercise price, E. That is

$$P \leq PV(E) \tag{10.8}$$

Since an American put can be exercised at any time before its expiration date, its corresponding upper bound is given by

$$P \leq E \tag{10.9}$$

That is, an American put cannot sell for more than its exercise price.

The lower bound   The lower bound for a European put is analogous to the lower bound on a European call. The European put must sell at least for the present value of its exercise value. That is

$$P \geq PV(E) - S \tag{10.10}$$

In contrast to an American call which is worth more unexercised ('alive') than exercised ('dead'), an American put may be worth more exercised than unexercised. It must be that an American put is worth at least as much as, and possibly more than, a European put with similar terms. The prices of two puts cannot, therefore, be strictly equal. Hence, the lower bound for the value of an American put will be equal to its intrinsic value, or

$$P = E - S \tag{10.11}$$

The lower bounds for European and American puts are shown in Figure 10.10. Notice that the lower bound for an American put lies

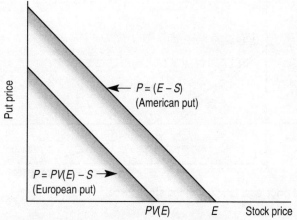

Fig 10.10 Lower bounds for European and American puts

above the European bound. This difference between American and European puts has important implications for pricing, since different models will be required to incorporate the possibility of early exercise in the case of American puts.

The relationship between changes in the price of the underlying stock and the value of an American put option written on it is shown in Figure 10.11. As in the case of a call option, the value of a put changes smoothly, as the price of the underlying stock changes as shown by the put price line.

However, unlike call options, the value of a put increases at a rate that varies from −1 to zero because the value of a put is inversely related to the value of the underlying stock. When the value of the underlying stock is very high relative to the exercise price of the put, i.e. the put is deep out-of-the-money, the value of the put approaches zero and the rate of change (delta) will be close to zero. As the value of the underlying stock approaches zero, i.e. the put is deep in-the-money, the value of the put approaches its exercise price, E, and the delta approaches −1.

Put call parity

Put-call parity refers to the relationship between the price of a put and the price of a call written on the same stock and with the same exercise price and expiration date. It can be shown that the payoff of a European call at its expiration date can be replicated by a long position in the underlying stock and a put written on the same stock.[3] Now, if that be the case, then the prices of puts and calls must clearly be related.

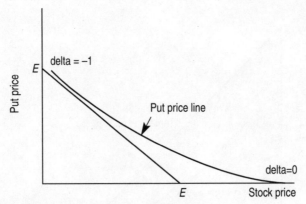

Fig 10.11 Put price as a function of the stock price

---

[3] H.R. Stoll, 'The relationship between put and call option prices,' *Journal of Finance*, December 1969.

To derive the put-call relationship, consider a portfolio consisting of long position in the stock and a European put written on the stock and short position in a European call written on that stock. Assume that the exercise price E and the term to expiration T on both the call and the put are the same. Now, at maturity the stock price will be either greater than E, less than E or equal to E. Table 10.1 shows the possible payoffs to the portfolio under each of these states.

Table 10.1 Possible payoffs for the put-call parity portfolio			
	$S > E$	$S = E$	$S < E$
Long stock	S	$S = E$	S
Long put	0	0	$E - S$
Short call	$E - S$	0	0
	E	E	E

It is clear that irrespective of the state of nature at maturity, the portfolio will be worth $\$E$ at maturity. This is, therefore, a risk free portfolio. Hence, its value today can be calculated by discounting it at the current risk free rate of interest r for the term of the option. That is

$$S + P - C = \frac{E}{(1 + r)^T} \qquad (10.12)$$

where r is the interest rate per period, S is the stock price, P is the price of the European put, C is the price of the European call and E is the exercise price. Equation (10.12) is called the put-call-parity equation because it relates the price of a European call to the price of a European put written on the same stock with the same exercise price and the time to expiration. It states that the call price minus the put price must equal the current stock price minus the present value of the strike price discounted back from the option expiration date using the risk free rate of interest. Equation (10.12) can be rearranged to give the price of a European put if the price of its corresponding call is known or vice versa. Thus,

$$P = C - S + PV(E) \qquad (10.13)$$

$$C = S + P - PV(E) \qquad (10.14)$$

Put call parity can also be used as a basis for the creation of several synthetic strategies. For example, Equation (10.12) can be expressed as

$$Long\ call + Short\ put = Long\ stock + Borrowing \qquad (10.15)$$

where 'Borrowing' equals the present value of the option's strike price, i.e. $PV(E)$. Equation (10.15) can be rearranged to produce synthetic long positions in each of the three basic assets as shown below.

$$Long\ call = \ Long\ put + Long\ stock + Borrowing \qquad (10.16)$$

$$Long\ put = \ Long\ call + Short\ stock + Lending \qquad (10.17)$$

$$Long\ stock = Long\ call + Short\ put + \ Lending \qquad (10.18)$$

where 'Lending' equals the present value of the option's strike price, i.e. $PV(E)$.

Factors affecting the value of stock options

There are six factors that affect the price of a stock option. These are

1 Current stock price
2 Exercise price
3 Time to expiration
4 Volatility
5 Risk-free rate of interest
6 Dividends.

In this section we consider the general effect of each of these variables on the price of stock options.

The effect of current stock price on the value of a stock option is straightforward. We showed in Figures 10.9 and 10.11 respectively that call options increase in value as the underlying stock price rises, whereas put options become more valuable as the stock price decreases.

A call option becomes more valuable as the stock price increases because, *ceteris paribus*, the holder of the call stands to gain more on exercise of the option. Put options, on the other hand, become more valuable as the stock price decreases since the holder stands to gain more on exercise of the option.

The longer the time to expiration, the greater the value of the option. That is because a longer dated option gives all the exercise opportunities of a short-dated option plus more. The long-dated option is, therefore, always worth at least as much as the short-dated option.

Volatility is an estimate of variability in the underlying stock price over the term of the option. Since volatility cannot be directly observed, it must be estimated from historical data or implied from option prices. It is defined as the variance of stock price changes. Higher volatility implies greater variability in the price of the underlying stock and, hence, greater potential for a higher option payoff. That is because unlike a long position in the underlying stock, the payoff of a long position in the option depends on price changes in one direction only. Thus, the holder of a call option benefits from price increases in the underlying stock but has limited downside exposure to a fall in the price of the underlying stock. Similarly, the holder of a put gains from a fall in the price of the underlying stock but has limited downside exposure to a rise in the price of the underlying stock. More volatility is, therefore, good for both the holders of calls and puts.

The risk free rate of interest, r, is the least intuitive of all the factors affecting the value of an option. As we will note in the next section, stock options are valued assuming a risk-neutral world. In such a world, as r increases, the growth rate of the stock price also increases. A higher r, however, means that the present value of any future payoff received by the option holder decreases. In the case of calls, while the first effect tends to increase the value of the call, the second effect tends to decrease the value. However, the first effect always dominates the value of a call resulting in a positive relationship between r and the value of a call. In the case of puts, the combined effect creates a negative relationship between r and the put price.

Finally, dividend payouts have the effect of reducing the stock price on the ex-dividend date. That means the value of a call will decrease after a dividend payout while the value of a put will increase.

VALUATION OF STOCK OPTIONS

In the previous sections, we examined the structure of option prices implied by the lack of arbitrage opportunities in an efficient market. We were able to define the boundaries within which stock option prices must fall to avoid arbitrage. We also identified the variables that affect the value of stock options. We now focus on the exact valuation of calls and puts written on common stock. It will be noted that in order to derive an exact option pricing formula we will need to make more restrictive assumptions than were needed to define the boundaries of option prices.

The valuation of stock options has fascinated researchers at least since the beginning of this century. The first recorded attempt to derive an explicit option valuation model was made by a French mathematician, Bachelier, in the year 1900 in his doctoral thesis. Although his work remained largely unknown for many years, we now know that his research lay the foundation for the modern option pricing theory. However, like many researchers after him, Bachelier's approach was flawed. The major problem faced by researchers trying to devise an explicit valuation formula for stock options was that their models required input parameters that could not be observed directly. These included the probability distribution for the price of the underlying stock at option expiration and the appropriate risk-adjusted interest rate to be used in discounting the expected option payoff back to the present. It was not until 1973 that these problems were overcome and an exact stock option valuation formula was developed.

In this section we will describe two important approaches to valuing stock options. These are the Black and Scholes model and the binomial model. The Black and Scholes model is a continuous time model that uses the concept of a hedge portfolio to derive an exact valuation formula for European calls and puts. The binomial model provides an alternative approach to valuing stock options that is consistent with Black and Scholes. It is a discrete time model and is more intuitive.

The Black and Scholes pricing model

In a seminal paper Fisher Black and Myron Scholes (1973) provided the first general equilibrium solution for the valuation of stock options. Their model is based on the key insight that a riskless hedge can be formed between the option and the underlying stock. They demonstrated that a riskless hedge can be created and maintained using call options and the underlying stock in proper proportions. The fact that a riskless hedge may be formed between the call and the underlying stock has an important implication and that is the price of the risky call can be derived without knowing the expected rate of return on the underlying stock. In other words, the value of the call relative to the stock is not influenced by investor preferences.

To derive an exact option pricing formula for the valuation of European calls and puts, Black and Scholes use the following assumptions:

- trading takes place continuously
- investors can freely buy and sell securities short
- the short-term risk-free rate of interest, r, is known and is constant over time
- the underlying stock pays no dividends
- the markets are frictionless, i.e. there are no transaction costs in buying or selling the stock or the option
- the stock price follows a random walk in continuous time with a variance rate proportional to the square of the stock price. Thus, the distribution of possible stock prices at the end of any finite interval is lognormal.

226

The concept of an instantaneous hedge

In Figure 10.7 above we showed the lower bound for the price of a call option written on a non-dividend paying stock. This lower bound was given by the price of the underlying stock less the present value of the strike price. In Figure 10.9 we illustrated the actual price line of a call option at some point prior to its expiration. We noted that for calls that are deep out-of-the-money, call price changes are insensitive to stock price movements (delta = 0), whereas for calls that are deep in-the-money the call price changes dollar for dollar (delta = 1) with the stock price.

Suppose the current stock price is S_0 and the current call price is C_0 as given by the price line shown in Figure 10.12. The slope of the price line at point a indicates the sensitivity of the call price to small instantaneous changes in the current stock price. Now, for an infinitesimal change in the price of the stock, ΔS, the call price will change by ΔC. Notice that the size of ΔC will depend on the slope of the call price line at point a. If we let h be the slope of the price line at point a (also known as the hedge ratio), then

$$\Delta C = h\Delta S \qquad (10.19)$$

Now consider forming a portfolio consisting of H shares of stock and a call written on that stock. For an infinitesimal change in the price of the stock, ΔS, the value of h shares will increase by $h\Delta S$, while the value of the call will decrease by ΔC. The net change in the value of the portfolio will, however, be zero because the (positive) change in the price of the stock is perfectly offset by the (negative) change in the price of the call. This essentially is the concept of a perfect instantaneous hedge that is at the heart of the Black and Scholes model for option pricing. It is important to note that this portfolio is hedged only if the changes in the underlying stock price are infinitesimal. More importantly, this portfolio

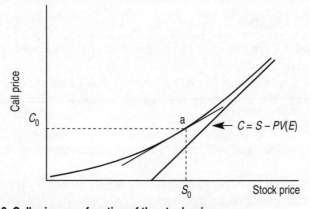

Fig 10.12 Call price as a function of the stock price

is risk free only over a small instant in time. However, since Black and Scholes assume continuous trading and frictionless markets, i.e. no transaction costs, it is possible to maintain the hedge portfolio by continuously revising the number of stocks according to the (changing) slope of the price line. As we will note below, Black and Scholes were thus able to demonstrate that a riskless hedge can be created and maintained using call options and the underlying stock in prescribed proportions, i.e. dictated by the hedge ratio, h. Since the hedge portfolio thus created is riskless then, if perfect substitutes yield the same rate of return, the rate of return on the hedge portfolio must be equal to the risk free interest rate. As we will note below, this forms the equilibrium condition from which the call price can be obtained.

Black and Scholes approach – the basic concept

We follow the approach developed in Chapter 3 to derive the Black and Scholes model. Consider forming a hedge portfolio consisting of stock and call options on that stock. If we let

N_S = Quantity of stock in the hedge portfolio

N_C = Quantity of call options in the hedge portfolio

then the value of the hedge portfolio, H, at any time is given by

$$H = N_C C + N_S S \qquad (10.20)$$

where H is the value of the hedge portfolio, S is the price of the stock and C is the price of a call to purchase one share of the stock.

In a short instant of time, where N_S and N_C are fixed, the only source of change in Equation (10.20) is the change in the price of the stock and the option. Using basic calculus the change in the value of the hedge position, dH, is given by the derivative of Equation (10.20)

$$dH = N_C dC + N_S dS \qquad (10.21)$$

where dC and dS are changes in the price of the stock and the call option respectively.

By the last assumption described above (that of random walk in continuous time), the stock price is assumed to follow an Ito process:

$$dS = \mu S dt + \sigma S dz \qquad (10.22)$$

where dz is a Weiner process and μ and σ are drift rate and volatility respectively.

Because the stock is assumed to follow a continuous Ito process and the option is assumed to be a function of the stock price and time, therefore, we can employ Ito's lemma to express the change in the call price, dC, as

$$dC = \left(\frac{\partial C}{\partial S} \mu S + \frac{\partial C}{\partial t} + \frac{1}{2} \frac{\partial^2 C}{\partial S^2} \sigma^2 S^2 \right) dt + \frac{\partial C}{\partial S} \sigma S dz \qquad (10.23)$$

Notice that both S and C are affected by the same underlying source of uncertainty, namely dz. In other words, the underlying Weiner process for S and C are the same. It follows that by choosing an appropriate portfolio consisting of the stock and the call, the only source of uncertainty in Equation (10.23), dz, can be eliminated at least instantaneously.

Consider a portfolio consisting of a short position in one call ($Nc = -1$) and a long position in the stock of $\frac{\partial C}{\partial S}$, then Equation (10.21) yields

$$dH = \left(-\frac{\partial C}{\partial t} - \frac{1}{2} \frac{\partial^2 C}{\partial S^2} \sigma^2 S^2 \right) dt \qquad (10.24)$$

All stochastic terms in Equation (10.23) have been eliminated in Equation (10.24). Now if the quantities of the stock and the option are adjusted continuously in the prescribed way as stock and option prices change over time, then the return on the hedge portfolio becomes certain. To avoid arbitrage, therefore, this portfolio must earn the risk free rate of interest. That is

$$dH = rHdt \qquad (10.25)$$

where r is the risk free interest rate.

Substituting (10.20) and (10.24) into (10.25) results in the fundamental Black and Scholes partial differential equation for the value of the call option:

$$\frac{\partial C}{\partial t} + rS \frac{\partial C}{\partial S} + \frac{1}{2} \frac{\partial^2 C}{\partial S^2} \sigma^2 S^2 = rC \qquad (10.26)$$

The solution to a particular option valuation problem using Equation (10.26) will depend on the boundary conditions. For European call and put options the required boundary conditions of (10.26) are those at the expiration date of the option. For such options Black and Scholes were able to derive a closed form analytical solution by transforming (10.26) into the heat equation from physics for which the solution is known.

For a European call option the Black and Scholes pricing formula is given by

$$C = SN(d1) - Ee^{-rT} N(d2) \qquad (10.27)$$

where

$$d1 = \frac{\ln\left(\dfrac{S}{E}\right) + \left(r + \dfrac{1}{2}\,\sigma^2\right)T}{\sigma\sqrt{T}}$$

and

$$d2 = d1 - \sigma\sqrt{T}$$

C = current value of a call
S = current price of stock
E = exercise price of the option
e = 2.7183
T = time to expiration of the option
r = continuously compounded riskfree interest rate per period
σ^2 = instantaneous variance of the stock price

The terms $N(d1)$ and $N(d2)$ are the cumulative probability for a unit normal variable z.[4] That is it is the probability

$$N(d1) = \int_{\infty}^{d1} f(z)dz$$

where $f(z)$ is distributed normally with mean zero and standard deviation of one.

From Equation (10.27) we note that the value of the call is equal to the stock price, S, minus the discounted value of the exercise price, Ee^{-rT}, each weighted by a probability. The stock price is weighted by $N(d1)$ which is also the hedge ratio. For each call written, the riskless hedge portfolio contains $N(d1)$ shares of stock. On the other hand the discounted value of the exercise price is weighted by $N(d2)$ which can be interpreted as the probability that the option will finish in-the-money.

The value of a European put, P, can be derived in a similar way to a European call. The result is

$$P = Ee^{-rT}N(-d2) - SN(-d1) \tag{10.28}$$

where P is the value of a European put and $d1$ and $d2$ are as defined above.

For American style option contracts, where there is some chance of early exercise, it is not possible to derive analytical solutions unless it can be, a priori, proved that a rational investor will not exercise the option before its expiry date. It can be shown that in the case of a non-dividend paying stock it is never optimal to exercise an American call option before its expiration date. In this case, therefore, the European

---

[4] That is, $N(d)$ is the probability that a normally distributed random variable, X, will be less than or equal to d.

call option pricing formula can be used. An American put option, on the other hand, has a chance of early exercise and therefore the valuation problem must be solved using numerical techniques such as an iterative binomial method.

Example
Although Equation (10.27) looks daunting it has an intuitive explanation as given above and can be used relatively easily, It depends on observable parameters such as the current stock price, S, the exercise price, E, the risk free rate of interest, r, and the volatility which can be estimated from market data using simple statistical techniques. To demonstrate its application, let

S = $100
r = 0.10 or 10%
E = $100
T = 1 year
σ = 25%

Using this information we can compute the value of the call as

$$C = SN(d1) - Ee^{-rT} N(d2)$$

where
$$d1 = \frac{\ln\left(\frac{S}{E}\right) + \left(r + \frac{1}{2}\sigma^2\right) T}{\sigma\sqrt{T}}$$

$$d1 = \frac{\ln\left(\frac{100}{100}\right) + (0.10 + 0.5(0.25)^2)\,(1)}{0.25\sqrt{1}}$$

$$= \frac{0.0 + 0.131}{0.25} = 0.525$$

and
$$d2 = d1 - \sigma\sqrt{T}$$
$$= 0.525 - 0.25 = 0.275$$

Substituting these values into the call option formula, we have

$$C = SN(0.525) - Ee^{-rT} N(0.275)$$

Recall that $N(d1)$ and $N(d2)$ are cumulative probabilities for a unit normal variable. Therefore $N(d1)$ is the cumulative probability from minus infinity to +0.525 standard deviations above the mean which is zero for the standard normal variable. A ready reckoner for the area under the normal curve appears as Appendix 1 of this book which shows the cumulative probability from $-\infty$ to 0.525 to be approximately 0.70. Repeating the same procedure for $N(d2)$ we get 0.608.

231

Substituting these probabilities into the call option formula we get

$C = \$100(0.70) - \$100(2.7183)^{-(0.10)(1)} (0.608)$

$= \$70 - \$100(0.9048)(0.608) = \$14.98$

The binomial stock option pricing model

In Chapter 3 we derived an alternative approach to value options known as the binomial model.[5] The binomial approach uses the key Black and Scholes insight of riskless hedge in a discrete, as opposed to continuous, time framework. Specifically, whereas the price of the underlying stock within the Black and Scholes framework can assume any number of possible values in any finite period of time – making the mathematics of the model difficult to grasp – the binomial model assumes only two possible values for the underlying stock price over any finite time period. The binomial model is sometimes referred to as the two-state pricing model. The model assumes that the stock price follows a multiplicative binomial process in discrete time.

There are many features of the binomial model that make it extremely valuable. Indeed, what began as a modelling trick has become a very important and versatile pricing tool particularly for market practitioners. The model is mathematically much simpler than the Black and Scholes model and affords a better insight into the economic principles of option pricing – an area much obscured by the use of complex mathematics within the Black and Scholes framework. What is remarkable, however, is that despite being simple, the binomial approach is fully consistent with the Black and Scholes approach. As will be noted later, the Black and Scholes model is a limiting case of the binomial model in which the price changes in the underlying stock occur over infinitesimally small periods of time.

A ONE-PERIOD OPTION PRICING MODEL

This section develops a simple approach[6] to price an option with one period to expiry to buy one share of the underlying stock currently trading at S. We will assume that at the end of one period the price of

---

[5] The binomial approach to option valuation was first discussed by William Sharpe, Professor of Finance at Stanford University and later developed by Cox, Ross and Rubinstein (1979).

[6] For a detailed derivation the reader is referred to Chapter 3.

this stock can go up by a factor of u to Su (with probability q) or fall by a factor of d to Sd (with probability $1 - q$). Thus, there are only two possibilities for the end-of-period stock price. To make matters simple we also make the following assumptions:

- investors can borrow or lend at the risk-free rate
- markets are frictionless and competitive
- constant risk-free interest rate
- no dividend payments.

Now, consider an option to buy one share of stock with a current price, S, of $100. Suppose the option has one period to expiry[7] and that at the end of this period the stock price can go up by 25 percent to $125 or fall by 25 percent to $75. What would a call option written on this stock with an exercise price, E, of $100 cost today? To answer this question we employ the key insight provided by Black and Scholes that the payoff structure of this particular call option contract at its expiration can be exactly duplicated by a levered portfolio consisting of a specific proportion of the underlying stock and certain amount of one-period borrowing. If we can construct such a portfolio and show that it is risk free under all scenarios, we can determine a unique price for the option.

Given our assumptions about the future price of the underlying stock we can easily determine the end-of-period range of values for the call option in our example. Since we have assumed that the underlying stock can only assume two possible values at the option's expiration, it follows that the call option can also have only two possible values at the expiration date. Thus, if the stock price at expiration turns out to be Su the option will be worth

$$C_u = \text{Max } (Su - E, 0)$$

$$= \text{Max } (125 - 100, 0) = \$25$$

Similarly, if the stock price at expiration turns out to be Sd, the option will be worth

$$C_d = \text{Max } (Sd - E, 0)$$

$$= \text{Max } (75 - 100, 0) = \$0$$

The end-of-period values for the stock and the call at the end of the period are depicted in Figure 10.13.

Now consider forming a riskless hedge portfolio consisting of one short call option and h shares of the underlying stock. The initial cost of establishing the position will be hS minus the option premium, C, received from writing one call, i.e. $hS - C$. The end-of-period values of

---

[7] The period is arbitrary.

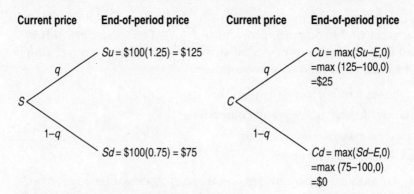

Current price **End-of-period price** **Current price** **End-of-period price**

$Su = \$100(1.25) = \$125$

q

S

$1-q$

$Sd = \$100(0.75) = \$75$

$Cu = \max(Su-E,0)$
$=\max (125-100,0)$
$=\$25$

q

C

$1-q$

$Cd = \max(Sd-E,0)$
$=\max (75-100,0)$
$=\$0$

Fig 10.13 End-of-period stock and call values

the position will be either $hSu - Cu$ if the stock price moves up to Su or $hSd - Cd$ if the stock price moves down to Sd as shown in Figure 10.14. This portfolio will be riskless only if the end-of-period payoffs are the same irrespective of whether the stock price moves up to Su or down to Sd. This condition can written as

$$hSu - C_u = hSd - C_d \qquad (10.29)$$

The proportion of stock or the hedge ratio, h, can be implied from this equation. Solving for h we obtain

$$h = \frac{C_u - C_d}{Su - Sd} \qquad (10.30)$$

The hedge ratio for our example will therefore be

$$h = \frac{\$25 - \$0}{\$125 - \$75} = 0.50$$

A hedge ratio of 0.5 means that for every call option sold we need to buy half a share of the underlying stock to ensure that the differences in the payoffs of the two positions are exactly equal. The end-of-period values for this portfolio will be $37.50 irrespective of whether the stock price rises to $125 or falls to $75 as shown in Table 10.3.

Table 10.2 End-of-period payoffs of the hedge portfolio

	End-of-period stock price = $125	End of period stock price = $75
Value of ½ share held long	$62.50	£37.50
Value of one call sold	−$25.00	$0.00
Net Portfolio Value	$37.50	$37.50

By choosing h such that the end-of-period values of the portfolio are the same irrespective of whether the stock price moves up or down, we have established a risk-free or 'hedged' position. To avoid arbitrage, the initial cost of establishing this position $hS - C$ must, therefore, grow at the risk-free rate to be equal to the end-of-period value of the hedge portfolio. That is:

$$(hS - C)(1 + r) = hSu - C_u \qquad (10.31)$$

Rearranging (10.31) gives us the value of the call:

$$C = \frac{hS(1 + r) + C_u - hSu}{(1 + r)} \qquad (10.32)$$

Equation (10.32) can be simplified by substituting h from Equation (10.30)

$$C = \frac{C_u \left(\frac{(1 + r) - d)}{u - d} \right) + C_d \left(\frac{u - (1 + r)}{u - d} \right)}{1 + r} \qquad (10.33)$$

If we let

$$p = \frac{(1 + r) - d}{u - d}$$

and

$$1 - p = \frac{u - (1 + r)}{u - d}$$

then

$$C = \frac{[C_u p + C_d (1 - p)]}{1 + r} \qquad (10.34)$$

Using Equation (10.34) for our base case example we have

$$C = \frac{\$25 \left[\frac{(1 + 0.10) - 0.75}{1.25 - 0.75} \right] + \$0 \left[1 - \frac{(1 + 0.10) - 0.75}{1.25 - 0.75} \right]}{1.1} = \$15.91$$

where

$S = \$100$
$u = 1.25$
$d = 0.75$
$r = 0.10$ or 10% for the term of the call

Notice that this value compares reasonably well with our earlier value of $14.98 that was derived using the Black and Scholes model. As we will note later, the binomial model will approach the Black and Scholes model as we increase the number of binomial steps or intervals.

As noted in Chapter 3, p can be regarded as the hedging probability. It has the properties of a probability because it is always between zero and one. In fact it can be shown that p is the value q would assume in equilibrium if investors were risk neutral. For example, a risk neutral investor would require only the risk-free rate on a stock investment of S that will grow to Su with probability q and fall to Sd with probability $(1 - q)$ at the end of the period. That is

$$S(1 + r) = Suq + (1 - q)Sd$$

or

$$q = \frac{(1 + r) - d}{u - d} \qquad (10.35)$$

Thus, for a risk neutral investor $p = q$ and Equation (10.33) can be interpreted as the expectation of the call option's discounted future value in a risk neutral world.[8] Parameters u and d represent the volatility of the underlying stock price.

Equation (10.34) has a number of notable features:

1 It does not depend on q, the probability of an upward price movement. This means that even if investors disagree in their subjective probabilities about an upward or downward movement in the stock price, they will still agree on the value of the call relative to its other parameters; S, u, d, E and r.

2 The value of the call option does not depend on investors' attitude to risk. The only assumption is that investors prefer more wealth to less.

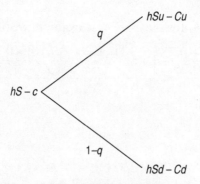

Fig 10.14 The payoff for a risk-free hedge portfolio

[8] As noted in Chapter 3, this does not imply that in equilibrium the required rate of return on call is the risk-free rate.

3 The only random variable on which the option value depends is the price of the underlying stock.

We were able to value a call option because of our ability to construct a properly proportioned hedge portfolio that gave exactly the same pay-offs irrespective of the price movement in the underlying stock.[9] Arbitrage arguments were then used to prove that the call price given by our method was the fair market price for the option. We were able to construct the hedge portfolio fairly easily because we assumed that the underlying stock price could assume only two values at option's expiry date. This assumption is clearly unrealistic but it allowed us to demonstrate the economic principles of options valuation. The following section develops a multiperiod binomial approach to option pricing.

MULTIPERIOD BINOMIAL OPTION PRICING

The one-period binomial option pricing technique described above is clearly unrealistic because it assumes that the stock price can only have two end-of-period values. When the period between the option's purchase date and its expiry is months or even years, this assumption will result in serious mispricing. However, if we divide this period into smaller intervals a more realistic description of stock price movements can be obtained.[10] The question of option valuation now becomes a multiperiod problem. In terms of the terminology used when discussing Bernouli trials in Chapter 3, the problem is simply equivalent to playing a game of chance with multiple trials. As noted previously, we can still use the same arbitrage arguments to value an option. However, in this case, since each portfolio corresponding to a single sub-interval, has a shorter life than the life of the option, the hedge portfolio must be periodically rebalanced to take into account any price changes as well as the option's remaining life.

Let us first consider a call option with two periods before expiration. Suppose that the current price of the underlying stock is S dollars and that over each period it can either go up by a factor of u with probability q or down by a factor of d with probability $(1 - q)$. Thus, at the end of the first period, the stock price will either be Su or Sd dollars. At the end of the second period (in this case corresponding to

[9] Or, equivalently, the duplicating portfolio that generates exactly the same pay-offs as the underlying call option.

[10] In the limit, if these intervals were to be the shortest possible time interval, say a micro-second, the binomial process becomes a diffusion process.

option's expiry date) the stock price can again either go up by u or down by d. At this point, therefore, the stock will either be Suu (if it goes up both times), Sud (if it goes up in one period and down in the other) or Sdd (if it goes down both times). As pointed out in our description of Bernouli trials in Chapter 3, the order of a sequence of outcomes is irrelevant. Thus, $Sud = Sdu$.

Purchasing an option with two periods to expiry is analogous to playing the game of chance twice. The drawing of a black ball in that case can be likened to the event of rising stock prices and the drawing of a white ball to the event of falling stock prices. The price of a call option on the above stock can be similarly denumerated.

Let C be the current price of the call with two periods to expiration. At the end of period one it can either be worth C_u or C_d depending on whether the stock price goes up or down. At its expiry, the call will be worth C_{uu} if the stock rises in both periods, C_{ud} if the stock goes up in one period and down in the other and C_{dd} if the stock price falls in both periods.

The possible movements in the stock price and the related option prices are depicted in Figure 10.15 assuming the current stock price, S = \$100, exercise price, E = \$100, u = 1.25, d = 0.75 and r = 10%.

First, we use Equation (10.34) to derive the value of the option at the end of the current period. It will be C_u or C_d depending on whether the stock price goes up or down and will be given in each case by:

$$C_u = \frac{C_{uu}p + C_{ud}(1-p)}{1+r} \tag{10.36}$$

and

$$Cd = \frac{C_{du}p + C_{dd}(1-p)}{1+r} \tag{10.37}$$

Again we can construct a hedge portfolio consisting of one short call and hS shares of the underlying stock such that the end-of-period pay-offs are the same irrespective of whether the stock price moves up or down. The functional form of the hedge ratio remains unchanged. To compute the hedge ratio we simply use Equation (10.30) with the new values of C_u and C_d. Note that in the case of an option with more than one period to expiration, the hedge ratio will need to be readjusted for each period to maintain the equivalence of the positions.

Since the hedge ratio has the same functional form in each period, the current value of the call in terms of C_u and C_d will still be

$$C = \frac{C_u p + C_d(1-p)}{1+r}$$

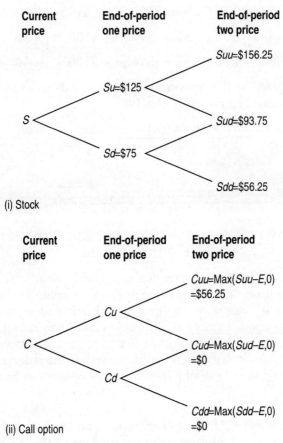

Fig 10.15 **Stock price movements and related option prices**

Substituting (10.36) and (10.37) into this equation and noting that $C_{du} = C_{ud}$ we obtain

$$C = \frac{[C_{uu}p^2 + C_{ud}(1 - p)2p + C_{dd}(1 - p)^2]}{(1 + r)^2}$$ (10.38)

Equation (10.38) is the two-period equivalent of the one-period pricing formula given by Equation (10.34). The terms within the brackets of Equation (10.38) are a binomial expansion of the terms within the brackets in Equation (10.34). It can be interpreted as the expected two-period payoffs discounted at the risk free rate. The expectation is based on hedging probabilities p and $(1 - p)$. Referring to Figure 10.15 we can now compute the value of the call two periods before expiration. At the time of expiration the stock price will be either $Suu = \$100\ (1.25)(1.25) = \$156.25$, $Sud = \$100\ (1.25)(0.75) = \$93.75$ or $Sdd = \$100\ (0.75)(0.75) = \$56.25$. The call prices associated with these stock prices will be

$$C_{uu} = \text{Max } [Suu - E, 0] = \text{Max } [\$156.25 - \$100, 0] = \$56.25$$

$$C_{ud} = \text{Max } [Sud - E, 0] = \text{Max } [\$93.75 - \$100, 0] = \$0$$

$$C_{dd} = \text{Max } [Sdd - E, 0] = \text{Max } [\$56.25 - \$100, 0] = \$0$$

The current price of the option with two periods to expiration can now be obtained using Equation (10.38)

$$C = \frac{[C_{uu}p^2 + C_{ud}(1-p)2p + C_{dd}(1-p)^2]}{(1+r)^2}$$

noting that

$$p = \frac{(1+r) - d}{u - d} = \frac{1 + 0.10 - 0.75}{1.25 - 0.75} = \frac{0.35}{0.50} = 0.70$$

$$C = \frac{[\$56.25(0.70)^2 + \$0(1 - 0.70)2(0.70) + \$0(1 - 0.70)^2]}{(1+0.10)^2} = \$22.78$$

The two-period case can be extended to a multi-period case using the same recursive procedure. By starting at the expiration date and working backwards we can write the general valuation formula for a call option with n-periods to expiration. The n-period generalization of the binomial model is simply the probability of each final outcome multiplied by the value of that outcome discounted at the risk free rate for n-periods. The general form of payoff for a call option can be written as

$$\text{Max } [Su^j d^{n-j} - E, 0]$$

where n is the total number of time periods up to expiration and j is the number of upward movements in the stock price ($j = 0,1,2,..n$). The general form of the probabilities of each payoff is given by the binomial distribution

$$\frac{n!}{n!(n-j)!} \, p^j (1-p)^{n-j}$$

Multiplying the payoffs by the probabilities and summing across all possible payoffs we have

$$C = \sum_{j=0}^{n} \frac{n!}{n!(n-j)!} \, p^j (1-p)^{n-j} \frac{\text{max}[Su^j d^{n-j} - E, 0]}{(1+r)^n} \tag{10.39}$$

which gives the complete general binomial valuation formula.

STOCK INDEX OPTIONS

OTC options on stock market portfolios were offered by insurance companies in the mid-1970s for investors in mutual funds. The exchange traded options on stock indexes did not develop until 1983 when CBOE began to offer options on S&P 100 Index. Exchange traded index options have become the most heavily traded of the stock options. Stock index options allow users to assume asymmetric exposure to an index or to hedge a portfolio of stocks.

The OTC market for stock index options, while not as active as the exchange traded market, has grown both in size and importance particularly since it allows investors to buy and sell customized index options. In particular, whereas the exchange traded index options are restricted to certain basic strategies, OTC index options encompass a wide variety of strategies and structures. For example, barrier index options, range index options and Asian index options can be bought and sold on major stock indexes in the OTC market.

A call on a stock index gives its holder the right to buy a specific 'fraction' of the underlying index at a pre-specified exercise price E. A put option, on the other hand, gives the holder the right to sell a specific 'fraction' of the index at a pre-specified exercise price. Whereas an American call can be exercised at any time up to its expiration date, a European call may be exercised only at maturity. The payoff at maturity of a long position in a stock index call is given by

$$\max(I - E, 0) \tag{10.40}$$

where I = value of the stock index
E = exercise price

The payoff at maturity of a long position in a stock index put is given by

$$\max(E - I, 0) \tag{10.41}$$

The common approach to valuation of stock index options assumes that the stock index follows a geometric Weiner process which would result in the Black and Scholes model described above. While this is a more reasonable assumption for stock indexes in which the price changes are continuous without a jump than it is for individual stocks, it results in a technical inconsistency because if individual stock prices are assumed to follow a log normal process then an index consisting of those stocks cannot also follow a lognormal process. That is because the sum of lognormal variables does not have a lognormal distribution. Moreover, in applying the Black and Scholes model to value stock index options, we must also take into account dividend payouts on individual stocks comprising the index. For broad based stock indices such as the S&P 500 Index, in which the dividend payments are spread throughout the year, it can be shown that a constant dividend yield provides a good approximation of the actual dividend stream.[11] For European options on such indexes, we can use a modified Black and Scholes model derived by Merton (1973) which incorporates a constant dividend yield.

$$C = Se^{-qT} N(d1) - Ee^{-rT} N(d2) \qquad (10.42)$$

where

  S = value of the index
  q = continuous dividend yield
  E = exercise price

$$d1 = \frac{ln\left(\dfrac{S}{E}\right) + \left(r - q + \dfrac{\sigma^2}{2}\right) T}{\sigma\sqrt{T}}$$

and

$$d2 = d1 - \sigma \sqrt{T}$$

The corresponding European put can be valued using the following formula

$$P = Ee^{-rT} N(-d2) - Se^{-qT} N(-d1) \qquad (10.43)$$

Equations (10.42) and (10.43) are suitable when the underlying index is broad based. However, if the composition of the index is not broad based, then these formulas will provide erroneous pricing. To value options on such indexes, we either need to modify the Black and Scholes model to incorporate dividend payments or, alternatively, we need to use the binomial approach to price stock index options. The binomial model can accommodate any number of discrete dividend payments. It also has the advantage of correctly valuing the American calls and puts on stock indexes.

Valuation of American stock options

For American-style stock options, where there is a possibility of early exercise, no analytical valuation model exists. It can be shown that in the case of a non-dividend paying stock it is never optimal to exercise an American call option before its expiration date. In this case, therefore, we use the European call pricing model. In the case of American put options and American call options written on dividend paying stock, the valuation involves the use of numerical techniques. The binomial model described above provides a simple way to price American options.

---

[11] See Brenner, Courtadon and Subrahmanyam (1987).

To value American-style options using the binomial model described above we need to compare the option value derived at each node with the early exercise value, given the stock price at that node. The exercise value at each node is simply max($S - E$, 0) for calls and max($E - S$, 0) for puts. If the early exercise value is higher than the call or the put value, then the computed call or put value is replaced with the early exercise value. We continue with this procedure until we obtain the today's option value (node 0). Notice that at the last node the option value is simply the exercise value.

EXOTIC STOCK OPTIONS

Exotic options are complex options that typically incorporate several option features. The most popular exotic stock options include look-back options, barrier options and binary options.

Look-back stock options

A look-back call option provides its holder with a payoff that is equal to the difference between the highest stock price, H, during the term of the option less the exercise price, E. That is:

$$C_{LB} = \max(H - E, 0) \tag{10.44}$$

A look-back put option, on the other hand, has a payoff at maturity given by:

$$P_{LB} = \max(E - H, 0) \tag{10.45}$$

Look-back options can be viewed as American-style options because the option holder is guaranteed the most advantageous exercise value. However, in the case of look-back options, the highest payoff is guaranteed, whereas in the case of American-style options there is no benefit of hindsight. It can be shown that it never pays to exercise an American-style look-back option prior to the expiration date. Both American and European calls can, therefore, be analytically valued. The value of a look-back call is given by:[12]

$$C_{LB} - Se^{(D-r)t} N(d1) - Ee^{-rt} N(d2)$$

$$+ Se^{(D-r)t} \lambda \left[e^{-D[t + \frac{2ln(S/E)}{\sigma 2}]} N(d3) - N(-d1)] \right] \tag{10.46}$$

where

---
[12] See Goldman, Sosin and Gatto (1979).

S = stock price

D = dividend rate

E = current minimum stock price

$\lambda = \dfrac{0.5\sigma^2}{b}$

$$d1 = \frac{ln\left(\dfrac{S}{E}\right) + (D + 0.5\sigma^2)t}{\sigma\sqrt{t}}$$

$$d2 = d1 - \sigma\sqrt{t}$$

$$d3 = \frac{(D - 0.5\sigma^2)t}{\sigma\sqrt{t}}$$

t = time to expiration

r = risk-free interest rate

σ = volatility.

Notice that the first two terms are the value of a standard call with an exercise price equal to the current minimum value of the underlying stock.

Barrier stock options

Barrier options are options whose existence is conditional on the underlying stock price not hitting the barrier price. A down-and-out call is a barrier option that expires (or 'extinguishes') if the price of the underlying stock falls below a specified barrier (or 'out') price. An up-and-out call is a barrier option that expires if the underlying stock price rises above the specified barrier price. These options are also referred to as knock-out options. Down-and-in calls and up-and-in puts are examples of knock-in options.

Barrier options tend to be cheaper than standard options since there is a possibility that the option will expire worthless before expiration. The value of a down-and-out call is given by:

$$C_{DO} = Se^{(D-r)t}\,N(d1) - Ee^{-rt}\,N(d2) - Se^{(D-r)t}\left(\frac{H}{S}\right)^{2(Y+1)}N(d3)$$

$$+ Ee^{-rt}\left(\frac{H}{S}\right)^{2Y}N(d4) + R\left(\frac{H}{S}\right)^{Y+\lambda}N(d5)$$

$$+ R\left(\frac{H}{S}\right)^{Y-\lambda}N(d6) \qquad\qquad (10.47)$$

where

244

S = stock price
D = dividend rate
r = risk-free interest rate
σ = volatility
E = exercise price
H = barrier price
R = rebate, if any, received on termination

$$d1 = \frac{ln\left(\frac{S}{E}\right)}{\sigma\sqrt{t}}\,(1 + Y)\sigma\sqrt{t}$$

$$d2 = d1 - \sigma\sqrt{t}$$

$$d3 = \frac{ln(H^2/SE)}{\sigma\sqrt{t}} + (l + Y)\sigma\sqrt{t}$$

$$d4 = d3 - \sigma\sqrt{t}$$

$$d5 = \frac{ln\left(\frac{H}{S}\right)}{\sigma\sqrt{t}} + \lambda\sigma\sqrt{t}$$

$$d6 = d5 - 2\lambda\sigma\sqrt{t}$$

$$Y = \frac{D}{\sigma^2} - \frac{1}{2}$$

$$\lambda = \sqrt{Y^2 + \frac{2r}{\sigma^2}}$$

Since the purchase of a down-and-out call and a down-and-in call with the same barrier price, exercise price, and time to expiration is equivalent to purchasing a standard call option, we can work out the value of a down-and-in call simply by deducting the value of a down-and-out call from a standard call option.

Binary stock options

Binary or 'digital' options are characterized by a binary, i.e. positive or zero, payoff. The positive payoff for a binary option is determined in advance. The likelihood of achieving this payoff is, however, uncertain. The fixed payoff is conditional on the underlying stock price reaching the strike or trigger price level. For example, a digital call on S&P 500 with a strike or trigger price, E, and a fixed payoff of P will have a payoff at maturity as shown in Figure 10.16.

The value of a digital call depends on the probability that the stock price will exceed the strike price E. This probability can be computed

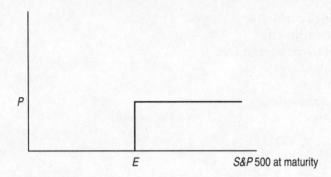

Fig 10.16 Payoff for a digital call

in the risk-neutral framework of Black and Scholes. Given the probability, $N(d1)$, that the stock price will exceed price, E, at maturity, the value of the digital call is:

$$Pe^{-rt} N(d2) \qquad (10.48)$$

where

$$d2 = \frac{\ln\left(\dfrac{S}{E}\right) + \left(r - \dfrac{1}{2}\,\sigma^2\right)t}{\sigma\sqrt{t}}$$

e = 2.7183
r = risk-free interest rate
t = time to expiration

Notice that $N(d2)$ is the probability that the stock price will be greater than the exercise price at expiration. It is important to note that when using Appendix 1 to find out the probability $(z < d2)$ we need to obtain the complement of the given probability. That is because the normal probability table at Appendix 1 finds the area under the unit normal density function from minus infinity up to the limit $d2$. To compute the probability that the stock price will be greater than the exercise price, E, we must take the complement or

$$\text{Prob } (S_T \geq E) = 1 - \text{Prob } (S_T < E)$$
$$= 1 - \text{Prob } (Z < d2)$$

Thus, for example, if $d2$ was equal to 2.0, the probability from Appendix 1 for $Z < d2$ is 0.9772. In order to obtain the probability that the stock price at maturity, S_T, will exceed E we take the complement:

$$\text{Prob } (S_T \geq E) = 1 - \text{Prob } (Z < d2)$$
$$= 1 - \text{Prob } (Z < 2.0)$$
$$= 1 - 0.9772$$
$$= 0.022$$

SUMMARY

Equity options have been traded in the over-the-counter market for over fifty years. The market for these options took off significantly following the publication of the seminal Black and Scholes option pricing model and the almost simultaneous trading of options on the CBOT. Equity options allow investors to take a geared view on the price of an underlying stock, an index on a basket of stocks. Exotic options such as look-back, barrier and binary options allow investors to assume structured positions.

Equity options are the easiest to value since these are based on a single state variable – the underlying stock price. European calls, European puts and American calls on non-dividend paying stocks can be valued using the Black and Scholes model. To value American puts and American calls on dividend paying stock we must use numerical techniques for valuation. The binomial approach is shown to be an easy and flexible technique to value more complex equity options.

References

Black, F. and Scholes, M., 'The Pricing of Options and Corporate Liabilities', *Journal of Politicial Economy*, May–June 1973, pp. 637–59.

Boyle, R., 'Options: A Monte Carlo Approach', *Journal of Financial Economics*, 4, May 1977, pp. 323–38.

Boyle, P. and Emmanuel, D., 'Discretely Adjusted Option Hedges', *Journal of Financial Economics*, September 1980, pp. 259–82.

Brennan, M. and Schwartz, E., 'The Valuation of American Put Options', *Journal of Finance*, May 1977, pp. 449–62.

Brenner, M., Courtadon, G., and Subramanyam, M., 'The Valuation of Index Options', Working paper No. 414, New York University, March 1987.

Cox, J. and Ross, S., 'The Valuation of Options for Alternative Stochastic Processes', *Journal of Financial Economics*, January–March 1976, pp. 145–66.

Cox, J., Ross, S. and Rubinstein, M., 'Option Pricing: A Simplified Approach', *Journal of Financial Economics*, September 1979, pp. 229–63.

Cox, J. and Rubinstein, M., Option Markets, Englewood Cliffs, N.J.: Prentice Hall, 1985.

Drezner, Z., 'Computation of the Bivariate Normal Integral', *Mathematics of Computation*, 32, January 1978, pp. 277–9.

Feller, W., *An Introduction to Probability Theory and its Applications*, Vol 1, 3rd edn, New York: John Wiley and Sons, 1968.

Figlewski, S., Silber, W. and Subramanyam, M., *Financial Options*, New York University, Irwin, 1990.

Geske, R., 'The Valuation of Compound Options', *Journal of Financial Economics*, 7, March 1979, pp. 63–81.

Geske, R. and Roll, R., 'On Valuing American Call Options with the Black-Scholes European Formula', *Journal of Finance*, 1984, pp. 443–55.

Geske, R. and Johnson, H., 'The American Put Option Valued Analytically', *Journal of Finance*, December 1984, pp. 1511–24.

Goldman, B., Sosin, H. and Gatto, M. 'Path Dependent Options: Buy at the Low and Sell at the High', *Journal of Finance*, 34, December 1979, pp. 1111–27.

Harvey, C.R. and Whaley, R.E., 'S & P 100 Index Option Volatility', *Journal of Finance*, 46, September 1991, pp. 1551–61.

Jarrow, R.H. and Rudd, A., *Options Pricing*, New York: Richard D. Irwin, 1983.

Johnson, H. 'Options on the Maximum or the Minimum of Several Risky Assets', *Journal of Financial and Quantitative Analysis*, 22, September 1987, pp. 277–83.

Latane, H. and Rendleman, R., 'Standard Deviation of Stock Price Ratios Implied by Option Premia', *Journal of Finance*, 31, May 1976, pp. 369–82.

Margrabe, W., 'The Value of an Option to Exchange One Asset for Another', *Journal of Finance*, 33, March 1978, pp. 177–86.

Merton, R., 'The Theory of Rational Option Pricing', Bell *Journal of Economics and Management Science*, Spring 1973, pp. 141–83.

Rendleman, R. and Bartler, B., 'Two-State Option Pricing', *Journal of Finance*, December 1979, pp. 1093–1110.

Roll, R., 'An Analytic Valuation Formula for Unprotected American Call Options on Stocks with Known Dividend', *Journal of Financial Economics*, November 1977, pp. 251–8.

Rubinstein, M., 'The Valuation of Uncertain Income Streams and the Pricing of Options', Bell *Journal of Economics*, Autumn 1976, pp. 407–25.

Rubinstein, M., *Exotic Options*, Working paper, University of California at Berkeley, November, 1990.

Smith, C., 'Option Pricing Review', *Journal of Financial Economics*, January–March 1976, pp. 1–51.

Stoll, H.R., 'The Relationship between Put and Call Option Prices', *Journal of Finance*, December 1969, pp. 802–24.

Whaley, R., 'On the Valuation of American Call Options on Stocks with Known Dividends', *Journal of Financial Economics*, June 1981, pp. 207–12.

11

PRINCIPLES OF FINANCIAL ENGINEERING

Characteristics of building blocks

Basic interrelationships of building blocks

Combining basic derivatives to engineer
new products

Combining forwards, swaps and options

Combining basic options

Static versus dynamic structures

Summary

Just as the spread of the industrial revolution in the first half of the nine-teenth century resulted in the evolution of mechanical engineering as a distinct discipline concerned with the design and development of indus-trial machinery, exactly in the same manner, it would seem, the financial revolution of the past quarter of a century is heralding the evolution of financial engineering as a distinct discipline that is concerned with the design and development of financial products. While the main stimulant in the former case was the invention of the steam engine, the main stimu-lant in the latter case has been the development of derivatives. Basic derivative products such as forwards, futures, swaps and options have allowed the financial industry to offer complex asset and liability man-agement products. Alongside the traditional instruments such as bonds, FRNs and CDs, these new off-balance-sheet products form the basic building blocks for financial engineering.

The main objectives of financial engineering can be summed up as:

- To create synthetic assets and liabilities that may not be otherwise available, such as reverse floaters, capped FRNs, yield curve notes, etc.
- To replicate an existing product at a cheaper cost or a higher return (the act of arbitrage)
- To provide 'tailored' asset and liability risk management solutions

In this chapter we develop a framework for creating structured assets and financial strategies through financial engineering.

CHARACTERISTICS OF BUILDING BLOCKS

To understand the process of engineering financial products, it is essen-tial to study the basic characteristics of the various building blocks that are used to create such products. We begin our analysis with two of the basic cash instruments, bonds and FRNs. We then go on to analyze the three basic 'off-balance sheet' or derivative instruments – forwards, swaps and options.

Bonds

A **bond** is characterized by three sets of cash flows: initial investment, periodic coupons and the final redemption. Ignoring credit risk, all three sets of cashflows are known with certainty on day one. The cash flows of a bond are illustrated in Figure 11.1 from the perspective of an investor.

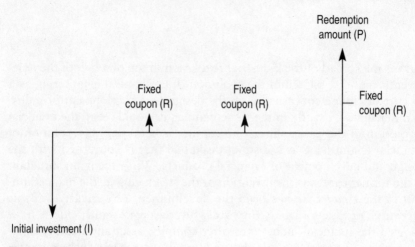

Fig 11.1 A fixed-rate bond

Floating rate notes

A **floating rate note** (FRN), like a bond, is also characterized by three sets of cash flows: initial investment, periodic coupons and the final redemption. Unlike the bond in which all three sets of cash flows are fixed and known with certainty, the periodic coupons in a floating rate note are (except for the first coupon), by definition, not known in advance and depend on the evolution of short-term interest rates on future coupon reset dates. The cash flows of an FRN are illustrated in Figure 11.2 from the perspective of an investor.

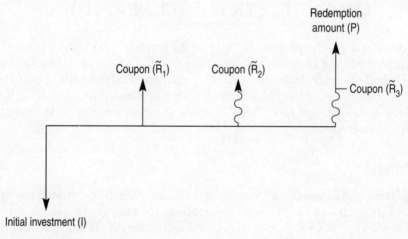

Fig 11.2 A floating rate note

Forward contracts

A **forward contract**, as we noted in Chapter 4, is an agreement between two parties to buy or sell an underlying security at a future date at a price that is agreed today. Forward contracts are the oldest of the derivative contracts and are also the simplest. These contracts exist on a variety of underlyings including commodities, deposits, bonds, foreign currencies, etc. The important feature of a forward contract is the lag in time between the agreement to trade and the trade itself. Forward contracts provide a mechanism to obtain protection against, or gain exposure to, future price movements in the underlying. A forward rate agreement (FRA) provides a mechanism to obtain protection against future interest rate changes. For example, an investor expecting to make a six-month investment in three months' time can lock-in the currently implied six-month interest rate (R) expected to prevail in three months' time by selling a 3×9 FRA in which it agrees to make a notional deposit for a period of six months beginning in three months' time at the agreed upon rate, R, against a notional loan for the same period at the prevailing six-month reference rate at maturity. Now, even though the underlying contract is based on a notional deposit and loan, only the difference between the agreed rate (the 'contract rate') and the actual six-month reference rate in three months' time (the 'settlement rate') changes hands. The cash flow of a forward rate agreement at its maturity date is illustrated in Figure 11.3.

By selling an FRA, the investor is guaranteed a fixed return on a future investment. However, by selling the FRA, the investor also foregoes the opportunity of earning a higher return should the reference interest rate end up higher than the contracted forward rate. In general, the exposure profile to buyers and sellers of forward contracts as a function of the price of the underlying instrument will be as illustrated in Figure 11.4.

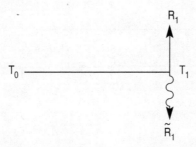

Fig 11.3 A forward rate agreement

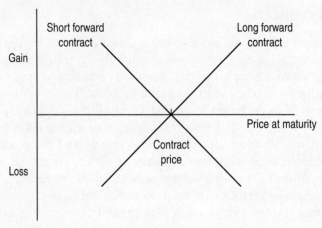

Fig 11.4 Exposure profile of forward contracts

Swaps

A **swap** is an agreement between two parties to exchange interest obligations denominated in a single currency (interest rate swaps) or in two currencies (cross currency swaps). In the case of an interest rate swap, one series of interest payment is typically fixed (R) whereas the other series is based on a floating rate index – usually LIBOR ($\tilde{R}$). The cashflows of a 'vanilla' interest rate swap are depicted in Figure 11.5 from the standpoint of the counterparty that receives a series of fixed interest payments against making a series of payments based on a floating rate index and where both payments are based on the same notional principal amount.

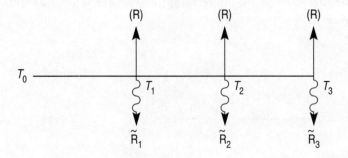

Fig 11.5 An interest rate swap

The exposure profile of an interest rate swap is illustrated in Figure 11.6.

Options

Both forward and swap contracts generate symmetric exposure in that the parties to these contracts stand to gain or lose depending on the performance of the underlying. Options, on the other hand, have an asymmetric or 'truncated' payoff. That is because an option contract gives its holder the right, but not the obligation, to buy or sell an underlying instrument. For this privilege, the purchaser pays a premium to the seller of the option who has an obligation to sell or buy the underlying instrument should the purchaser exercise the option. A call, that gives its purchaser the right to buy the underlying instrument at an agreed exercise price, and a put, that gives its purchaser the right to sell the underlying instrument at an agreed exercise price, are the two basic option structures. The exposure profiles of these two types of options both for buyers and sellers are illustrated in Figure 11.7.

Notice that the exposure profile of an option buyer is the mirror image of the exposure profile of an option seller. That is akin to the exposure profile of forward contract buyers and sellers. However, the main difference between options and forward contracts is the asymmetry of exposure in the case of options. Whereas the option buyer has the potential to make an unlimited gain, his risk is limited to the upfront premium paid for the option. The seller faces the reverse situation.

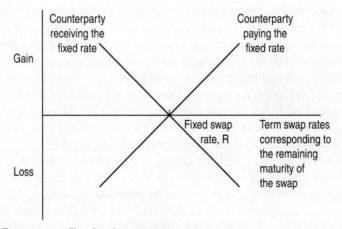

Fig 11.6 Exposure profile of an interest rate swap

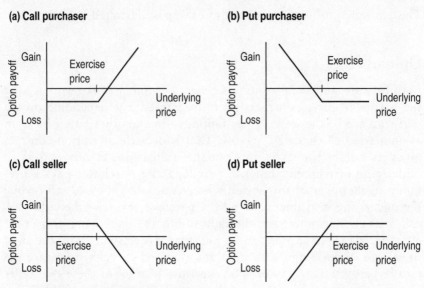

Fig 11.7 Exposure profile of calls and puts

BASIC INTERRELATIONSHIPS BETWEEN BUILDING BLOCKS

Before we show how combinations of the basic building blocks described above result in new products, structures or strategies, it will be useful to study the interrelationships that exist among these products. Let us begin by analyzing an interest rate swap. A careful look at Figure 11.3 showing the cash flow structure of a forward rate agreement and Figure 11.5, showing the cash flow structure of an interest rate swap reveals that there is a similarity between the two instruments with one exception. Whereas a forward rate agreement is a single period contract involving a single (net) payment at maturity, an interest rate swap (like other swaps) is a multiperiod contract involving (net) payments at periodic intervals. Indeed, it is easy to show that an interest rate swap is no more than a portfolio of forward rate agreements bundled together. This is clearly illustrated in Figure 11.8.

Notice that we labelled the contract rates in the case of the FRAs with subscripts 1 to 3 to highlight the fact that in the case of FRAs, the contract rate for each contract will be different[1] to reflect the term of the forward contract as well as the shape of the yield curve. In effect, each contract rate is that interest rate which gives a present value of

---

[1] Except when the yield curve is flat.

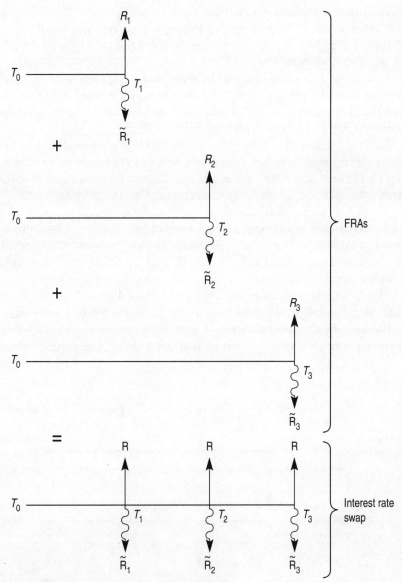

Fig 11.8 Interest rate swap as a portfolio of FRAs

zero for the FRA. In the case of an interest rate swap, however, the fixed rate, R, is constant. Since the floating payments in both cases are assumed to be based on the same index, they will have the same present value. To avoid opportunities for arbitrage, the fixed swap rate, R, must therefore be the rate that gives the same present value for the swap as that for the three forward rate agreements combined together.

Receiving R_1, R_2 and R_3 at time T_1, T_2 and T_3 under three forward rate agreements is, therefore, equivalent to receiving the swap rate, R, at time T_1, T_2 and T_3. Hence, swaps can be replicated by a portfolio of forward rate agreements.

An interest rate swap can also be replicated using cash instruments. To see this, consider the cash flows of a long bond (illustrated in Figure 11.1) and the cash flows of an FRN sold short (the reverse of the long position shown in Figure 11.2) as illustrated in Figure 11.9.

Buying a fixed rate bond and selling an FRN of similar maturity short clearly replicates the cash flows of an interest rate swap. The initial investment and final redemption amounts, by construction, cancel each other leaving net cash flows that mimic an interest rate swap.

We noted earlier that an interest rate swap is essentially a portfolio of forward rate agreements that can also be replicated by long and short positions in bonds and FRNs. It is easy to show that forward rate agreements can, in turn, be replicated by single period or single coupon bonds and FRNs.

At first, options seem to be the only instrument discussed in this chapter that differ fundamentally from cash and forward contracts. However, even option payoffs can be replicated, at least in theory, by a dynamic strategy involving a riskless security such as Treasury bills and the underlying secu-

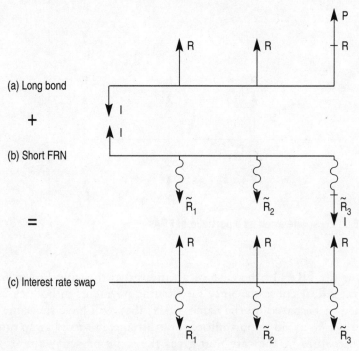

Fig 11.9 An interest rate swap as a combination of a bond and an FRN

rity on which the option is written. Besides, puts and calls can be combined to create forward contracts. This is illustrated in Figure 11.10. Buying a call and selling a put is equivalent to buying a forward contract on the underlying security where the strike rates on calls and puts are the same as the contract rate of the forward contract. Similarly, selling a call and buying a put replicates a short position in a forward contract. This relationship is also referred to as the put-call-parity.

At this point, it would seem that since all the basic derivatives can be replicated using cash market instruments, these products are redundant. Indeed, in efficient and frictionless markets derivatives will be unnecessary. In practice, of course, markets are not perfect and frictions such as taxes, transaction costs and regulatory restrictions abound. The interrelationships highlighted above show that derivatives provide an unprecedented toolkit to assume cash market positions in fundamentally different ways. For example, derivatives provide an efficient vehicle to shift risks and synthesize returns. The range of products that have been developed over the years by combining the basic building blocks described above is truly mind-boggling. As we will note in the next section, most of these 'new' products are merely new combinations of the basic building blocks described above.

COMBINING BASIC DERIVATIVES TO ENGINEER NEW PRODUCTS

In this section we will show how the structure of the basic derivatives – forwards, swaps and options – together with the interrelationships among them has been exploited over the years to engineer new securities, structures and strategies. Knowledge of how these products are engineered makes reverse engineering a trivial pursuit.

Combining bonds, FRNs and basic derivatives

Over the past ten years investors have been offered a dazzling array of structured investment products. While many of these products have not withstood the test of time, some, such as capped FRNs, dual currency bonds, callable bonds and inverse floaters have become a near permanent feature of capital markets. In this section we will show how these securities are engineered by combining a basic security with derivatives.

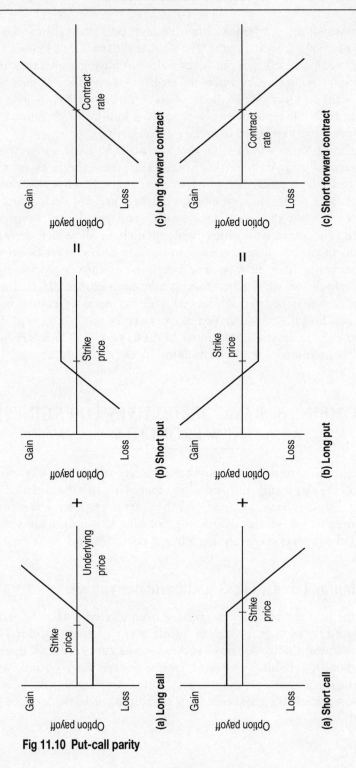

Fig 11.10 Put-call parity

Capped FRNs

A **capped FRN** is a floating rate security whose interest is capped at a certain level. Since investors stand to earn lower returns should the reference interest rate fix at a level above the cap, a capped FRN provides a higher spread than would be the case with a non-capped floater for equivalent credit risk. A capped FRN is simply constructed by combining a straight FRN with a short cap (an option on the reference interest rate). The premium received from the sale of the option is used to provide the enhanced spread to the investor. The payoff of a straight FRN on coupon dates is given by the reference interest rate, say, LIBOR. The payoff of a cap sold short at expiration is given by

$$\min(Cap\ Rate - LIBOR, 0)$$

The combined payoff of the FRN and the short cap, from the investor's standpoint, is

$$LIBOR + \min(Cap\ Rate - LIBOR, 0)$$

or simply

$$\max\ (LIBOR,\ Cap\ Rate)$$

This is graphically illustrated in Figure 11.11.

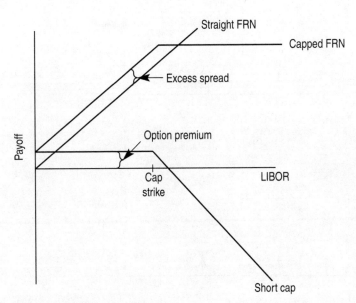

Fig 11.11 A capped floater

Dual currency bonds

Dual currency bonds have enjoyed wide success since they were first launched in Euromarkets in 1981. While most of the public deals have been aimed at Swiss franc investors, a large number of private placements have been aimed at Japanese investors. In its simple form, a **dual currency bond** is issued in one currency while the redemption takes place in another currency. The coupons, usually fixed, are paid in the issuing currency. For example, a Swiss franc bond that pays fixed Swiss franc interest is redeemed in US dollars at a fixed exchange rate.

A dual currency bond is, therefore, a combination of a straight fixed rate bond denominated in say, Japanese yen, plus a forward currency contract that, effectively, converts the redemption proceeds of the yen bond into, say, US dollars. This is shown in Figure 11.12.

Callable Bonds

A **callable bond** gives the issuer the right to redeem the bond prior to its maturity date. A callable bond is a simple combination of the straight non-callable bond and an option on interest rates that the investor has granted to the issuer in order to earn an enhanced yield. The issuer may call the bond if the term interest rates for the residual

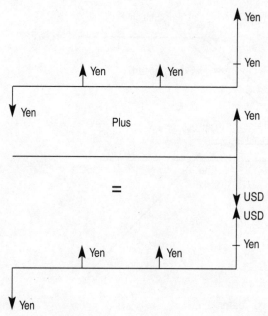

Fig 11.12 A dual currency bond

maturity of the bond are lower than the fixed rate on the bond. The issuer, in turn, can provide the enhanced yield on the bond in anticipation of a fall in term interest rates or simply by selling an interest rate option (receiver swaption in this case) to receive a premium that is passed on to the investor in the form of an enhanced coupon for the interest rate risk that is inherent in a callable asset. This is shown in Figure 11.13.

It is easy to show that a puttable bond, which gives the investor the right to seek early redemption, can be similarly constructed by embedding an interest rate option (a payer swaption) in a straight bond.

Inverse floater

An **inverse floater**'s payoff, as its name suggests, is inversely related to the reference rate such as LIBOR. Thus, rising interest rates reduce the floating coupon on the FRN whereas falling interest rates have the reverse effect. An inverse floater is a combination of a straight FRN plus an interest rate swap. If the inverse floater is not geared, its coupon is expressed as $(X-\bar{R})$ where X is a fixed rate which is equal to twice the term fixed rate that the issuer would achieve through the swaps market against LIBOR $(\bar{R})$ flat. The components of an inverse floater are shown in Figure 11.14. The notional principal of the swap needed to convert a straight floater into an inverse floater has to be twice the principal amount of the FRN.

From the issuer's standpoint, therefore, an inverse floater is equivalent to a straight FRN plus an interest rate swap that is geared two times. That is,

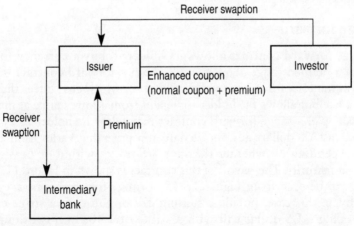

Fig 11.13 A callable bond

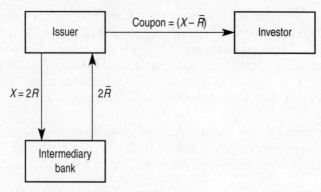

Fig 11.14 The structure of an inverse floater

Inverse floater = Straight FRN + [2 × Interest rate swap]

$$= \tilde{R} + 2(R - \tilde{R})$$

$$= \tilde{R} + (2R - 2\tilde{R})$$

$$= \tilde{R} + (X - 2\tilde{R})$$

$$= X - \tilde{R}$$

COMBINING FORWARDS, SWAPS AND OPTIONS

The basic derivatives described in this book can be combined in a variety of ways to create hybrid structures. In this section we will describe some of the important hybrid structures that have been engineered by combining forwards, swaps and options.

Range forward

A range forward contract allows its holder to buy a currency forward within a defined range. This is unlike both a forward contract – which locks in the forward price – and a call option which guarantees the maximum price but allows the holder to benefit from a lower price at maturity. For example, a range forward contract may allow its holder to buy sterling against US dollars at a future date at a price that varies from 1.40 to 1.60 depending on whether the spot \$/£ trades within or outside this range at maturity. The payoff of this contract is shown in Figure 11.15.

As can be seen from Figure 11.15, a range forward contract is created by, in this case, buying a sterling call option with a strike of 1.60 and selling a US dollar call with a strike of 1.40. In this example we assume that the premium cost of buying the sterling call is offset by the

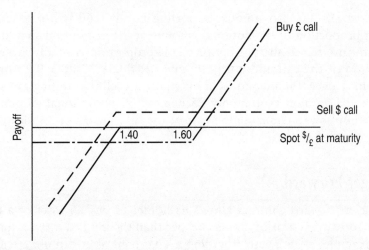

Fig 11.15 Range forward contract

premium income from selling the dollar put. Indeed, a prime motivation for the creation of a range forward contract is its ability to reduce
(or eliminate) the cost of buying a call option. Most call buyers are
concerned about the rising value of the currency they need to buy in
future. To minimize the cost of purchasing protection against such a
rise, they can give up part of the benefit that arises from a fall in the
value of the currency they need to buy in future. In our example, the
holder of the range forward contract gives up the potential benefit of
sterling falling below 1.40 against the dollar.

Participating forward

A participating forward also allows its holder to reduce the cost of
buying protection against the rise in the value of a currency by agree-
ing to share the benefit of a lower currency value or expiry. Unlike a
range forward in which the holder sells an out-of-money put to reduce
the cost of buying a call, a participating forward involves selling the
put at the same strike as the call. If the call strike is out-of-the-money
then, in this case, the put strike must be in-the-money. Since an in-the-
money put is more valuable than an out-of-the-money call written at
the same strike the holder will need to write the put for only a portion
of the notional amount of the call to reduce or eliminate the cost of
purchasing the call. Let us consider the example described above.
Suppose the six-month forward $/£ is 1.50. A sterling call with a strike
of 1.60 is, therefore, out-of-the-money. Now suppose the investor buys
a sterling call to protect against sterling rising above 1.60. Suppose this

call cost $0.50. Also suppose a sterling put at 1.60 will pay $2.00. What proportion of the notional amount of the call option should the investor use to sell the put option? This proportion is simply given by the ratio of the call and put premium, i.e. $0.50/$2.00 = 0.25 or 25 percent. Hence, the investor will only need to sell the sterling put with a notional amount that is only 25 percent of the notional amount of the call option to eliminate the cost of the call. Figure 11.16 illustrates this example.

Trigger Forward

A trigger forward contract allows its holder to buy an asset or a currency forward at a price that is cheaper than the implied forward price. For example, a US investor holding a Thai baht asset can use a trigger forward contract to protect against a large depreciation in Thai baht while benefiting from high Thai baht returns. To illustrate, suppose a U.S. investor holds a one year Thai baht asset yielding 10 percent per annum. The investor is concerned about the possibility of Thai baht depreciating against the dollar. The conventional solution would be to purchase US dollars forward or to buy a US dollar call/Thai baht put. Given the low historical volatility of Thai baht against the US dollar, the investor may be reluctant to pay the forward premium to lock-in the US dollar return. To show how a trigger forward contract can be used to generate potentially higher return than would be the case if a forward contract is used to hedge against currency risk, consider the following information:

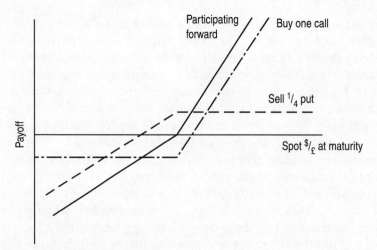

Fig 11.16 Participating forward

1-year Thai baht interest rate = 10%
1-year US dollar interest rate = 5%
Spot THB/USD = 25.0
One-year forward THB/USD = 26.19

The interest rate differential between the two currencies implies a forward premium of 1.19 (i.e. 4.76 percent). Using a conventional forward contract would effectively reduce the asset to a US dollar asset. Under a trigger forward contract the investor is able to buy US dollars forward at, say, the current spot of 25.00 if the spot FX at maturity trades below, say, 26.19 (forward FX). If the spot FX at maturity trades at or above 26.19, the investor will buy US dollars at 26.19. In other words, the worst case FX to purchase US dollars in one year's time is 26.19, which is the same as the forward FX. The best case FX is 25.00 which generates a premium of 4.76 percent over an equivalent US dollar asset. To enter into a trigger forward contract, the investor needs to pay an up-front premium. This is usually significantly lower than the forward premium.

It is easy to show that a trigger forward contract is a combination of an off-market forward contract struck, in our case, at today's spot plus a short binary US dollar call, struck at currently implied forward FX – 26.19 in our case. This is graphically shown in Figures 11.17 and 11.18.

Figures 11.17 and 11.18 can now be combined into the payoff of a trigger forward as shown in Figure 11.19.

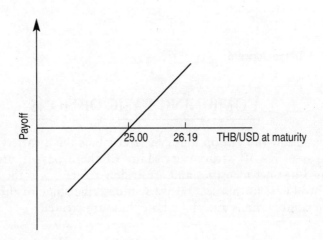

Fig 11.17 Off-market forward

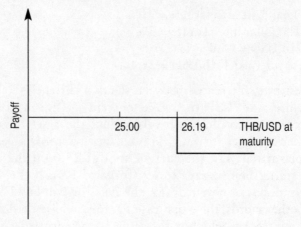

Fig 11.18 Binary call

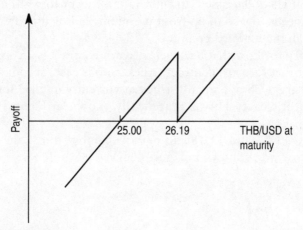

Fig 11.19 Trigger forward

COMBINING BASIC OPTIONS

The basic call and put options can be combined in a variety of ways to create new payoff structures. Many of these payoff profiles have assumed distinct identities and are widely treated as if these were distinct products. In this section we will describe some of the important option combinations and show how these are created.

Bull spread

The bull spread is a directional strategy. For example, if an investor expects the price of a stock to go up somewhat but is not sure of his bullish expectation, the bull spread allows him to make limited gain at low cost and limited downside risk. The bull spread involves the purchase of a call at a low exercise price (E_1) and the sale of a call at a higher exercise price (E_2) as shown in Figure 11.20(a). The same payoff can be achieved by buying a put at the low exercise price as shown in Figure 11.20(b). The premium paid for the call (put) is partly offset by the premium received from the sale of another call (put).

Bear Spread

The bear spread strategy is used by investors who are bearish, to some extent, on an underlying stock. As in the case of a bull spread, the investor can buy and sell puts or calls to create a limited gain payoff at a low cost as shown in Figure 11.21.

Straddles

Straddles, like strangles, butterflies and condors discussed below, are essentially volatility strategies. That is, the investor may be convinced that the price of the underlying asset will move but may be unsure about the direction of the movement. Since a call pays if the prices rise

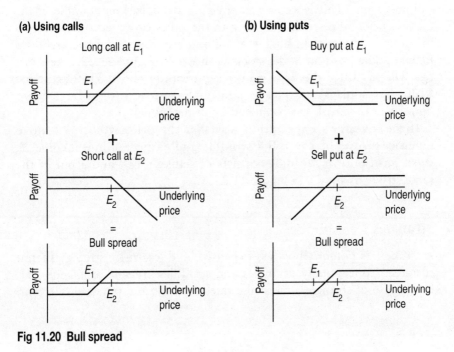

Fig 11.20 Bull spread

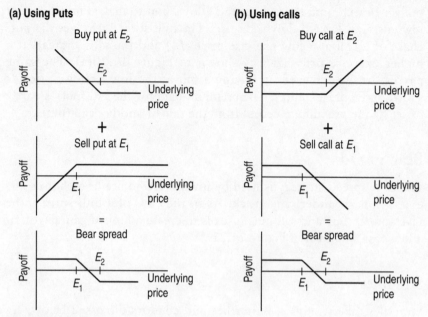

(a) Using Puts

Buy put at E_2

(b) Using calls

Buy call at E_2

+

Sell put at E_1

+

Sell call at E_1

=

Bear spread

=

Bear spread

Fig 11.21 Bear spread

and a put pays if prices fall, a simple strategy to benefit from a move in either direction of an underlying price is to combine the purchase of a call and a put. This is known as buying a straddle. For example, if the current price of a stock is $100 and the investor expects the price to move up or down then buying a call and a put at, say, $100 creates a long straddle position in the stock as shown in Figure 11.22. The strategy will pay off if the price moves significantly above $100 or below $100. A straddle is an expensive strategy because it involves buying two options, only one of which can end up in-the-money.

If the investor's expectation was that the price would not move much in future, he can sell a straddle and earn premium income. A short position in a straddle consists of selling a call and a put at the same strike, as shown in Figure 11.23.

Strangles

A strangle is potentially a less expensive and less risky strategy than a straddle. Conceptually, strangles and straddles are similar except that, in the case of strangles, the strike rates for calls and puts are different.

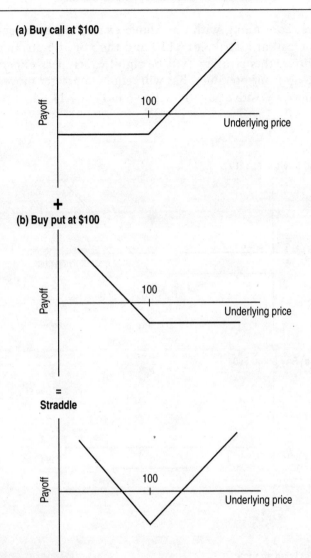

(a) Buy call at $100

+

(b) Buy put at $100

=

Straddle

Fig 11.22 Long straddle

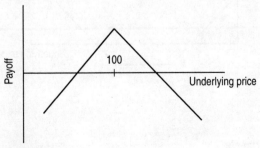

Fig 11.23 Short straddle

For instance, continuing with our above example, our investor can purchase the call at a strike of \$110 and the put at a strike of \$90. *Ceteris paribus*, this strategy will be significantly less expensive in terms of the up-front premium, but will require a greater movement in price to achieve a positive payoff as shown in Figure 11.24.

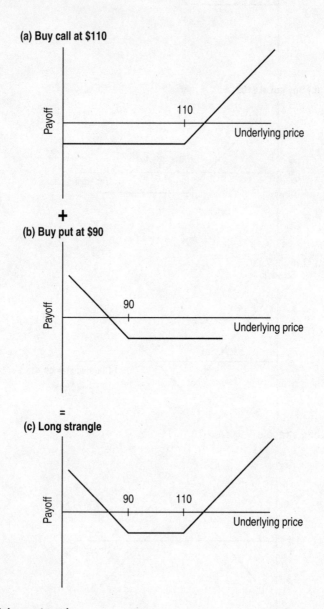

Fig 11.24 Long strangle

A short strangle can be created by selling a call and a put at different strikes.

Butterflies

The butterfly strategy, like straddles and strangles, is a volatility rather than a directional play but is less risky than either of the two. It is like a straddle but with 'bent wings' on either side (hence 'butterfly'). The butterfly strategy can be created by combining calls or puts as shown in Figure 11.25. Using calls, an investor will need to sell a call at a lower strike, E_1, buy two calls at a higher strike, E_2, and sell a call at a still higher strike, E_3.

A long butterfly spread is the mirror image of the short butterfly spread.

Condors

As in the case of strangles versus straddles, a condor is a strategy to reduce the cost of buying a butterfly by changing the strikes of the middle call to be apart. Continuing with our butterfly spread example, a condor is created as shown in Figure 11.26.

STATIC VERSUS DYNAMIC STRUCTURES

In this chapter, our objective was to show how, by combining various derivatives and other securities, we can create structures that are often sold as packages. While the range of structures that can be created by combining basic derivatives is large indeed, there are a number of structured products that cannot be replicated from basic derivatives alone. Many such products require continuous (dynamic) hedging and are, therefore, best handled by professional market makers. Some of the popular products in this category would be quanto swaps, index-amortizing structures, contingent premium structures etc.

SUMMARY

Generic derivatives can be viewed as building blocks that can be combined to create more complex derivatives, structured assets and structured liabilities. Financial engineering is the process through which these complex structures are created. The objectives of financial engineering include the creation of synthetic assets and liabilities that

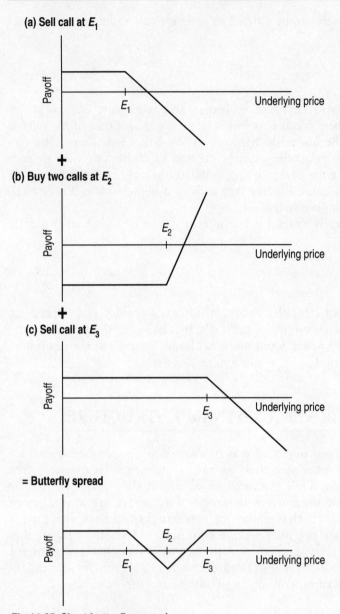

(a) Sell call at E_1

Payoff

E_1

Underlying price

+

(b) Buy two calls at E_2

Payoff

E_2

Underlying price

+

(c) Sell call at E_3

Payoff

E_3

Underlying price

= Butterfly spread

Payoff

E_2

E_1 E_3

Underlying price

Fig 11.25 Short butterfly spread

may not be otherwise available; replication of an existing product at a cheaper cost or a higher return; and creation of tailored asset and liability products. To create complex packages from generic derivatives, it is important to understand the interrelationships among various building blocks.

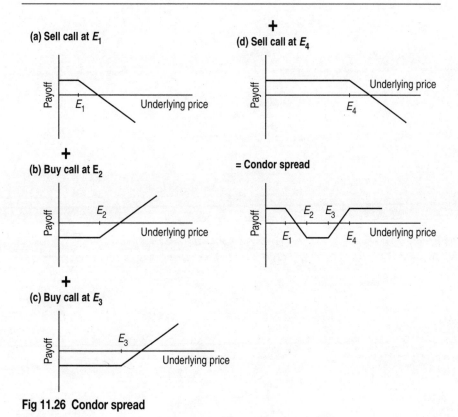

Fig 11.26 Condor spread

References

Bullen, H.G., Wilkins, R.C. and Woods III, C.C., 'The Fundamental Financial Instrument Approach: Identifying the Building Blocks', *The Handbook of Financial Engineering*, New York: Harper Business, 1990.

Miller, M., 'Financial Innovation: The Last Twenty Years and the Next', *Journal of Financial and Quantitative Analysis*, 1986, pp. 459–71.

Smith, C.W. and Smithson, C.W., 'Financial Engineering: An Overview', *The Handbook of Financial Engineering*, New York: Harper Business, 1990.

Smith, D.J., 'The Arthimetic of Financial Engineering', *Journal of Applied Corporate Finance*, 1, Winter 1989, pp. 49–58.

Smithson, C.W. and Chew, D.H., 'The Use of Hybrid Debt in Managing Corporate Risk', *Journal of Applied Corporate Finance*, 1992, pp. 79–89.

Tufano, P., 'Financial Innovation and First Mover Advantages', *Journal of Financial Economics*, 1989, pp. 213–40.

12

SYNTHETIC SECURITIES

Synthetic bonds and FRNs

Structured securities

How are structured notes created?

Currency linked structured securities

Interest rate linked structured securities

Equity linked notes

Summary

The evolution of over-the-counter (OTC) derivatives over the past two decades has resulted in a variety of derivatives-driven synthetic securities both straight and structured. While there have been a number of public issues with embedded derivatives over the years, private placements dominate this market, both in terms of size and diversity of structures. In this chapter we will examine a variety of synthetic securities.

SYNTHETIC BONDS AND FRNs

One of the most important applications of interest rate swaps has been the creation of synthetic fixed and floating rate assets. Interest rate swaps are widely used to transform a fixed rate bond into a floating rate asset and vice versa. The ability to synthesize desired interest rate exposure allows investors to separate credit and market risk decisions. The swaps market also allows investors to exploit arbitrage opportunities across credit and interest rate markets.

Synthetic FRNs

A synthetic FRN is created by purchasing a fixed rate asset and simultaneously entering into an interest rate swap to transform the fixed cash flows into floating cash flows. To illustrate, suppose you can purchase a five-year bond paying a fixed coupon of 10 percent on a semi-annual basis at par. To convert this bond into a synthetic FRN you will need to enter into a five-year interest rate swap in which you pay a fixed rate of 10 percent semi-annually against receiving, say, six-month LIBOR plus or minus a spread. Since you will be required to pay fixed against receiving floating, you need to know the offered rate for the five-year swap. Suppose the five-year offer is 9 percent against six-month LIBOR flat quoted on the same basis as the bond (i.e. semi-annual with similar day count convention). That means you should expect to receive the six-month LIBOR + 100 basis points under the swap. The structure of this transaction is shown in Figure 12.1. Notice that the notional principal amount of the swap corresponds to the par amount of the bond[1].

---

[1] It is possible to structure the swap to take into account the differences between par and market values.

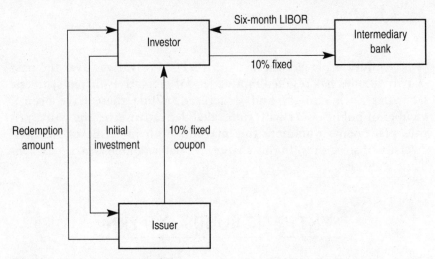

Fig 12.1 Creating a synthetic FRN

It is also possible to synthetically create an FRN from a foreign currency bond. For example, a US dollar based investor can purchase a Thai baht bond and simultaneously enter into a cross-currency swap to convert the fixed rate Thai baht asset into a floating rate US dollar asset. Suppose you can purchase a two-year Thai baht bond paying 11 percent semi-annually at par. Suppose you invest THB 250 million in the bond. To convert this fixed rate Thai baht bond into a floating rate US dollar asset you will need to enter into a USD/THB cross currency swap in which you pay fixed THB at 11 percent semi-annually against receiving six-month US dollar LIBOR plus or minus a spread. Suppose the current two-year Thai baht swap is offered at 10 percent (semi-annual). That means you should expect to receive six-month US dollar LIBOR plus, say, 90 basis points[2] against paying 11 percent semi-annually in Thai baht. Assuming the current spot of 25.00, the notional amounts for the swap are THB 250 million and USD 10 million. The initial, periodic and final cash flows of the structure are shown in Figure 12.2.

It is also possible to create a synthetic FRN from other, possibly hybrid, securities such as convertible bonds and structured notes. For example, in the case of a convertible, the intermediary bank will effectively purchase the embedded call option in addition to providing a vanilla interest rate swap to convert fixed coupons into floating coupons. The up-front premium generated from the sale of the call is used to increase the coupon or the spread.

---

[2] The 10 basis points difference between the Thai baht spread is assumed to arise on account of interest differential between Thai baht and US dollar.

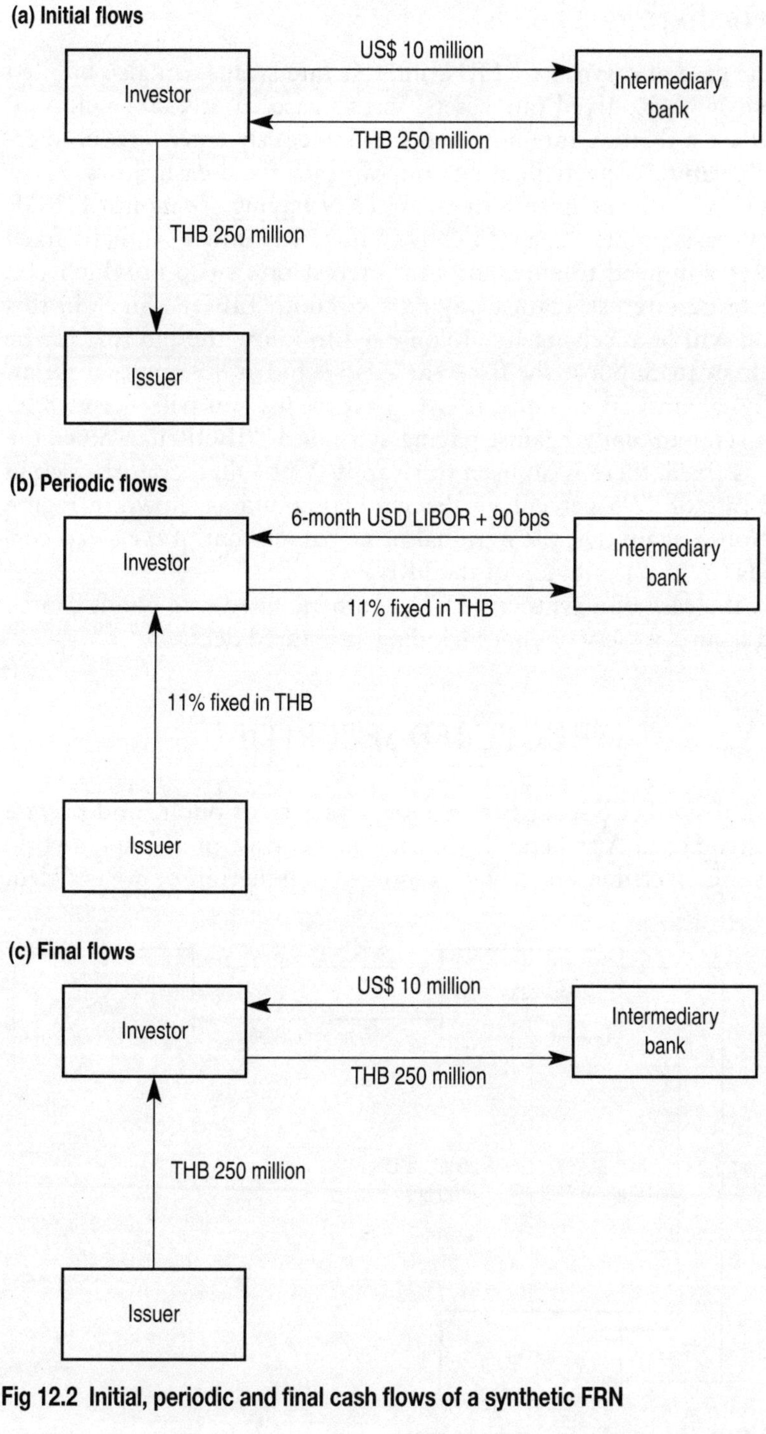

(a) Initial flows

(b) Periodic flows

(c) Final flows

Fig 12.2 Initial, periodic and final cash flows of a synthetic FRN

Synthetic fixed rate bonds

As in the case of a synthetic FRN, interest rate swaps can also be used to create synthetic fixed rate assets. In this case, an investor will need to purchase a floating rate note and simultaneously enter into an interest rate swap to convert floating coupons into fixed cash flows. Now, suppose you can purchase a five-year FRN paying six-month LIBOR plus 100 basis points at par. To convert this FRN into a synthetic fixed rate asset you need to enter into an interest rate swap in which you receive fixed interest against paying six-month LIBOR. Since in this case you will be receiving fixed you need to know the bid side of the five-year swap. Suppose the five-year swap is bid at 8.95 percent (semi-annually) against six-month LIBOR. That means you will receive 8.95 percent semi-annually against paying six-month LIBOR flat. Since the margin is fixed, there is no need to swap it. You will, therefore, lock in a fixed rate of 9.95 percent on the synthetic bond as shown in Figure 12.3. Notice again that the notional principal amount of the swap corresponds to the par amount of the FRN.

As in the case of a synthetic FRN, synthetic fixed rate bonds can be created from a variety of debt including structured debt.

STRUCTURED SECURITIES

Structured synthetic securities include a variety of public and private debt instruments. A structured security may consist of a simple hybrid such as a convertible bond or a complex combination of a basic debt

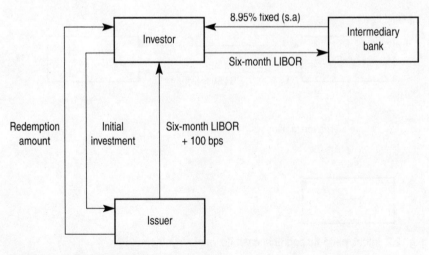

Fig 12.3 Creating a synthetic fixed rate asset

security with embedded derivatives. While structured securities are offered both in public and private debt markets, the latter tends to predominate. While structured securities are not new to investors[3], these instruments have grown phenomenally both in size and diversity over the past two decades, especially the last one. It is no accident given that the derivatives market has essentially evolved over the same period.

Structured securities allow investors to:

(a) increase current yield by assuming higher market risk
(b) increase potential yield by accepting a lower current yield
(c) act on specific market views
(d) access markets that may otherwise be closed
(e) achieve more effective diversification

In general, structured securities are created by combining a basic debt security with a simple or structured derivatives. The linkages thus created can take any of the following forms:

• absolute level plays
• spread plays across markets
• spread plays across indices
• yield curve shape plays
• correlation plays

In this section we will analyze some of the important categories of structured securities. These include currency, equity and interest rate linked structured securities.

HOW ARE STRUCTURED NOTES CREATED?

Before we describe some of the important structured asset categories let us understand how a structured security is created. A structured security has, in general, two components: an underlying straight security (such as an MTN, bond, FRN or CD) and a vanilla or structured derivatives as shown in Figure 12.4.

The issuer does not usually assume any market risk and ends up with a straight bond or FRN. The attraction for an issuer to issue a structured note is usually a lower funding cost.

---

[3] For example, a gold indexed bond was issued by Rand Kardex Corporation of USA as early as 1925 in which the redemption amount was linked to gold prices.

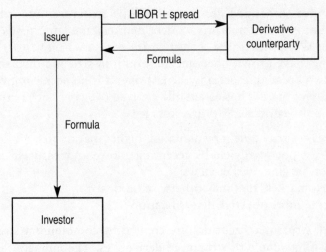

Fig 12.4 Structured securities

CURRENCY LINKED STRUCTURED SECURITIES

Currency linked structured securities usually involve a play either on the direction of an exchange rate or its volatility over a period of time.

Index currency option note (ICON)

An index currency option note allows investors to take a protected view on the direction of an exchange rate. For example, if you believe that US dollar is going to appreciate against DM over the next twelve months, you can buy an ICON that pays a lower coupon but whose redemption is linked to the performance of $/DM at maturity.

Example
Amount: $10 million
Tenor: 12 months
Current 12 month yield: 7%
Coupon: 5%
Strike: 1.50

$$Redemption: Par + max \left[par \left(\frac{(FX_1 - strike)}{FX_1} \right) \right]$$

where FX_1 is $/DM at maturity. If $/DM trades above 1.50 at maturity, the redemption will be above par as shown in Figure 12.5. If, on the other hand, $/DM trades below 1.50 the redemption is set at par. For the investor, the downside is limited to achieving a lower yield of 5 percent instead of the

284

market yield of 7 percent on a similar security. The difference of 2 percent in the yield represents the cost of purchasing the embedded dollar call/DM put.

Variations

Index currency option notes can be structured to assume other views. For example, to reduce the cost of the option the redemption amount can be capped at a certain level. The premium can also be reduced by embedding a barrier option that, for example, knocks out once the underlying FX trades at a certain level. ICONS can also be created using average rate (or 'Asian') options. Clearly, ICONS can be used to express both a bullish or a bearish view on a currency.

Currency range notes

A currency range note allows investors to assume the view that the currency will trade within or outside a certain range. Range notes are essentially volatility plays on a currency. Consider the following range play on $/DM.

Example
Amount: $10 million
Tenor: 12 months
Current 12-month yield: 7%
Coupon: (i) 9% if $/DM trades within the range
       (ii) 4% if $/DM trades outside the range
Range: 1.45 – 1.55 at any time during the term of the note
Redemption: Par

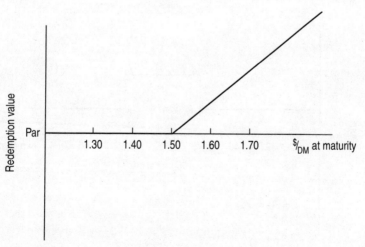

Fig 12.5 Redemption value of an ICON

If, throughout the term, $/DM trades within the defined range of 1.45 to 1.55 the investor stands to earn an above market yield of 9 percent. If, on the other hand, $/DM trades outside the range at any time during the next twelve months, the yield is lower than would be achieved on a straight twelve-month security of comparable credit risk as shown in Figure 12.6.

Variations
Range notes can be structured such that the yield is linked to the range at maturity rather than throughout the term of the note (European range note). Such notes can also be used to express the view that the underlying currency will most likely trade outside rather than inside the defined range. It is also possible to link the yield to more than one range (Ladder range note).

INTEREST RATE LINKED STRUCTURED SECURITIES

Interest rate linked structured securities allow investors to take a view on interest rates in a variety of forms including:

- level plays
- cross market index plays
- yield curve shape plays

A prime example of a structured level play is the inverse floater in which the investor assumes that the short-term interest rates will fall. Other structured securities include bull notes, cross index (quanto) notes and yield curve notes.

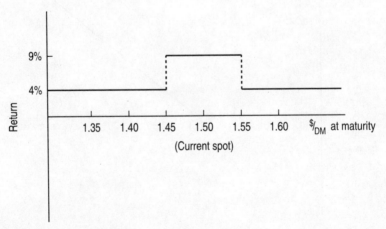

Fig 12.6 Return on a range note

Bull note

A bull note, as its name implies, allows investors to take a view on a fall in term interest rates or a rise in bond prices.

Example:
Amount: $10 million
Tenor: 12 months
Current 12 month yield: 7%
Current 5 year swap: 8%
Coupon: 6%
Redemption:
Par + (8.25% – 5 year swap rate) subject to a minimum of 95%

Thus, if at the end of twelve months the five-year swap rate trades below 8.25 percent the investor stands to make an above-market return on a twelve-month investment. If, on the other hand, the 5-year swap rate trades above 8.25 percent, the investor will earn a below-market yield. Notice that if the five-year swap rate trades above 8.25 percent, the redemption value falls below par. To provide protection against a significant fall below the par level, an interest rate option is used to create a floor of 95 percent in this case.

Variations
A bear note is a variation on the bull note and allows investors to assume a bearish view on the underlying market. In both the bull and the bear notes, if the investor view is strong, the structure can be geared to maximize the potential yield pick-up.

Cross index basis (quanto) notes

A cross index note allows investors to benefit from the difference in the shapes of yield curves in two different currencies. Suppose the six-month US dollar and sterling forward curves are as depicted in Figure 12.7.

Suppose a US dollar investor wishes to invest in a floating rate asset for three years. The current six-month dollar LIBOR is 5 percent while the implied forward curve suggests that the LIBOR will rise over the investment period, the investor may not be convinced. Now consider the sterling forward LIBOR curve. The current six-month sterling LIBOR is 8 percent but the forward curve implies that it is going to fall in future. Suppose an investor believes that short-term sterling interest rates are not likely to fall as much as is implied by forward rates. These two expectations of the investor can be combined to create a security that allows him to take the view that the expected tightening of the spread between short-term dollar and sterling interest rates is not going to materialize at the expected rate. The structure of the cross index basis note is shown in Figure 12.8.

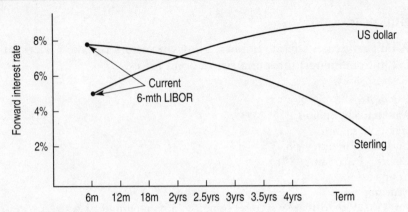

Fig 12.7 Forward curves

Under the structure, the investor receives a coupon that is linked to sterling LIBOR but payable in US dollars. Therefore, the investor does not assume any currency risk. The investor has a certain yield pick-up of 1 percent for the first interest period (8% – 2% = 6% – 5% = 1%). In the subsequent interest periods, however, the coupon will depend on the level of sterling LIBOR. The investor is assuming the risk that the differential between sterling and dollar LIBORs will narrow over time. Notice that the issuer is fully hedged.

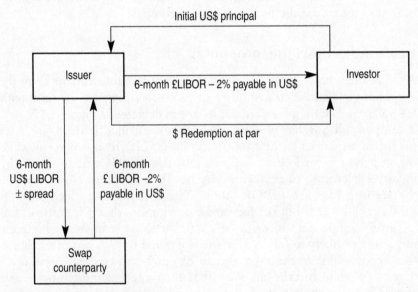

Fig 12.8 Structure of cross index note

Yield curve note

Yield curve notes allow investors to take a view on the shape of the yield curve. For example, an investor expecting a steepening of the curve may wish to receive a return that is linked to the longer end of the yield curve. Investors can also take a view on the shape of the curve by linking the return to the spread between any two points of the curve.

EQUITY LINKED NOTES

Equity linked notes allow investors to take a view on the performance of a single stock, a basket of stocks or a stock index without having to trade the underlying equity. The popularity of equity linked structured notes has grown enormously over the years because of their flexibility and cost effectiveness as well as their ability to provide exposure to markets that may otherwise be closed to a particular investor. Like currency linked notes, equity notes usually involve a play either on the direction of a stock or an index or their volatility.

Equity index note

An equity index note allows investors to assume exposure to a stock market through the purchase of a note. For example, if you believe that FTSE is going to rise above 3500 over the next twelve months, you can purchase an equity index note whose redemption is linked to the performance of FTSE.

Example:
Amount: $10 million
Tenure: 12 months
Current FTSE: 3000
Strike: 3300
Coupon: 5%
Current 12-month yield: 7%

$$Redemption: Par + \max \left[Par \left(\frac{(FTSE_1 - Strike)}{FTSE_1} \right), 0 \right]$$

If, at maturity, FTSE trades above the strike level of 3300 you stand to gain as shown in Figure 12.9. If, on the other hand, FTSE trades below 3300, your minimum coupon as well as the par redemption are guaranteed.

Notice that the FTSE-linked payoff is simply obtained by embedding a FTSE call struck at 3300 in the underlying note.

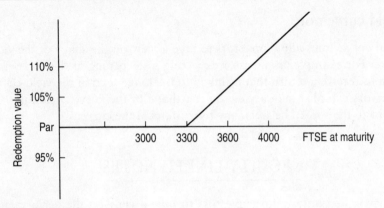

Fig 12.9 Equity note

Equity range note

As in the case of currency range notes, an equity range note allows investors to take a view on the volatility of an underlying stock or an index. For example, if you believe that FTSE is going to trade between 3100 to 3400 over the next twelve months, an equity range note can be constructed that provides an above-market yield if FTSE trades within the defined range over the next twelve months. You will earn a below market yield if FTSE trades outside the defined range.

SUMMARY

The emergence of derivatives has resulted in a variety of synthetic securities – both straight and structured. While there have been a number of derivatives-driven public issues, the market is dominated by structured private placements. One of the important applications of interest rate swaps is in the area of synthetic fixed and floating rate assets. The ability to synthesize interest rate exposure allows investors to separate credit and market risk decisions. Structured synthetic securities allow investors to create complex risk and return profiles that may not possible through straight assets. Investors can link asset returns to commodity prices, interest rates, interest rate spreads, equity prices, currencies or a combination of any of these markets.

References

Finnerty, J.D., 'The Case for Issuing Synthetic Convertible Bonds', *The Handbook of Financial Engineering*, New York: Harper Business, 1990.

Finnerty, J.D., 'An Overview of Corporate Securities Innovation', *Journal of Applied Corporate Finance*, 1992, pp. 23–39.

Smith, D.J., 'The Artithmetic of Financial Engineering', *Journal of Applied Corporate Finance*, 1, Winter 1989, pp. 49–58.

13

PORTFOLIO MANAGEMENT

Asset switching

Performance restructuring

General principles of portfolio management

The role of derivatives in asset portfolio management is one of the least studied areas at present. Yet, their use in portfolio management makes derivatives the most important development for portfolio managers they have ever experienced. While there is an array of areas in which derivatives can be used in asset management, in this chapter we will focus on the following aspects:

- asset switching
- performance restructuring, and
- risk management

ASSET SWITCHING

We noted in Chapter 12 how interest rate swaps are used to create synthetic bonds and FRNs. In a portfolio context, interest rate and currency swaps can be used to alter the exposure profile of the portfolio without having to buy or sell securities. This approach has several advantages some of which are as under:

1. Flexibility: given the size and liquidity of the swaps market, converting a portion of the portfolio from fixed to floating or vice versa is very easy.
2. Cost effectiveness: swaps can be particularly cost effective when the bid-offer spread for the underlying securities is wide.
3. The use of swaps and other derivatives allows investors to delink credit and market risk decisions.

PERFORMANCE RESTRUCTURING

For institutional investors, the use of options has thus far been primarily restricted to three areas that are essentially tactical in nature. These are:

- purchase of call options to gain leverage
- purchase of put options to lock-in gains
- selling of covered calls to improve return on sluggish assets

Recent advances in options trading as well as portfolio management techniques have resulted in a shift towards the use of options in a portfolio context. In particular, the use of options as protective insurance has assumed critical importance for those investors who must meet investment criteria that go beyond the efficient frontier.

GENERAL PRINCIPLES OF PORTFOLIO MANAGEMENT

The modern portfolio theory is predicated on the principle of diversification. Two parameters that capture the return and risk characteristics of a portfolio of securities are the mean and the variance of returns.

Technically, the principle of diversification means that whereas the return on a portfolio of assets is simply a weighted average of the return on the individual assets, the variance of the portfolio is not, in general, a simple weighted average of the variance of each security. This results in the most powerful feature of diversification: the ability of combinations of securities to reduce risk. More specifically:

(a) When two securities' returns are perfectly positively correlated, the portfolio risk, measured by the standard deviation of return, is the weighted average of the standard deviations of the component securities. Diversification, in this case, does not help.
(b) When two securities' returns are perfectly negatively correlated, it is possible to combine them in such a manner that all risk is eliminated.
(c) When two securities' returns are uncorrelated, portfolio risk is substantially reduced.

When managing a portfolio, investors consider the tradeoff between portfolio risk and return. Higher return is accompanied by higher risk and vice versa as shown in Figure 13.1.

Using option contracts to restructure performance

We noted above that an investment manager can manage a portfolio using the trade off between risk and return to match its risk appetite and other financial objectives. In particular, we noted that risk can be reduced by using the principle of diversification. There may be occasions when this framework does not lead to the achievement of portfolio objectives. For example, in addition to the general objective of maximizing return while minimizing the risk, an investor may be required to ensure a minimum return on the portfolio. This is, for example, true for pension funds who are required to ensure a minimum payoff to meet their actuarial payouts.

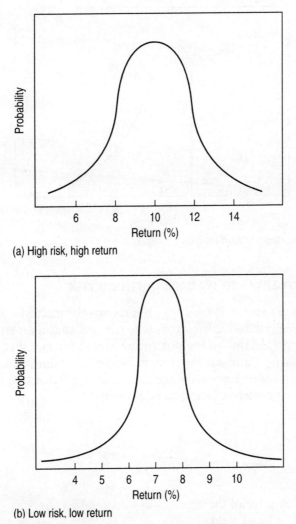

(a) High risk, high return

(b) Low risk, low return

Fig 13.1 Portfolio risk and return

We noted the insurance-like characteristics of option contracts in Chapter 3. This feature can be used to truncate the returns of a portfolio of securities as shown in Figure 13.2.

In this case, the investor purchases a put to ensure that the value of the portfolio does not fall below a certain level. To achieve this protection, the investor has to either give up part of the upside in return or accept a lower current return. It is also possible to create other payoff patterns by using various option strategies described in Chapter 11. It is also possible to use dynamic hedging strategies to replicate options that may not be traded.

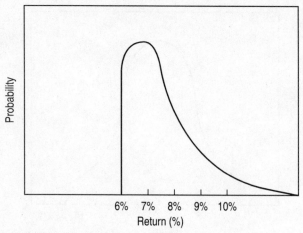

Fig 13.2 Truncated portfolio returns

Using derivatives to manage portfolio risk

Derivatives provide a flexible way to manage the interest rate risk of a fixed-income portfolio. Investors face the risk that interest rates will rise, causing a decline in the portfolio value. One measure of a fixed income security's interest rate risk is its modified duration. Modified duration measures the percentage change in the value of a bond for a given change in interest rates and is given by:

$$D_m = -\frac{dP}{P} \, dY \tag{13.1}$$

$$= -D \frac{dY}{1 + Y} \tag{13.1}$$

where   P = price of the bond
              Y = bond yield
              D = duration of the bond

Equation (13.1) implies that, for a given change in yields, the percentage change in a bond's price is proportional to its duration.

Modified duration is only an approximation of the percentage change in bond price for a given change in its yield. In reality, this measure only holds for very small changes in yield. For large changes in yield, modified duration will not hold. That is because, as shown in Figure 13.3, duration is a linear measure of interest rate sensitivity of a bond. The true price-yield relationship is not linear. A greater precision in measuring a bond's price sensitivity can be achieved by assessing the degree of convexity.

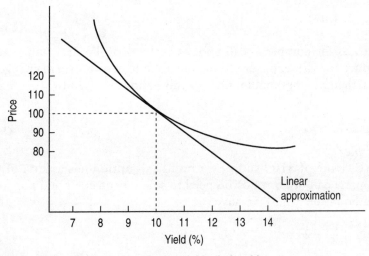

Fig 13.3 Duration approximation of price yield relationship

Convexity is defined as the second derivative of the bond price with respect to a change in yield and is given by

$$\text{Convexity} = \frac{1}{2} \frac{d^2P}{dY^2} \frac{1}{B} \qquad (13.2)$$

Notice that the concepts of duration and convexity are akin to the concepts of delta and gamma in the option terminology. Indeed, it is possible for a portfolio manager to use bond options to control duration and convexity of a bond portfolio.

Managing duration risk

To use options in the management of duration we need to develop expressions for bond option price changes as a function of yield changes. This is simply given by the first derivative of option price with respect to a change in yield. That is

$$\frac{\delta C}{\delta Y} = \frac{\delta C}{\delta P} \frac{dP}{dY} = \Delta \frac{dP}{dY} \qquad (13.3)$$

where
  C = call price
  P = bond price
  Δ = call delta

The combined dollar exposure of a bond and an option position is given by

297

$$\frac{dP}{dY} \ (1 + n\Delta)$$

(13.4)

where n is the number of call options in the portfolio. If the objective is to reduce the risk exposure of the portfolio to zero for small changes in yields, then, the optimal number of call options is given by

$$n = -\frac{1}{\Delta}$$

(13.5)

Example
With a strike of $100 suppose a bond call option has a delta of 0.5, how many call options do you need to sell to protect a bond portfolio? Using Equation (13.5) we have

$$n = -\frac{1}{0.5} = 2$$

That is, purchasing two bond options with a strike of $100 for each bond held in the portfolio provides a delta hedge. As shown in Figure 13.4, however, a delta neutral hedge does not provide protection for large changes in the price of the underlying bond. It does, however, reduce the variability significantly.

Managing convexity

To manage convexity, we need to develop an expression for the dollar value of convexity. This is given by:

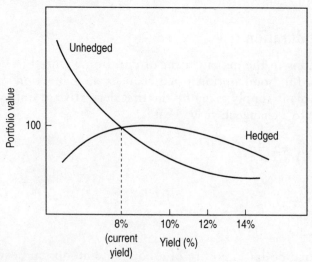

Fig 13.4 Hedging duration risk with bond options

298

$$\frac{d^2P}{dY^2}(1 + n\Delta + fn\gamma) \tag{13.6}$$

where

$$f = \frac{\left(\dfrac{dP}{dY}\right)^2}{\left(\dfrac{d^2P}{dY^2}\right)}$$

and

$$\gamma = \frac{\partial\,\Delta}{\partial P}$$

To neutralize duration and convexity risks simultaneously, we need to solve the following two equations simultaneously:

$$n_1\,\Delta_1 + n_2\,\Delta_2 = -1$$

and

$$n_1\,(\Delta_1\,f_1\,\gamma_1) + n_2\,(\Delta_2 + f\gamma_2) = -1$$

where subscripts 1 and 2 refer to two bond options with different strike prices.

SUMMARY

This chapter has highlighted the role of derivatives in asset portfolio management. Investors can use derivatives in asset switching, performance restructuring and risk management. The use of derivatives in portfolio management is driven by flexibility, cost effectiveness and delinking of credit and market risks.

References

Bookstaber, R., 'The Uses of Options in Performance Structuring', in Investment Management, ed. Frank J. Fabozi, Cambridge: Ballinger, 1989.

Fischer, B. and Rouhani, R., 'Constant Proportion Portfolio Insurance and the Synthetic Put Option: A Comparison;' in Investment Management, ed. Frank J. Fabozi, Cambridge: Ballinger, 1989.

Stoll, H. and Whaley, R., Futures and Options, Current Issues in Finance, 1993.

Walmsley, J., The New Financial Instruments, John Wiley, 1988.

APPENDIX 1

AREA UNDER THE NORMAL CURVE

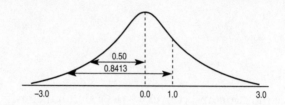

(i)   Z<o

	0	1	2	3	4	5	6	7	8	9
-3.	.0013									
-2.9	.0019	.0018	.0018	.0017	.0017	.0016	.0015	.0015	.0014	.0014
-2.8	.0026	.0025	.0024	.0023	.0023	.0022	.0021	.0021	.0020	.0019
-2.7	.0035	.0034	.0033	.0032	.0031	.0030	.0029	.0028	.0027	.0026
-2.6	.0047	.0045	.0044	.0043	.0041	.0040	.0039	.0038	.0037	.0036
-2.5	.0062	.0060	.0059	.0057	.0055	.0054	.0052	.0051	.0049	.0048
-2.4	.0082	.0080	.0078	.0075	.0073	.0071	.0069	.0068	.0066	.0064
-2.3	.0107	.0104	.0102	.0099	.0096	.0094	.0091	.0089	.0087	.0084
-2.2	.0139	.0136	.0132	.0129	.0125	.0122	.0119	.0116	.0113	.0110
-2.1	.0179	.0174	.0170	.0166	.0162	.0158	.0154	.0150	.0146	.0143
-2.0	.0228	.0222	.0217	.0212	.0207	.0202	.0197	.0192	.0188	.0183
-1.9	.0287	.0281	.0275	.0268	.0262	.0256	.0250	.0244	.0239	.0233
-1.8	.0359	.0351	.0344	.0336	.0329	.0322	.0314	.0307	.0300	.0294
-1.7	.0446	.0436	.0427	.0418	.0409	.0401	.0392	.0384	.0375	.0367
-1.6	.0548	.0537	.0526	.0516	.0505	.0495	.4085	.0475	.0465	.0455
-1.5	.0668	.0655	.0643	.0630	.0618	.0606	.0594	.0582	.0571	.0560
-1.4	.0808	.0793	.0778	.0764	.0750	.0735	.0721	.0708	.0694	.0681
-1.3	0.968	0.951	.0934	.0918	.0901	.0885	.0869	.0853	.0838	.0823
-1.2	.1151	.1131	.1112	.1093	.1075	.1056	.1038	.1020	.1003	.0985
-1.1	.1357	.1335	.1314	.1292	.1271	.1251	.1230	.1210	.1190	.1170
-1.0	.1587	.1562	.1539	.1515	.1492	.1469	.1446	.1423	.1401	.1379
-.9	.1841	.1814	.1788	.1762	.1736	.1711	.1685	.1660	.1635	.1611
-.8	.2119	.2090	.2061	.2033	.2005	.1977	.1946	.1921	.1894	.1867
-.7	.2420	.2389	.2358	.2327	.2296	.2266	.2236	.2206	.2177	.2148
-.6	.2743	.2709	.2676	.2643	.2611	.2578	.2546	.2514	.2483	.2451
-.5	.3085	.3050	.3015	.2981	.2946	.2912	.2877	.2843	.2810	.2776
-.4	.3346	.3400	.3372	.3336	.3300	.3264	.3228	.3192	.3156	.3121
-.3	.3821	.3783	.3745	.3707	.3669	.3632	.3594	.3557	.3520	.3483
-.2	.4027	.4168	.4129	.4090	.4052	.4013	.3974	.3936	.3897	.3859
-.1	.4602	.4562	.4522	.4483	.4443	.4404	.4364	.4325	.4286	.4247
-.0	.5000	.4960	.4920	.4880	.4840	.4801	.4761	.4721	.4681	.4641

(ii) Z>o

	0	1	2	3	4	5	6	7	8	9
.0	.5000	.5040	.5080	.5120	.5160	.5199	.5239	.5279	.5319	.5359
.1	.5398	.5438	.5478	.5517	.5557	.5596	.5636	.5675	.5714	.5753
.2	5793	.5832	.5871	.5910	.5948	.5987	.6026	.6064	.6103	.6141
.3	.6179	.6217	.6255	.6293	.6331	.6368	.6406	.6443	.6480	.6517
.4	.6554	.6592	.6628	.6664	.6700	.6736	.6722	.6808	.6844	.6880
.5	.6915	.6950	.6985	.7019	.7054	.7088	.7123	.7157	.7190	.7224
.6	.7257	.7291	.7324	.7357	.7389	.7422	.7454	.7486	.7517	.7549
.7	.7580	.7611	.7642	.7673	.7704	.7734	.7764	.7794	.7823	.7852
.8	.7881	.7910	.7939	.7967	.7995	.8023	.8051	.8078	.8106	.8133
.9	.8159	.8186	.8212	.8238	.8264	.8289	.8315	.8340	.8365	.8389
1.0	.8413	.8438	.8461	.8485	.8508	.8531	.8554	.8577	.8599	.8621
1.1	.8643	.8665	.8686	.8708	.8729	.8749	.8770	.8790	.8810	.8830
1.2	.8849	.8870	.8888	.8907	.8925	.8944	.8962	.8980	.8997	.9015
1.3	.9032	.9049	.9066	.9082	.9099	.9115	.9131	.9147	.9162	.9177
1.4	.9192	.9207	.9222	.9236	.9251	.9265	.9279	.9292	.9306	.9319
1.5	.9332	.9345	.9357	.9370	.9382	.9394	.9406	.9418	.9429	.9441
1.6	.9452	.9463	.9474	.9484	.9495	.9505	.9515	.9525	.9535	.9545
1.7	.9554	.9564	.9573	.9582	.9591	.9599	.9608	.9616	.9625	.9633
1.8	.9641	.9649	.9656	.9664	.9671	.9678	.9686	.9693	.9700	.9706
1.9	.9713	.9719	.9726	.9732	.9738	.9744	.9750	.9756	.9761	.9767
2.0	.9772	.9778	.9783	.9788	.9793	.9798	.9803	.9808	.9812	.9817
2.1	.9821	.9826	.9830	.9834	.9838	.9842	.9846	.9850	.9854	.9857
2.2	.9861	.9864	.9868	.9871	.9875	.9878	.9881	.9884	.9887	.9890
2.3	.9893	.9896	.9898	.9901	.9904	.9906	.9909	.9911	.9913	.9916
2.4	.9918	.9920	.9922	.9925	.9927	.9929	.9931	.9932	.9934	.9936
2.5	.9938	.9940	.9941	.9943	.9945	.9946	.9948	.9949	.9951	.9952
2.6	.9553	.9955	.9956	.9957	.9959	.9960	.9961	.9962	.9963	.9964
2.7	.9965	.9966	.9967	.9968	.9969	.9970	.9971	.9972	.9973	.9974
2.8	.9974	.9975	.9976	.9977	.9977	.9978	.9979	.9979	.9980	.9981
2.9	.9981	.9982	.9982	.9983	.9984	.9984	.9985	.9985	.9986	.9987

INDEX